THE TIME OF CATASTROPHE

This book brings together a distinguished, interdisciplinary group of scholars who offer a set of frameworks and a critical language for examining conventional understandings of catastrophe and the catastrophic. Framed around the ideas of Agamben, Kant and Benjamin, the volume demonstrates how the question of 'catastrophic time' is in fact a question about something much more than the frequency of disasters in our so-called 'Age of Catastrophe'.

Pervasive reporting of events has brought us back to the catastrophe as central to governing. This imaginative collection refuses to define catastrophe as exceptional, or by its limits in time and space. The chapters pose the times of catastrophe as multiple, integrating catastrophic events with the everyday and with how we envision futures. The authors creatively cross critical theory with historical and cultural analyses, generating a rich research agenda and teaching us all why we ought to turn to disaster to understand governing.

Susan Sterett, Virginia Tech, USA

The Time of Catastrophe poses critical questions about how we think about events, conditions, and practices that have located humanity on the threshold of total destruction. The chapters develop exciting and innovative bridges between theory and everyday life, and offer compelling new possibilities for understanding the past, present, and future.

Sylvia Schafer, University of Connecticut, USA

This timely collection shifts from the places of human catastrophes to a consideration of their temporality. Innovative and challenging, the collection considers how catastrophes are endured, remembered, and projected. Far from being a moment in time, whether inside or outside history, the chapters in this book establish the catastrophes as trajectories: passages in time that mark our era.

Ronen Shamir, Tel-Aviv University, Israel

To Ben, with hope that he will live in better times (A.S.)

The Time of Catastrophe
Multidisciplinary Approaches to the Age of Catastrophe

Edited by

CHRISTOPHER DOLE
Amherst College, USA

ROBERT HAYASHI
Amherst College, USA

ANDREW POE
Amherst College, USA

AUSTIN SARAT
Amherst College, USA

BORIS WOLFSON
Amherst College, USA

ROUTLEDGE
Routledge
Taylor & Francis Group
LONDON AND NEW YORK

First published 2015 by Ashgate Publishing

2 Park Square, Milton Park, Abingdon, Oxfordshire OX14 4RN
711 Third Avenue, New York, NY 10017

Routledge is an imprint of the Taylor & Francis Group, an informa business

First issued in paperback 2018

British Library Cataloguing in Publication Data
A catalogue record for this book is available from the British Library

The Library of Congress has cataloged the printed edition as follows:
Dole, Christopher.
The time of catastrophe : multidisciplinary approaches to the age of catastrophe / by Christopher Dole, Robert Hayashi, Andrew Poe, Austin Sarat and Boris Wolfson.
pages cm. -- (Law, justice and power)
Includes bibliographical references and index.
ISBN 978-1-4724-6836-9 (hardback : alk. paper) -- ISBN 978-1-4724-6837-6 (ebook) -- ISBN 978-1-4724-6838-3 (epub) 1. Disasters. 2. Political psychology. I. Title.
HV553.D65 2015
363.34--dc23

2015012406

ISBN: 978-1-4724-6836-9 (hbk)
ISBN: 978-1-138-38406-4 (pbk)

Contents

List of Figures

List of Contributors

David W. Bates, Rhetoric, University of California, Berkeley received his PhD in European History from the University of Chicago, where he specialized in the French Enlightenment and the Revolutionary period. Since coming to Berkeley in 1999, he has been working on two main research tracks: one on the history of legal and political ideas, and the other on the relationship between technology, science, and the history of human cognition. His recent book, *States of War: Enlightenment Origins of the Political*, explores the invention of an autonomous idea of political community in natural law thinkers, from Grotius and Hobbes to Locke, Montesquieu, and Rousseau. His forthcoming book, entitled *Human Insight: An Artificial History of Natural Intelligence* focuses on the problem of insight, or radical novelty, at the intersection of theories of knowledge, media networks, machine technologies, concepts of the body, and practices of industrial organization.

Carolyn J. Dean is Professor of History at Yale University. She was previously John Hay Professor of International Studies at Brown, where she served as interim director of the Watson Institute for International Studies and as Senior Associate Dean of the Faculty from 2005–2011. She is the author of several books, most recently *Aversion and Erasure: The Fate of the Victim after the Holocaust* (Cornell, 2010), and the recipient of several fellowships including an ACLS and a Guggenheim.

Lewis R. Gordon is Professor of Philosophy and Africana Studies, with affiliations in Asian and Asian American Studies, Caribbean and Latino/a Studies, and Judaic Studies, at UCONN-Storrs; European Union Visiting Chair in Philosophy at Université Toulouse Jean Jaurès, France; and Nelson Mandela Visiting Professor of Politics and International Studies at Rhodes University, South Africa. His most recent book is *What Fanon Said: A Philosophical Introduction to His Life and Thought*. His website is: http://lewisrgordon.com and he is on twitter at: https://twitter.com/lewgord.

Joseph Masco, Professor of Anthropology and of the Social Sciences in the College at the University of Chicago writes and teaches courses on science and technology, U.S. national security culture, political ecology, mass media, and critical theory. He is the author of *The Nuclear Borderlands: The Manhattan Project in Post-Cold War New Mexico* (Princeton University Press, 2006), which won the 2008 Rachel Carson Prize from the Society for the Social Studies of Science and the 2006

Robert K. Merton Prize from the Section on Science, Knowledge and Technology of the American Sociological Association. His work as been supported by the American Council of Learned Societies, The John D. and Catherine T. MacArthur Foundation, The Wenner-Gren Foundation, and the National Endowment for the Humanities. His current work examines the evolution of the national security state in the US, with a particular focus on the interplay between affect, technology, and threat perception within a national public sphere.

Elizabeth Stewart is a Associate Professor of English at Yeshiva University. She holds a PhD from NYU in comparative literature. Her areas of specialty are Modernism, critical theory, psychoanalysis, and postcolonial/world literature. She teaches courses in British, American, and European Modernism ("Modernisms," "Modern and Postmodern Literature: Crosscurrents"); modern and contemporary literature ("Coetzee and South African Literature," "Faulkner and Morrison: Myths of America"); non-Western literature ("Trauma, Memory, Magic", "Contemporary World Fiction", "Diaspora Literature"); "Literature and Psychoanalysis;" interrelations of literature and the visual arts ("Literature and Art in the Age of Photography"); literature and philosophy ("Nietzsche," "German Jewish Writers"); individual modern authors ("Kafka and the Modern"); critical theory ("Interpreting Texts"); and science fiction. She is author of *Catastrophe and Survival: Walter Benjamin and Psychoanalysis* (Continuum, 2009),and editor and translator of *Lacan in the German-Speaking World* (SUNY, 2004); and has published articles on Walter Benjamin, Friedrich Nietzsche, Jacques Derrida, and J.M. Coetzee. She has also been awarded an NEA Translation Grant for her work in translation.

Editors

Christopher Dole is Associate Professor of Anthropology at Amherst College
Robert Hayashi is Associate Professor of American Studies at Amherst College
Andrew Poe is Assistant Professor of Political Science at Amherst College
Austin Sarat is William Nelson Cromwell Professor of Jurisprudence & Political Science and Associate Dean of the Faculty at Amherst College
Boris Wolfson is Associate Professor of Russian at Amherst College

Acknowledgments

This book is the product of a seminar series at Amherst College during the 2013–14 academic year. Our thinking about catastrophe was enriched by our participation in a reading group on the subject and by Amherst College's 2013–14 Copeland Colloquium. We are grateful to the following colleagues who participated in those groups, Joanna Dyl, Lawrence Douglas, Luca Grillo, Kimberly Lowe, Pooja Rangan, and Simon Stow.

When Is Catastrophe?: An Introduction

Christopher Dole, Robert Hayashi, Andrew Poe, Austin Sarat, and Boris Wolfson

Why Ask?

When is catastrophe? This would appear to be a question with a clear answer. If we understand a catastrophe as a calamitous event that causes widespread destruction and suffering, there should be no need to pose such a question. There should be no need to ask, for instance, *when* the Indian Ocean earthquake struck, creating a tsunami that would lead to more than 200,000 deaths (December 26, 2004—for those who have forgotten); or *when* a poisonous gas leak at the Union Carbide plant in Bhopal, India killed thousands of nearby residents (December 2–3, 1984); or *when* Hurricane Katrina made landfall on Louisiana's Gulf Coast (August 29, 2005). How could this question—"When is catastrophe?"—be anything other than rhetorical? If catastrophes are, by definition, exceptional events of such a magnitude that worlds and lives are dramatically overturned, a catastrophe would seem to be an event that admits no uncertainties with regards to its timing. *The Time of Catastrophe* poses this seemingly straightforward question anew, arguing that there is much to be gained by interrogating the temporal conceits of conventional understandings of catastrophe and the catastrophic.

If, as we argue, the meaning of catastrophe turns in fundamental ways around temporal presumptions—a sense of time and history being ruptured, a characteristic eventfulness, an emphasis on the "here and now," an urgency of response and anxiety of anticipation– then the conditions of our collective existence seem to have grown, of late, particularly dire. News of large-scale disasters and impending catastrophes multiply day by day—news that heralds irreparable ecological devastation, the unbounded ravages of infectious disease, the geological and atmospheric precariousness of "nature," the mounting toll of civil wars and non-state political violence, and so forth. Alongside these present dangers, catastrophes also seem to command a monopoly over every imaginable future, such that the idea of a future catastrophe has become a real force in the ordering of lives and worlds in the present. Catastrophe has taken hold as both a backdrop to and condition for the intimate terrain of our everyday lives—as schoolchildren are taught to prepare for massacres and natural disasters, local police departments train and equip for terrorist attacks, communities come into existence to share strategies and scenarios to "prep" for the "next disaster," and new forms of leisure and media consumption grow around wildly varying visions of the world's destruction. In short, the language of catastrophe and disaster has established itself as a defining idiom of life and survival in the contemporary world.

Yet, why focus on the temporality of catastrophe when the human suffering and material destruction of large-scale disaster seem so much more pressing? As we argue in this introduction, and the chapters in this volume demonstrate, it is imperative that we consider experiences of suffering and destruction precipitated by disaster in conjunction with the temporal conventions associated with catastrophe, or what we regard as "catastrophic time." In other words, *The Time of Catastrophe* makes a case for recognizing the central importance of "catastrophic time" for the study of catastrophe, a concern that should not be regarded as secondary to the human and material loss associated with catastrophes. With a multi-disciplinary group of contributors gathered to make our case, this volume seeks to demonstrate how the question of "catastrophic time" is in fact a question about something much more than the frequency of disasters in our so-called "Age of Catastrophe."[1]

Indeed, to take seriously the temporal entanglements of catastrophe requires confronting fundamental questions that span from the everyday intimacies of suffering and loss to the place of our species within the geological time of planetary history. "When is catastrophe?" is therefore a question that is at once generative and protean. For our purposes, there are three facets to this question that we consider in this introduction, as a means of organizing the conversations to come. First, we introduce the question of catastrophe's temporality as a call to recognize the specificity of catastrophic time—that the temporality of catastrophe is in fact multiple, and varies within and across geographical, social, and historical contexts. Appreciating the multiplicities and specificities of catastrophic time will help us grapple with a persistent question that runs through the literature on and of catastrophe: does catastrophe belong within history or, as an event that obliterates the very coordinates of time, does it stand outside of history? Secondly, whereas many scholars have regarded disasters as moments of revelation, whereby typically unrecognized societal processes come into view,[2] we explore the implications of reversing this formulation to question the capacity of catastrophic time, or the temporal urgency of disaster, to obscure the processes that created the conditions for large-scale disaster, the forms of governance at play in seemingly exceptional events, the "slower" destructiveness of structural violence and ecological degradation, and the possibility that catastrophe may in fact be a

1 See, among many others, Peter Gray and Kendrick Oliver, *The Memory of Catastrophe* (Manchester: Manchester University Press, 2004); John Ebert, *The Age of Catastrophe: Disaster and Humanity in Modern Times* (Jefferson, NC: McFarland, 2012).

2 See Kai Erikson, *Everything In Its Path: Destruction of Community in the Buffalo Creek Flood* (New York: Simon and Schuster, 1976); Gary A. Kreps, "Disaster and the Social Order," *Sociological Theory* 3 (1985): 49–64; Anthony Oliver-Smith, "Anthropological Research on Hazards and Disasters," *Annual Review of Anthropology* 25 (1996): 303–29; Susanna Hoffman and Anthony Oliver-Smith (eds), *Catastrophe and Culture: The Anthropology of Disaster* (Santa Fe: School of American Research Press, 2004).

permanent condition of the everyday. Lastly, we consider how the question "When is catastrophe?" is inescapably a question about the future. Although "catastrophic time" would seem to be a temporality fixed to the present (the "present" tense, after all, is the tense of disaster, the urgent response to the here and now), contributors to this volume insist that we recognize the ways that catastrophe and catastrophic time also speak in the mode of futurity. Taken together, *The Time of Catastrophe* raises a range of fundamental questions about catastrophe that have yet to be sufficiently articulated. As we will consider in more detail below, the problem of catastrophe's temporality remains poorly elaborated in the enormous body of writing dedicated to the theme of catastrophe. With this in mind, we seek to pose the most basic of questions: "When is catastrophe?"

In raising this question, we enter into an astonishingly long and rich history of thought on calamity, crisis, disaster, apocalypse, and any number of allied concepts. Beyond the deep theological history that cuts across, and at times unites, a range of religious traditions that have taken up catastrophe and apocalypse,[3] much attention has been given to the vital role played by catastrophe in shaping a range of European philosophical traditions. The Lisbon earthquake of 1755, for instance, is widely regarded as a defining moment in the development Enlightenment thought. From exchanges between Rousseau and Voltaire about the sort of God who could inflict such destruction in the world, to a young Immanuel Kant's budding interest in seismology and the sublime qualities of the earthquake's destruction, the Lisbon earthquake is understood as having set the course for debates about rationality, progress, and modernity to which we remain deeply indebted.[4] More generally, as Kevin Rozario has written, "The most potent philosophies of the last two centuries"—including Hegel, Marx, and Darwin—"have insisted that improvement or 'progress' unavoidably moves through catastrophic rhythms of destruction and reconstruction, ruin and renewal."[5] Approached in this light,

3 See M. van de Wetering, "Moralizing in Puritan natural science: Mysteriousness in earthquake sermons," *Journal of the History of Ideas* 43 (1982): 417–438; David G. Roskies, *Against the Apocalypse: Responses to Catastrophe in Modern Jewish Culture* (Cambridge, Mass: Harvard University Press, 1984); Jane Anna Gordon and Lewis R. Gordon, *Of Divine Warning: Reading Disaster in the Modern Age* (Boulder, CO: Paradigm Publishers, 2009); Eric Ormsby, *Theodicy in Islamic Thought: The Dispute Over Al-Ghazali's Best of All Possible Worlds* (Princeton: Princeton University Press, 2014).

4 See Rita Goldberg, "Voltaire, Rousseau, and the Lisbon Earthquake," *Eighteenth Century Life* 13 (1989): 1–20; Russell Dynes, "The Dialogue between Voltaire and Rousseau on the Lisbon Earthquake: The Emergence of a Social Science View," *International Journal of Mass Emergencies and Disasters* 18 (2000): 97–115; Marie Helene Huet, *The Culture of Disaster* (Chicago: University of Chicago Press, 2012); Svend Erik Larsen, "The Lisbon Earthquake and the Scientific Turn in Kant's Philosophy," *European Review* 14 (2006): 359–67.

5 Kevin Rozario, *The Culture of Calamity: Disaster and the Making of Modern America* (Chicago: University of Chicago Press, 2007), 3.

the history of European philosophical thought can be read as but an extended reflection on catastrophe.

In addition to being a concept that runs through—if not underlies—a complex field of theological and philosophical inquiry, the concept of catastrophe has also been a popular means for exploring the distinctive conditions of modernity. Here, the religious connotations of catastrophe give way to a secular discourse characterized by its efforts to rationalize catastrophe otherwise than through an idiom of divine retribution.[6] Catastrophes, in this context, gain meaning in relation to the emergence of particularly modern political, economic, and technological orders.[7] Along with providing an idiom for enumerating the unique dangers of modernity, catastrophe has also been widely regarded as playing an essential role in facilitating societal transformations associated with modernity, especially in terms of the capacity of disasters to enable large scale political-economic change.[8] Across these examples, catastrophe comes into view as a paradigmatic example of the "creative destructiveness" of modernity.

In both its scale and specificity, catastrophe can thereby be understood as vital to the constitution of social and political orders.[9] In other words, as much as a disaster marks the ending of a particular order, it also inaugurates new forms of communal and political life[10] and is, therefore, intimately bound up with issues of law and governance.[11] In this context, the humanitarian crisis (in terms of both the response to emergency and preparations for a future disaster) has emerged

6 Marie Helene Huet, *The Culture of Disaster* (Chicago: University of Chicago Press, 2012); Ernest Gilman, *Plague Writing in Early Modern England* (Chicago: University of Chicago Press, 2009).

7 Kenneth Hewitt, "The Idea of Calamity in a Technocratic Age," in *Interpretations of Calamity*, ed. K. Hewitt (Boston: Allen and Unwin, 1983), 2–32; Ulrich Beck, *Risk Society: Towards a New Modernity* (London: Sage, 1992); Ulrich Beck, *World at Risk* (Cambridge, UK: Polity, 2009); Charles CharPerrow, *Normal Accidents: Living With High-Risk Technologies* (New York: Basic Books, 1984).

8 C. Cohen and E. Werker, "The Political Economy of 'Natural' Disasters," *Journal of Conflict Resolution* 52 (2008): 795–819; Adriana Petryna, *Life Exposed: Biological Citizens after Chernobyl* (Princeton: Princeton University Press, 2002); Vincanne Adams, *Markets of Sorrow, Labors of Faith: New Orleans in the Wake of Katrina* (Berkeley: University of California Press, 2013); Naomi Klein, *The Shock Doctrine: The Rise of Disaster Capitalism* (New York: Picador, 2008).

9 Kevin Rozario, *The Culture of Calamity: Disaster and the Making of Modern America* (Chicago: University of Chicago Press, 2007); Mike Davis, *Ecology of Fear: Los Angeles and the Imagination of Disaster* (New York: Metropolitan Books, 1998).

10 Kim Fortun, *Advocacy after Bhopal: Environmentalism, Disaster, New Global Orders* (Chicago: University of Chicago Press, 2001); Dole, Christopher, "The House That Saddam Built: Protest and Psychiatry in Post-Disaster Turkey," *Journal of the Ottoman and Turkish Studies Association* forthcoming.

11 Austin Sarat, Lawrence Douglas, and Martha Umphrey (eds), *Law and Catastrophe* (Stanford: Stanford University Press, 2007); Ruth Miller, *Law in Crisis: The Ecstatic Subject of Natural Disaster* (Stanford: Stanford University Press, 2009); A. Ophir, "The

as a privileged setting for exploring the relationship between catastrophe and governance.[12] In tandem with this concern with the sociopolitical implications of large-scale disasters, scholars have also underscored the ways that the effects of disaster are not distributed equally within societies. Building on conceptualizations of catastrophes as social, symbolic, and technical processes,[13] many scholars have tracked the various ways that vulnerability and resilience are socially distributed within particular political-economic orders.[14]

Alongside this scholarly attention to the various social, political, and technological entanglements of catastrophe, the theme of catastrophe has also had a distinguished career within literature and the arts. From Camus's *The Plague* to Morrison's *Beloved*, Defoe's *A Journal of the Plague Year* to zombie thrillers and post-apocalyptic science fiction, catastrophe has long animated a range of literary

---

Sovereign, the Humanitarian, and the Terrorist," in *Nongovernmental Politics*, ed. M. Feher (New York: Zone Books, 2007), 161–82.

12 Mariela Pandolfi, "Contract of Mutual (In)Difference: Governance and Humanitarian Apparatus in Albania and Kosovo," *Indiana J of Global Legal Studies* 10 (2003): 369–81; Didier Fassin (ed), *Contemporary States of Emergency: The Politics of Military and Humanitarian Interventions* (New York: Zone Books, 2013); Michel Feher, *Nongovernmental Politics* (Cambridge: MIT Press, 2007); Craig Calhoun, "The Imperative to Reduce Suffering: Charity, Progress, and Emergencies in the Field of Humanitarian Action," in *Humanitarianism in Question: Politics, Power, Ethics*, M. Barnett and T. Weiss (eds) (Ithica: Cornell University Press, 2008), 73–97; Andrew Lakoff, "The Generic Biothreat, or, How We Became Unprepared," *Cultural Anthropology* 23 (2008), 399–428; Joseph Masco, "'Survival is Your Business': Engineering Ruins and Affect in Nuclear America," *Cultural Anthropology* 23 (2008), 361–98; Claudia Aradau and Rens van Munster, *Politics of Catastrophe: Genealogies of the Unknown* (New York: Routledge, 2011); Giorgio Agamben, *Homo Sacer: Sovereign Power and Bare Life* (Stanford: Stanford University Press, 1998); Giorgio Agamben, *State of Exception* (Chicago: University of Chicago Press, 2005).

13 Anthony Oliver-Smith and Susanna Hoffman (eds), *The Angry Earth* (New York: Routledge, 1999); Susanna Hoffman and Anthony Oliver-Smith (eds), *Catastrophe and Culture: The Anthropology of Disaster* (Santa Fe: School of American Research Press, 2004); E. L. Quarantelli, *What Is a Disaster? Perspectives on the Question* (New York: Routledge, 1998); Kai Erikson, *Everything in Its Path: Destruction of Community in the Buffalo Creek Flood* (New York: Simon and Schuster, 1976).

14 Eric Klinenberg, *Heat Wave: A Social Autopsy of Disaster in Chicago* (Chicago: University of Chicago Press, 2002); Ted Steinberg, *Acts of God: The Unnatural History of Natural Disaster in America* (Oxford: Oxford University, 2000); Charles Perrow, *The Next Catastrophe: Reducing Our Vulnerablities to Natural, Industrial, and Terrorist Disasters* (Princeton, N.J.: Princeton University Press, 2007); Michael Dyson, *Come Hell or High Water: Hurricane Katrina and the Color of Disaster* (New York: Basic Books, 2006); Joanna Dyl, *Seismic City: An Environmental History of San Francisco's 1906 Earthquake* (n.d.).

pursuits.[15] Here, catastrophe has served as a compelling vehicle for efforts to imagine the unimaginable, which is in turn a means for exploring the representational limits of language and aesthetics.[16] Relatedly, cinematic renderings of catastrophe and disaster have been regarded as distinctively revelatory spaces of imagination and fantasy,[17] an observation likewise applicable to news media and documentary accounts of disaster.[18] In turn, efforts to memorialize or commemorate disaster have attracted similar scholarly attention regarding their distinctive aesthetics of catastrophe.[19] As these examples begin to indicate, the theme of catastrophe animates a remarkably elaborate archive of imaginable ends to the present world, an archive that remains insufficiently explored.

Despite the fact that this selective overview leaves unaddressed the innumerable ways that catastrophe is used metaphorically to describe everything from one's health, to the health of one's relationships, to the conditions of one's personal finances, the range of themes discussed above demonstrates the capacity of the subject of catastrophe to draw together an enormously heterogeneous body of scholarly, literary, and creative work. Catastrophe is, in other words, a capacious concept. The challenge of delimiting catastrophe's meanings is made all the more difficult by the semantic ambiguities or inconsistencies of concepts like catastrophe, disaster, calamity, emergency, and apocalypse. Every attempt to establish a stable meaning, or draw distinctions between meanings, seems to generate additional

---

15 See James Berger, *After the End: Representations of Post-Apocalypse* (Minneapolis: University of Minnesota Press, 1999); Scott Juengel, "The Early Novel and Catastrophe," *Novel* 42 (2009): 443–50.

16 Maurice Blanchot, *The Writing of the Disaster* (Lincoln: University of Nebraska Press, 1986); Theodor Adorno, *Negative Dialectics* (New York: Continuum, 1983).

17 Susan Sontag, "The Imagination of Disaster," in *Against Interpretation, and Other Essays* (New York: Farrar, Straus & Giroux, 1966); Slavoj Žižek, *Welcome To the Desert of the Real!* (London: Verso, 2002); Slavoj Žižek, "Catastrophes Real and Imagined." *In These Times*, February 28, 2003, http://inthesetimes.com/article/56/catastrophes_real_and_imagined, accessed June 1, 2013.

18 Mary Ann Doane, "Information, Crisis, Catastrophe," in *Logics of Television*, P. Mellencamp (ed.), (Bloomington: Indiana University Press, 1990), 222–39; Pooja Rangan, *Immediations: Humanitarianism, Otherness, and the Documentary Logic of Intervention* (Durham: Duke University Press, n.d.).

19 Marita Sturken, *Tourists of History: Memory, Kitsch, and Consumerism from Oklahoma City to Ground Zero* (Durham: Duke University Press, 2007); Marita Sturken, "The Aesthetics of Absence: Rebuilding Ground Zero," *American Ethnologist* 31 (2008): 311–25; James Young, *At Memory's Edge: After-images of the Holocaust in Contemporary Art and Architecture* (New Haven: Yale University Press, 2000); Yuki Miyamoto, *Beyond the Mushroom Cloud: Commemoration, Religion, and Responsibility after Hiroshima* (New York: Fordham University Press, 2011); Jay Winter, *Sites of Memory, Sites of Mourning: The Great War in European Cultural History* (Cambridge and New York: Cambridge University Press, 1995); Simon Stow, "From Upper Canal to Lower Manhattan: Memorialization and the Politics of Loss," *Perspectives on Politics* 10 (2012): 687–700; Peter Gray and Kendrick Oliver, *The Memory of Catastrophe* (Manchester: Manchester University Press, 2004).

complexity. It is not surprising, then, that the study of catastrophe has not, or has yet to, constitute itself as a field of discourse. There is no canon to the study of catastrophe. And this volume has no aspirations of establishing one. We envision *The Time of Catastrophe* not as a comprehensive treatment of catastrophe, but, rather, as a provocation regarding the alluring and elusive temporal qualities of catastrophe and the catastrophic.

Catastrophic Times

There is no shortage of omens indicating that we live in catastrophic times. New disasters pile up almost daily—tsunamis, tornadoes, and earthquakes are growing ever more destructive; nuclear disasters appear imminent; civil wars and political conflict have produced the worst refugee crisis since World War II. Catastrophes—once the favored trope for literary, cinematic, and theoretical speculation—have seemingly become the mundane background of our daily lives. Setting aside the empirical question about whether there are, in fact, more disasters today than in the past, the suggestion that we live in a distinctively catastrophic era begs a more fundamental question. What, precisely, is the "time" of catastrophe that we want to speak of? In its conventional formulation, a catastrophe—from the Greek *κατά*, "down," and *στρέφειν*, "to turn"—is a sudden, destructive event that marks an ending or overturning of a pre-existing order. As such, a catastrophe is a radical break, a rupturing of the temporal continuity of history that heralds a destructive and unexpected ending. Yet, this seemingly straightforward temporality of catastrophe—what we refer to as the temporality of eventfulness—obscures a set of complicated and persistent questions about the multiplicity of temporalities at play in conceiving and making sense of the catastrophic.

If catastrophe is both a destruction of lives as well as a rupturing of time—such that a truly catastrophic event creates a break in time of such a magnitude that it introduces a new sense of historical time—the contributors to this volume challenge the very place of catastrophe and its temporality within human history. That is, does catastrophe belong in or to history? This question is, in part, also a question about perspective, as well as scale. On the one hand, from the point of view of those living a catastrophe, how does catastrophe fit into the temporal continuity of the present? And, by extension, how do we know if we are or are not living a catastrophe at this very moment—as some future observer may conclude (if the ominous projections about global climate change are fulfilled)? On the other hand, where does catastrophe belong within the scale of the history of our species, or even planetary history? While an earthquake that destroys a city and leaves thousands of people dead and injured is undoubtedly a catastrophic event, what is the meaning of this event in the geological time of the earth's tectonic activity? Should we locate catastrophic events within the temporal horizon of our species, or the historical coordinates of specific people and their social and singular lives?

In turn, how might the very nature of a catastrophic threat or event carry with it new conceptions of the scale of time and history?

The contributors to this volume push these questions in several significant directions, directions that in fact highlight the most pressing forms of catastrophe of the modern era—nuclear destruction, global climate change and ecological devastation, cultural loss, and genocidal violence. As we will see, each imagined end presumes its own distinctive "catastrophic time."

The development of the atomic bomb, for instance, introduced the possibility of sudden, total, and technologically mediated catastrophe. In particular, as the anthropologist Joseph Masco argues in his contribution to this volume, "The always-on-alert system of missiles-bombers-submarines armed with thermonuclear weapons made *not* launching a nuclear war a minute-to-minute calculus, and then naturalized that restraint as the basis of 'defense.' In psycho-social terms, this means that Americans have lived for more than half a century in the temporal space in which the missiles may have always already been launched—that is, within the 15-minute window offered by early warning systems" (p. 34). This distinctive temporality of catastrophe, as Masco argues, would become both the rationale for and setting of the emergence of a characteristic Cold War mode of citizenship. And with its emphasis on imminent threat and corresponding practices of preparedness training, this "catastrophic time" of nuclear disaster would prove itself to be surprisingly durable.

Although the language of "mutual assured destruction" may sound antiquated today, the Cold War temporality of nuclear destruction continues to organize visions of and responses to catastrophic futures. As Masco notes, the temporality of nuclear catastrophe has provided the blueprint for contemporary imaginings of ecological devastation and global catastrophe. "Nuclear crisis has," he writes, "come to structure our very idea of crisis, where the sudden shock of a total ending becomes the basis for thinking large-scale threat .... Our notions of catastrophe today have been crafted by the nuclear system, which invented a machinery and imaginary of ultimate endings" (p. 34). In addition to underscoring the ways that temporalities of catastrophe have their own histories, this point relatedly highlights the fact that as much as temporalities of catastrophe inherit older visions of worldly destruction, they also grow within a set of conditions unique to a given era.

To recognize this play between contextual specificity and historical continuity is to appreciate the variability and multiplicity of "catastrophic time." At any given moment, in any given place, multiple visions and temporalities of catastrophe are circulating. As the contributors to this volume repeatedly emphasize, varying conceptions of catastrophe profoundly shape the way in which one understands and relates to the world, simultaneously obscuring and generating alternate visions of possibility. In other words, while the temporality of nuclear danger may well inspire urgent concern and action with regard to the perils of global climate change, it also runs the risk of obscuring alternative ways of understanding the nature and implications of rapid ecological transformation.

Alongside these obscuring, or asynchronous, qualities of "catastrophic time," contributors to this volume are also interested in the ways that differing temporalities of catastrophe can enable novel perspectives. For instance, the "catastrophic time" animating the discourse of ecological crisis invites us to think differently about the place of humans within the catastrophic. Should massive *human* suffering and death be the limit within which we conceptualize catastrophe? Here, the historian of political and legal thought David Bates discusses the efforts of physiologists and neurophysiologists working in the early twentieth century to conceptualize the unity of biological life in the face of catastrophic threat. For these "theorists of the organism," a catastrophic assault was not to be conceived as some sort of "singular external interruption of some normal internal functioning" (p. 102). Rather, as Bates characterizes the work of the influential neurophysiologist Kurt Goldstein, "the life of an organism is a series of 'slight catastrophes' (*leichter Katastrophen*) that continually produce new adjustments and reorganizations" (p. 118). Approached in these terms—the biological terms of life and organism—catastrophes come to be seen as ongoing aspects of life itself. The organism survives not in spite of but through the experience of continual catastrophic threat. Although this organismic temporality of catastrophe may seem far removed from concerns about nuclear and ecological crisis, Bates provocatively suggests that we would be well served to recognize these scientists as serious political thinkers. Their efforts to theorize the organism articulate an alternative logic and temporality of catastrophe that diverges from the apocalyptic political thinking of the time, a logic that affords "the possibility that catastrophic disruption might be *integrated* into the sphere of politics, without permanently contaminating the genuine promise of human security and stability" (p. 103).

As these examples indicate, catastrophe poses a vexing representational problem. In this respect, each author confronts differently what Maurice Blanchot identified as the fundamental problem of "writing the disaster"—the problem of representing that which is, by its very definition, beyond comprehension. "The disaster" writes Blanchot, "is what escapes the very possibility of experience—it is the limit of writing. This must be repeated: the disaster de-scribes."[20] How, then, does one represent that which defies or exceeds representation? What is the best metaphor, model, or analogy for giving persuasive form to the unimaginable? In short, through what form does one "think the unthinkable"? As the contributors to this volume remind us, such representational questions are, in important regards, questions about the temporality of catastrophe. How do we give meaning to an event that destroys the very temporal coordinates of the present order? How do we position catastrophe in relation to history? Or, put otherwise, how do we insert the unthinkable into time?

---

20 Maurice Blanchot, *The Writing of the Disaster* (Lincoln: University of Nebraska Press, 1986), 7.

Carolyn Dean identifies two possible responses to these questions in her examination of critical debates about "photographs of catastrophe"—especially photographic depictions of Nazi concentration camps. On the one hand, photographs of catastrophe invite the viewer to engage the image as if it depicted some sort of trans-historical "human condition"—as "sacred" images that transcend the messiness of specific historical circumstances to render "human evil" in the "continuous time of human sinfulness" (p. 85). On the other hand, in Dean's reading of a counter-discourse on atrocity photography, the potential efficacy of representations of catastrophe—their ability to motivate action—depends on their capacity to render context and historical specificity. For these critics, only by emphasizing the actuality of specific catastrophes can one hope to prevent future catastrophes. Ultimately at stake in these debates is the temporal horizon of catastrophe. Should we regard photographs of atrocity as belonging to the "universal and infinite time of human evil" (p. 85), a temporality of catastrophe that ultimately de-historicizes and potentially obscures accountability? Or should they be regarded only in relation to the historical conditions of their production, a temporality that runs the risk of rendering the atrocities they depict as banal? As Dean's argument powerfully suggests, determining the temporal frame of such photographs plays a decisive role in determining whose lives are regarded as worthy of empathy and, hence, grievable.[21] In this regard, if Bates' chapter invites us to bracket the "human" in thinking about catastrophe, Dean underscores the varied ways in which the category of the human comes into focus in narratives of catastrophic endings.

The philosopher and Africana Studies scholar Lewis Gordon invites us to think in yet another register about the temporality of catastrophe. Moving through a set of examples of worlds that have ended (from Columbus's landing in the Bahamas in 1492, to the archeological record of hominid evolution, to stories from Greek antiquity), Gordon urges us to recognize that "catastrophic time" is at once the temporality of ruins—those "irreparable remains of a human construction that, by a destructive act or process, no longer dwells in the unity of the original."[22] Gordon's approach thereby suggests a relationship between catastrophe and history that cannot be adequately contained in narratives of cataclysmic events inaugurating new eras—stories, in other words, of radical breaks and fresh starts. Instead, to attend to catastrophe in the form of "cultural disaster"—which is not only the destruction of worlds and realities, but also the very conditions of meaning-making—we must envision a present that is haunted by catastrophic loss, a world "littered by ruins" of a reality that no longer exists and in which we live a "ruined existence" (p. 138). Put differently, Gordon offers us the perspective of the survivor, where to live on after "cultural disaster" is to be continually not-at-

21 See Judith Butler, Precarious Life: The Powers of Mourning and Violence (New York: Verso, 2003).

22 Robert Ginsberg, The Aesthetics of Ruins (Amsterdam, The Netherlands: Rodopi, 2004), xvii; cited in Gordon, this volume, p. 133.

home in the world. Here, time has not only "come to a halt," but time itself has been "ruined" (p. 133). Gordon's provocative reflections on catastrophe in the temporality of ruins offers a framework for thinking about "catastrophic time" that simultaneously complements and complicates the temporalities of both sudden, total nuclear destruction and the "slow, attritional" violence of global climate change

The chapters that comprise *The Time of Catastrophe* raise a series of questions about conventional formulations of catastrophe, questions that aim to draw into the open the specific temporal conceits of catastrophe and the catastrophic. Toward this end, contributors insist on the importance of recognizing the multiplicity of the temporality of catastrophe. The most immediate implication of this argument is that "catastrophic time"—with its characteristic urgency and eventfulness—does not unfold on a single, universal scale. It, too, exists within history, as it also has its own history. The insights offered by our contributors regarding both the multiplicity and specificity of catastrophic time point us in at least two important directions. On the one hand, to examine closely the temporalities of catastrophe is to raise fundamental questions about our place in the world, and especially the comparative brevity of human history in relation to the geological time of the planet. On the other hand, they offer the promise of providing critical insights into the assumptions about human dignity and human belonging that different temporalities of catastrophe encode.

Catastrophe and the Everyday

A prominent lineage of European critical theory regards the catastrophic as foundational to modern political and legal orders. Here, the work of Walter Benjamin holds a privileged position. For Benjamin, human history should not be conceived as a narrative of progressive development. Instead, it is imperative that we appreciate history as a continuing wreckage of catastrophic events, events organized not as a "chain of events" that lead toward ever more human freedom, but rather by a logic of violence.[23] As Bates characterizes this "catastrophic" view of history, "catastrophe [for Benjamin] did not punctuate some normal form of human life. Catastrophe was a permanent condition of unredeemed violence that was itself punctuated by the merely apparent forms of stable order" (p. 100).

Although the "apocalyptic tone" of Benjamin's work reflected well the sentiment of the era within which he was writing (particularly Germany of the 1930s), his conception of history and catastrophe has gained renewed attention since the events of September 11, 2001. In this context, it has provided the basic framework for examining the dynamics and practices of political sovereignty in

23 Walter Benjamin, "Theses on the Philosophy of History," In *Illuminations*, trans. Harry Zohn (New York: Schocken, 1968); Walter Benjamin, "Theologico-Political Fragment," in *Reflections*, trans. Edmund Jephcott (New York: Schocken, 1986).

the contemporary world. Especially through the work of philosophers Giorgio Agamben and Robert Esposito, Benjamin's thought has emerged again as an influential language for speaking about the foundational place of violence and catastrophe within modern political orders. As Bates describes these developments, "after years of debate about 'deliberative democracy,' the public sphere, and the politics of performative identity, political theorists and other intellectuals were now scrambling to make sense of the return of such issues as emergency executive power, the sovereign exception, and the political and ethical significance of 'just war'" (p. 104).

Such formulations of political authority—which locate catastrophe, disaster, and violence as intrinsic qualities of political orders—invite us to think in more critical terms about the seeming exceptionality of catastrophe. In so doing, *The Time of Catastrophe* challenges the presumed distinctiveness of catastrophe and the everyday. Rather than an overturning of order, how might we conceive of catastrophe as being continuous with, if not an extension of, the everyday? Indeed, what do we gain by conceiving of catastrophe as a permanent condition of the everyday?

In posing these questions, our interests overlap with a set of parallel scholarly efforts to conceptualize the "everyday" as an object of study and theorizing. Rather than presuming that the "everyday" provides some sort of stable backdrop or passive context to social lives, these scholars conceptualize it as a dynamic field that is actively produced and reproduced by relationships and forces commonly unrecognized in the mundane flow of habituated life.[24] Here, we are specifically interested in a set of scholarly conversations about the relationship between disaster and the everyday in settings marked by large-scale political violence. In her writing about political violence in India, for example, Veena Das has argued that outbursts of dramatic communal violence and everyday socialities of community life should be thought of in terms of continuity, rather than exceptionality. "[V]iolence was not set apart from sociality," she writes of the large-scale violence that erupted after the assassination of Indira Ghandi in 1984, "rather, the agency of the violence rendered the social as an entity to be 'made' rather than that which was given."[25] Explosive violence, in other words, is not to be set apart from the everyday, as an exception to either a pre-given or otherwise tranquil community life. At the same time, as Das argues, "[t]o say that the extreme violence was continuous with everyday life is not to say that it was the same, but rather that the everyday provided the grounds from which the event could be grown."[26]

---

24 See, among many others, Henri Lefebvre, *Critique of Everyday Life, Vol. 1* (London: Verso, 1991); Michel de Certeau, *The Practice of Everyday Life* (Berkeley: University of California Press, 1984); Dorothy Smith, *The Everyday World as Problematic: A Feminist Sociology* (Boston: Northeastern University Press, 1987); Michael Gardiner, *Critiques of Everyday Life* (New York: Verso, 2000).

25 Veena Das, *Life and Words: Violence and the Descent into the Ordinary* (Berkeley: University of California Press, 2007), 149.

26 Ibid.

Approaching catastrophe as continuous with the everyday takes us to an understanding of catastrophe defined less in terms of eventfulness than as a potentiality that inheres in the flow of social life. As Masco puts it, "the atomic revolution installed a catastrophic potential into everyday life" (p. 20)—a potentiality that has been extended with the emergence of a discourse of global climate change and ecological destruction. While Masco emphasizes the everyday potentiality of catastrophe, Elizabeth Stewart attends to the parallel psychic, affective, and sensorial registers of this relationship between catastrophe and the everyday. Stewart, a literary theorist, considers two crime dramas—Fritz Lang's 1931 film *M.* and the contemporary BBC drama series *Luther*—to explore the interlinked themes of law, community, and catastrophe. For Stewart, *M.* and *Luther* depict two fundamental ways that these themes implicate the everyday. On the one hand, they capture how the everydayness of the law operates as a "constant danger" and "permanent every day possibility" of violence—especially in those instances or contexts when law is suspended to protect the community from threat. On the other hand, *M.* and *Luther* also draw attention to how the political dynamic of sovereignty bears on the constitution of individual subjectivities. That is, the potential of law's violence stands as the condition of possibility for the subject's emergence, which thus renders the subject constitutively and subsequently dependent on "permanent catastrophe." For Stewart, *M.* and *Luther* thus serve as a productive entry for rethinking the relationship between catastrophe and the everyday.

Turning from Stewart's reading of the complex politico-psychic investments of catastrophe, Bates introduces us to efforts in the biological sciences to consider analogous questions regarding the relationship between catastrophe and the everyday, here framed in organismic terms. Rather than reading the catastrophic as a sign of some sort of "foundational violence," the "theorists of the organism" examined by Bates conceptualized catastrophe as an ongoing process of making and remaking unity. Invoking, again, Goldstein's notion of "slight catastrophes" (*leichter Katastrophen*), Bates describes how these scientists regarded "catastrophic situations" as a continually occurring presence; "the organism survives not in spite of but via the experience of *permanent catastrophe*" (p. 118).

In drawing a series of suggestive connections between physiological and political theory, Bates offers an alternate means for imaging the relationship between catastrophe and the everyday. While catastrophe may be a permanent condition of the present, it need not be conceived in terms of totalizing destruction. "Catastrophic disorder," writes Bates, "was not simply the result of a singular external interruption of some normal internal functioning. But neither was it the sign of some foundational violence inherent in the appearance of any 'order,' as the theorists of permanent catastrophe maintain. … Catastrophe was permanent in the sense that organisms (and by extension other vital unities) were always re-founding their order, and not merely protecting it, in response to the perpetual threat of dissolution" (p. 102). Rather than a moment of radical ending or rupture, catastrophe thus comes into view here as a perpetual process of generativity. "[T]he physiologically inspired sense of unitary life pointed to the catastrophe as something that illuminated both the fragility of these organismic unities and their vitality. Catastrophe was the constant risk of death, but it was also the opportunity for creativity and improvisation" (p. 102).

Framing the relationship between catastrophe and the everyday in these terms highlights a recurring tension between approaching catastrophe synchronically (as an event of a particular moment in time) as compared to diachronically (as part of a much larger set of historical processes). Each emphasis carries its own hazards. Focusing too closely on catastrophe synchronically risks obscuring the broader histories at play in any given event, such that debates about the role of individual agency dissolves into claims of the capriciousness of "natural" events. This was Rousseau's point when he argued that, in the aftermath of the Lisbon earthquake, "nature did not construct twenty thousand houses of six to seven stories there." In turn, focusing on catastrophe diachronically runs the risk of obscuring the distinctive implications of its eventfulness, such that the specificity of the catastrophic event dissolves into the undifferentiated flow of the everyday or is subsumed within the temporal scale of geological time and planetary history.

It is important to distinguish our concern with the everyday-ness of catastrophe from commonplace claims that disasters—as massive, destructive events—have become "routine" or "everyday" in this age of catastrophe. In fact, by drawing special attention to the variability and specificity of catastrophic temporalities, *The Time of Catastrophe* raises critical questions about the assumptions that underlie such claims. In what ways do conventional understandings of the routine or commonplace occurrence of catastrophes rely upon a set of temporal assumptions regarding the distinctiveness of the catastrophic event and the everyday? How does the temporality of emergency characteristic of the catastrophic create particular modes of seeing and attention? If, as Craig Calhoun has persuasively argued, the contemporary "emergency imaginary" is characterized by a temporality of urgency and immediacy that opposes the temporality of "critical reflection,"[27] how does "catastrophic time" obscure our capacity to recognize other forms of danger, or divert attention from the violence and exclusions of the "everyday"?

While these questions suggest lines of critique that lead otherwise than to banal proclamations about the prevalence of disaster in the contemporary world, it is nonetheless significant to take stock of the ways that catastrophe has moved with such force from the domains of film, literature, and theory onto the social terrain of everyday anxiety. Although it remains unclear if this era is in fact any more prone to disaster than an any other era, it is certainly true that the *idea* of catastrophe has taken hold as a pervasive idiom for imagining life and survival in the contemporary world. Indeed, the seeming routineness of large-scale disasters

27 Craig Calhoun, "The Imperative to Reduce Suffering: Charity, Progress, and Emergencies in the Field of Humanitarian Action," in *Humanitarianism in Question: Politics, Power, Ethics*, M. Barnett and T. Weiss (eds) (Ithica: Cornell University Press, 2008); see also Pooja Rangan, *Immediations: Humanitarianism, Otherness, and the Documentary Logic of Intervention* (Durham: Duke University Press, n.d.).

may speak less to the inherent dangers of the modern world than to the ascendance of a particular political rationality. More precisely, it may in fact indicate the emergence of catastrophe, disaster, and emergency as distinctive forms of future-oriented governance.

Catastrophe's Future

> To think the disaster (if this is possible, and it is not possible inasmuch as we suspect that the disaster is thought) is to have no longer any future in which to think it.
>
> Maurice Blanchot, *The Writing of the Disaster*[28]

To suggest that catastrophe inhabits the everyday as both a permanent condition and radical potentiality opens a series of additional questions regarding the "future" of catastrophe. What sorts of futures become imaginable in the name of catastrophe? And why has catastrophe become such a compelling vehicle for imagining the future? We are not, of course, the first to raise questions about catastrophe's future. To do so is to enter into an extended history of imaginings of the world's end—from the apocalyptic discourses of any number of religious traditions to recurring tropes of world annihilation that are a staple of literary and cinematic imaginations. *The Time of Catastrophe* enters this history to pose novel questions about the mutually conditioning qualities of catastrophe and futurity.

Lewis Gordon, for example, urges us to consider catastrophe not merely as a "ruined existence" but also as harboring a distinctive relationship to the future. For Gordon, "cultural disaster"—the destruction of a community's or society's system of signs that produce meaning and persons—represents both the loss of a contemporary reality as well as an assault on the future. "Cultural disaster," as Gordon argues, "leads to a rallying of forces against the future. It demands sacrifice of the young" (p. 138). In other words, the desire for cultural continuity in the face of a decaying capacity to imagine a future that resembles the present leads to the ossification of the present in the name of preservation; "the struggle for cultural continuity drags cultural practice out of the stream of mundane life to the level of sacrifice and fanatic devotion" (p. 138). With an eye toward both Greek mythology and contemporary consumer debt, Gordon provocatively argues that this "war on the future" is a burden borne with particular intensity by the youth. "The next generation is, in effect, forced to be the parents of those from whom they have descended by virtue of the debts they bear.... Implicit in such presumption is the same cultural fear pushed to subconscious levels: indebted to the past but without a future, what else do they sense, with fear and trembling, but the end of the world" (p. 141)?

---

28 Maurice Blanchot, *The Writing of the Disaster* (Lincoln: University of Nebraska Press, 1986), 2.

Elizabeth Stewart's contribution builds on a parallel set of concerns to suggest a pathway for building such a "coming community" in the wake of catastrophe. In addition to elaborating the psychic register of catastrophe's future implicit in Gordon's argument, Stewart indicates that our very ability to imagine the future is itself dependent on the catastrophic. In other words, at the same time that catastrophes threaten the future of the present, the future is itself unimaginable without an idea of the catastrophic. As Stuart argues, to build new (and better) futures for ourselves, we must therefore attend to both the ways that catastrophe structures political orders *and* the catastrophic dependencies that organize the psyches of individual subjects.

While Gordon and Stewart raise questions about the relationship between the catastrophic potentiality of the present and the capacity to imagine a livable future, other contributors reverse this relationship to pose additional questions about catastrophe's future. How might imaginations of future disaster bear upon the ordering and organization of the present? How can such a "catastrophic imagination" of the future shape and motivate conduct in the present? What does it mean to intervene on potential future catastrophes? To ask these questions is to highlight the ways that the temporality of catastrophe can also be understood as a site of governance. In so doing, *The Time of Catastrophe* draws attention to the configuration of catastrophe and futurity that has come to characterize late-modernity and how the management of the time of catastrophe has become such an orienting political problem of our times.

The concept of "disaster preparedness," for instance, captures well this relationship between governance and catastrophic futurity. As several scholars have recently argued, the rapid spread of the logic and practices of "disaster preparedness"—with its own forms of expertise and professionalism, its techniques of calculating probabilities and scenario-based trainings, its temporality of urgency and emergency, and so forth[29]—has emerged as a defining site of political governance. Contributors to this volume offer important insights into the conditions that gave rise to this future-oriented mode of governance. For example, Masco, as he traces the logic of catastrophic futurity as it was played out in the popular domain of Civil Defense training and Cold War efforts to prepare American citizens for nuclear crisis, introduces us to the historical crucible within which the contemporary relationship between disaster preparedness and governance was initially forged. Underscoring the political implications of this catastrophic futurity, Masco describes how, "the extraordinary achievement [of Civil Defense] was to turn contemplating the end of the nation-state into a form of

29 See Andrew Lakoff, "The Generic Biothreat, or, How We Became Unprepared," *Cultural Anthropology* 23 (2008), 399–428; Joseph Masco, "'Survival is Your Business': Engineering Ruins and Affect in Nuclear America," *Cultural Anthropology* 23 (2008), 361–98; Stephen Collier, "Enacting Catastrophe: Preparedness, Insurance, Budgetary Rationalization." Economy and Society 37 (2008): 224–250.

national building, constituting an affective relation to destruction as the terms of a new collective beginning" (p. 27).[30]

It is not difficult to recognize how this logic of catastrophic future-making continues to animate contemporary discourses of "disaster preparedness." Rather than viewing the future as but an extension of the progressive development of the present (which is characteristic of the historical imagination of the modern nation-state, and its reliance on the logic of probability and risk[31]), the discourse of "disaster preparedness" marks an effort to conceptualize and manage an unimaginable future. Claudia Aradau and Rens Van Munster, in one of the few instances in which scholars have focused on the temporal specificities of catastrophe, characterize this dynamic in the following terms: "[I]f risk and probability introduce an array of finite possibilities for the future, catastrophe challenges the limits of possibility. Catastrophe is a temporal concept that points towards an unexpected future and, as such, breaks with the ways in which the future has been apprehended in modernity."[32] Fantasies of catastrophic ends thereby fold into practices of governance to forge a temporality of catastrophe made up equal parts of anxiety, calculation, and control.

Bringing together an interdisciplinary group of prominent scholars, *The Time of Catastrophe* demonstrates the analytic productiveness of posing a seemingly straightforward, if not redundant question—"When is catastrophe?" The chapters that follow ask: How are we to regard "catastrophic time" in relation to the specificities of actual lives, as they unfold in particular places and times? What schemes of action and thought are embedded within the frenzy of destruction and the urgency for response characteristic of catastrophe's dominant temporality? How does the urgency of catastrophic time obscure our capacity to recognize the conditions that produced catastrophes or other destructive processes, or competing conceptions of time and history circulating at any given moment? If we conceive of a catastrophe as both a destruction of lives as well as a breaking of time, how are we to understand the relationship between the catastrophic and the historical? In turn, how are we to conceptualize the close, if not mutually constitutive, proximity of catastrophe and the everyday, without dissolving the specificity of each into the other? Taken together, our contributors develop a critical language for examining "catastrophic time," and in so doing offer a set of frameworks for examining the alluring and elusive temporal qualities of catastrophe and the catastrophic.

---

30 See also Joseph Masco, *The Theater of Operations: National Security Affect from the Cold War to the War on Terror* (Durham: Duke University Press, 2014).

31 See Ulrich Beck, *Risk Society: Towards a New Modernity* (London: Sage, 1992)

32 Claudia Aradau and Rens van Munster, *Politics of Catastrophe: Genealogies of the Unknown* (New York: Routledge, 2011), 10.

Chapter 1
Catastrophe's Apocalypse

Joseph Masco

Does the catastrophic reference a specific event, or a potentiality? Is it always finite and episodic, a transformational rupture, and thus discernible as the opposite of normative everyday life? Or can the catastrophic also structure the very nature of the contemporary world, referencing forms of violence that are difficult to locate precisely because they are so deeply embedded in modern institutions and modes of living that they appear both natural and unending? In his "Commandments in the Atomic Age" the German philosopher Gunther Anders was definitive on the subject: "Your first thought upon awaking be: 'Atom.' For you should not begin your day with the illusion that what surrounds you is a stable world."[1] For Anders, the central conundrum of modernity is how technological capabilities have come to exceed human perception and understanding. This enables wide-ranging forms of violence to proceed as simply instrumental developments, operating without a collective critical assessment or social recognition of the new forms, velocities, or scales of violence being unleashed. The atomic bomb is, for him, emblematic of this process as in the name of security it installs a new possibility for collective death, making the nuclear age the ultimate example of self-alienation through technological revolution. As Anders puts it:

> Your second thought after awaking should run: "The possibility of the Apocalypse is our work. But we know not what we are doing." ... [This is an] effect of the daily growing gap between our two faculties: between our *action* and our *imagination*; of the fact, that we are unable to conceive what we can construct; to mentally reproduce what we can produce; to realize the reality which we can bring in to being. For in the course of the technical age the classical relation between imagination and action has reversed itself ... . We humans are smaller than ourselves.[2]

We humans are smaller than ourselves. Here, the incommensurability between the ability to engineer a technologically mediated universe while simultaneously expanding human perception to recognize all the new potentials put in motion

1 Gunther Anders, "Commandment in the Atomic Age" in *Burning Conscience: The Case of the Hiroshima Pilot Claude Eatherly, told in his Letters to Gunther Anders* (New York: Monthly Review Press, 1961), 11.

2 Ibid.

within that emerging universe is stark. The finite human ability to both build things and to assess the world-making/world-breaking effects of those undertakings, undoes reason, and installs danger ever deeper into the everyday. This "lag" between human industry and comprehension can be highly consequential, substantially remaking society and environment without a conscious intent or plan to do so. Catastrophe becomes, for Anders, a potential that is embedded within a modern mode of living that is no longer able to evaluate or register alternative futures or assess the social, material, or moral effects of ongoing technological revolution. Thus, in the nuclear age, an unreflexive allegiance to technological "progress" installs an escalating minute-to-minute possibility of collective death, challenging the terms of modernist rationality itself.[3]

From this point of view, the atomic revolution installs a catastrophic potential into everyday American life, one that has not abated since the end of the Cold War arms race (and is mirrored by the emerging environmental and social force of other industrial commitments—notably petrochemicals). But this historical fact raises another set of important and even more difficult and subtle questions: How has the nuclear danger—now approaching its eighth decade—shifted our ability to see and consider catastrophe itself, altering American thought and perception across the generations? What discursive forms have evolved to negotiate and/or naturalize the minute-to-minute collective danger of nuclear catastrophe; that is, where can we see nuclear fear publicly articulated, socially managed, and psychologically contained? What can transcend or expose a social world so structured by the possibilities of its own ending that contemplating catastrophe becomes socially normative, or merely a form of entertainment, or even just boring? Above all, we must ask: how does the cultural preoccupation with a specific vision of catastrophe block perception of other dangers (particularly slower moving crises, like global warming) less tuned to our post-nuclear sensibilities, thereby encouraging their ultimate expression?

This chapter interrogates how key terms—disaster, crisis, catastrophe, and apocalypse—function to define specific kinds and scales of violence and to load distinct futurities into those appraisals. It considers how we visualize such dangers across three domains:

1. in popular film (where mass destruction has become a highly commodified idiom bringing together vast photographic and animator expertise to portray in ever more convincing detail images of the end);
2. in the official nuclear war fighting plans of the U.S. government (a program to end life on a massive scale in the name of national security); and

3 See Paul Erickson, Judy Klein, Lorraine Daston, Rebecca Lemov, Thomas Sturm, and Michael Gordin, *How Reason Almost Lost its Mind: The Strange Career of Cold War Rationality* (Chicago: University of Chicago Press, 2013); and Joseph Masco "The End of Ends" *Anthropological Quarterly* 85, no. 4 (2012): 1107–24.

3. in the contemporary articulations of climate crisis (a kind of violence produced by the cumulative historical force of capitalist consumption and petrochemical extraction).

In each case, we will examine the cinematic visions that often come to stand in for the complexity of real world violence in the U.S. As we will see, the "catastrophic" has become so over-determined today that it can block thought, becoming a highly aestheticized register for entertainment, politics, and visions of the future. If Anders is correct that there is a disconnect between action and imagination in the world today, it is important to examine any national-cultural "familiarity" with ultimate endings, and to consider the everyday practices across a nuclear, petrochemical, capitalist, militarist economy that in their collective planetary force also transform the terms of life on earth. This chapter ultimately locates a crisis in the very nature of crisis, considering how and when the fast and slow violences of the industrial age emerge as objects of public concern.[4]

Species at/of War

> In our obsession with antagonisms of the moment, we often forget how much unites all members of humanity. Perhaps we need some outside, universal threat to make us recognize this common bond. I occasionally think how quickly our differences worldwide would vanish if we were facing an alien threat from outside of this world.
>
> Ronald Reagan, *Address to the 42nd Session of the United National General Assembly in New York, September 21, 1987.*

> Today at the edge of our hope, at the end of our time, we have chosen to believe in each other. Today, we face the monsters that are at our door. Today we are cancelling the apocalypse.
>
> *Pacific Rim* (2013)

In director Guillermo Del Toro's 2013 summer sci-fi blockbuster, *Pacific Rim*, invaders from another dimension open a rift in the floor of the Pacific Ocean, sending gigantic creatures through the portal hell-bent on destroying humanity.[5] Striding out of the ocean depths as literal leviathans, these monsters have no language, no culture, no purpose, except that of a pure destruction. Set in the near future, the film imagines an oceanic regional effort to fight this overpowering otherworldly force, providing the context for righteous violence, multi-national

4 Rob Nixon, *Slow Violence and the Environmentalism of the Poor* (Cambridge: Harvard University Press, 2011).

5 Guillermo Del Toro (director), *Pacific Rim.* 132-minute feature film. (Warner Brothers and Legendary Pictures, 2013).

camaraderie, and heroic individual sacrifice. Defense comes in the form of nuclear-powered humanoid machines, allowing a martial arts contest of giant robots (*Mecha*) against giant monsters (*Kaiju*), both of which level city spaces and produce mass casualties without comment or concern. This is an old story, one that draws on twentieth century Japanese and American nuclear cinema (particularly the giant radioactive creature films, *Godzilla* and *Them!*) as well as *manga*, and its familiarity is precisely the source of its presumed pleasure.[6] Its remarkable conceit is to merge a Japanese popular culture genre of nuclear victimization with an American nuclear triumphalism via the personal charisma of a black military leader of uncertain nationality (played by Idris Elba) who quite literally promises to cancel the apocalypse. Viewers learn that the nonhuman invaders tried once before to colonize Earth, in the era of the dinosaurs, but found the climate inhospitable and have been waiting for human industrial activities to warm the atmosphere to a cozy level for their species—making *Pacific Rim* a nuclear narrative as well as a climate narrative, all in one. The suture here is thus not only between national nuclear cultures, but also between apocalyptic concepts. The film is an act of catastrophic *bricolage*, a cutting and pasting of twentieth-century disaster tropes to imagine a humanity unified by environmental destruction, nuclear technologies, and total war.

The implicit promise of the film is the delivery of a state-of-the-art technological depiction of a child's universe of super-powered beings and inter-dimensional conflict, enabling a war that does not need to be ideologically or morally assessed or defended. It relies on a total war as normality frame but locates itself at a moment of maximal precariousness for people. Depicting a world that has largely collapsed, with citizens living in the ruins of Pacific coast cities, as well as in the carcasses of the leviathans, *Pacific Rim* serves up for viewer enjoyment a "last battle" for a world already destroyed. The Japanese filmic genre, *Kaiju* (featuring highly imaginative species of monsters) is important in that it frequently offers up allegories of nature's revenge against the industrial world: for more than a half-century, its incredible creatures (some the imagined product of irradiated ocean ecologies) have made fictional war on Japanese urban life with an special attention to nuclear power plants (eerily prefiguring the tsunami that flooded the Fukushima-Daiichi nuclear power plant in 2012 to such tragic effect). Tellingly, one almost always identifies with the monsters in this genre, as the nonhuman becomes a vengeful subject quite justified in attacking urban populations for crimes against nature (articulating longstanding Japanese anxieties about war, the un-memorialized dead, and ecological costs of urban consumption). The *Kaiju* genre depicts a kind of nature outside of human control but directly tied to human

6 See Mick Broderick (ed.), *Hibakusha Cinema: Hiroshima, Nagasaki and the Nuclear Image in Japanese Film* (New York: Kegan Paul, 1996); David Kalat, *A Critical History and Filmography of Toho's Godzilla Series* (Jefferson: McFarland and Company, 2010); and Joyce Evans, *Celluloid Mushroom Clouds: Hollywood and the Atomic Bomb* (Boulder: Westview Press, 1999).

actions, constituting a distinctly non-American nuclear culture of ecological disruption, mutation, and revenge. *Pacific Rim* merges this genre with an American technological fetishism and nuclear powered militarism to create the imaginary grounds for trans-national, -ethnic, and -gender belonging. Del Toro's ambitious film is thus lusciously absurd at every level; it is a form of ideological, historical, and cinematic dada.

The timing of this film about (ending the) apocalypse also is well worth interrogating.[7] Depicting a world of total war relying on the human/machine interface of new military technologies (robots/drones), with a plot organized around suicide attacks, and demonic, all-but-unknowable others, the film casually evokes the U.S. War on Terror, which also relies on images of an unstoppable enemy that cannot be reasoned with, who is committed to relentless violence in perpetuity. But if the first decade of counter-terror has demonstrated anything, it is the power of this enemy formation combined with a discourse of imminent catastrophic danger (the "terrorist armed with a weapon of mass destruction" in President George W. Bush's memorable configuration) to mislead. The terrorist enemy, in practice, has proven not only to be those who crash planes into buildings, but also a vast field of misrecognition and projection, sweeping up fantasized threats with the spectacularly outgunned, the abjectly poor, noncombatants, and children in many parts of the world. Killing in the second decade of counter-terror, for attentive U.S. citizens, has lost is heroic narrative of revenge and righteousness, evoking more readily today crimes against humanity rather than a national regeneration through violence. The declaration of what White House officials have alternatively called "the war on terror," "the long war", or simply, "the new normal" committed the U.S. in 2001 to a permanent war mobilization against an implacable, and all but unlocatable, foe. But today, this concept of war has itself become catastrophic, constituting a vastly violent, radically undemocratic, and spectacularly expensive global mobilization that offers up no vision of victory, truce, or a return to peacetime. Instead, the counter-terror state now addresses the future itself as a domain of unending threat, constituting a permanent field of imminent crisis.[8]

The leviathans of *Pacific Rim* are thus offered as an attempt to lure viewers into a universe where nonhumans, spectacularly rendered through Computer Generated Imagery (CGI) but lacking motivation or complexity, can be killed without remorse, and the aesthetics of their death can be offered up as a source of both pleasure and social renewal. The commercial tag line of the film, delivered by the charismatic British actor Idris Elba (who also portrayed Nelson Mandela in 2013), is thus a hopeful comment on our historical moment but also fundamentally a lie: the film cannot cancel the apocalypse because it relies entirely on the promise of a total destruction to create its appeal and market. The film, despite its

7 Kathleen Stewart and Susan Harding, "Bad Endings: American Apocalypsis" *Annual Review of Anthropology* 28 (1999): 285–310.

8 Joseph Masco, *The Theater of Operations: National Security Affect from the Cold War to the War on Terror* (Durham: Duke University Press, 2014).

ambition to be something more, is an "us or them" depiction of total war played out at the species level. In the summer of 2013, a time of widespread crises across the domains of war, finance, politics, and the environment, it was impossible to avoid this cinematic promise of an end to the apocalypse, shouted globally via an aggressive advertising campaign, installing all of its infantile desires for righteous killing and total victory into public spaces already saturated by counter-terror, collapsing markets, and ecological crisis. *Pacific Rim*, and the larger apocalyptic cinema genre it engages, offers us insight into the familiarity of the catastrophic as a social text in the early twenty-first century. It invites us to consider how evoking the catastrophic, as well as claiming the ability to control and defer the catastrophic, has become the very basis for the political today, a core feature in American storytelling, politics, and visions of the future.

Del Toro, for example, cinematically enacts President Ronald Reagan's public fantasy about how Cold War antagonisms could be overcome simply by the arrival of a new existential danger in the form of an extraterrestrial invasion.[9] Competing national-subjects would then become unified species subjects in Reagan's vision, ending the Cold War nuclear standoff instantly in favor of planetary defense. What is naturalized and thus unaddressed in both Reagan and Del Toro's vision is the commitment to total war. Both assume that threat constitutes the social and rely on a species-level "friend/enemy" distinction to organize human life on a new scale (constituting through war a social revolution without a difference).[10] After the World Wars of the twentieth century, it is a remarkable project to transform total war—an engineered catastrophe—from absolute crisis into the normative basis for society. Rehearsing and fantasizing collective disaster in this way also ultimately works to ward off consideration of actual destruction, as violence is imaginatively transformed from irrevocable loss into the exclusive basis for community and belonging (mirroring the longstanding American ideology of the frontier).[11]

Spectacles of disaster are also mesmerizing, and, through constant repetition, have the power to block thought, and to colonize the concept of danger with specific images tuned for maximal political effect. CGI technologies have opened a universe of potentially limitless storytelling, constituting ever evolving and advanced technologies of visualization.[12] Hollywood's summer blockbuster concept is indebted to this technological revolution, which has been devoted almost entirely to depictions of war, crisis, and disaster, worked out in increasing resolution and

---

9 Ronald Reagan, *Address to the 42nd Session of the United National General Assembly in New York, September 21, 1987*. Available at: http://www.reagan.utexas.edu/archives/speeches/1987/092187b.htm, accessed December 1, 2014.

10 Carl Schmitt, *The Concept of the Political* (Chicago: University of Chicago Press, 2007).

11 See Richard Slotkin, *Regeneration Through Violence: The Mythology of the American Frontier, 1600–1860* (Norman: University of Oklahoma Press, 2000).

12 See Kristen Whissel, *Spectacular Digital Effects: CGI and Contemporary Cinema* (Durham: Duke University Press, 2014).

detail. Thus, a very real question involves how to consider the catastrophic and not be intellectually overwhelmed or neutralized by its spectacle.[13] American society has rehearsed certain forms of absolute crisis now for generations, making them (particularly the mushroom cloud) the very tools of state and nation-building, filling the conceptual space of the catastrophic with specific images and fears to the exclusion of other concerns and potentials.

In other words, the catastrophic remains a highly aestheticized and thus a highly politicized concept in the twenty-first century United States. But the wide ranging utility of the catastrophic narrative today also reveals its ideological over-determination, as the truly catastrophic leaves no remainder. We need to ask then why is the catastrophic so conceptually powerful—as the designation of an ultimate violence—at this historical moment that it displaces all other modalities of future making in the U.S.? At what cost comes this historically generated "familiarity" with the catastrophic, this intimacy, indeed pleasure, in end time thinking? And what does the "catastrophic" render invisible in its depiction of both everyday violences and total endings?

Pacific Rim's promise to make the catastrophic fun again by creating a species level war belies the lived reality of collapsing infrastructures, ecological imbalance, and the cumulative effects of the war machine in the twenty-first century, while simultaneously evoking each of these topical concerns to constitute a consumerist relation to the apocalyptic. It assumes that viewers are walking out of the theater into an unbroken world, thus allowing its vision of end-times to be experienced through the pleasures of the sublime and the relative security of everyday comfort. The catastrophic here is simulated in order not to provoke thought and action but rather to satiate and dull viewer sensibility—to contain and reduce thought about external threats, environmental crisis, and war. In terms of domestic box office, *Pacific Rim* was the 34th most successful film of 2013, enough to insure a sequel. Its moderate success (at odds with the popularity of *Kaiju* as filmic genre as well as its $200 million special effects production and the talent of its director), however, might well be considered diagnostic of an over-determination in the mass media of disaster today. Perhaps a shift is occurring in the very terms of catastrophic reasoning—marking a more general crisis in the nature of crisis—in the early twenty-first century. Driven by the proliferation (and repeated political exploitation) of claims on end times, this would mark a social exhaustion in the U.S. with efforts to regenerate the national community through (real and simulated) violence. Perhaps today we are witnessing nothing less than catastrophe's apocalypse.

What would this mean? A "catastrophe" is not the same as a "crisis" or the "apocalyptic." Each of these concepts evokes a different degree of violence,

13 See Sigmund Freud, "Thoughts for the Times on War and Death (1915)" in *Civilization, Society and Religion*. The Penguin Freud Library, Volume 12. (London: Penguin, 1991), 57–89; and Jacques Derrida, "No Apocalypse, Not Now (Full Speed Ahead, Seven Missiles, Seven Missives)" *Diacritics* 20 (1984): 20–31.

operates on a different temporal scale, and offers up a specific perspective on the future. Each also has a different relation to a normative everyday, by which I mean a predictable social space unmarked by radical surprise. Crisis implies a threat to a system or infrastructure, and precisely because it is not yet catastrophic presents an opportunity for maximal political urgency and utility. We talk about the political *crisis* of the federal government today because the gridlock of the two party system is not yet recognized to be a catastrophe; that is, an irrevocable violence. A crisis can be resolved to maintain the existing structure of a system, while a *catastrophe* involves the ruination of that system in some kind of permanent manner. Crisis is a potential, but catastrophe is a lived ending, an actual form of destruction. An *apocalypse*, however, evokes more than simply destruction; it also references a revelation, an intellectual uncovering of matter as it actually is, a revealing of some kind of previously inaccessible truth. An apocalypse produces new insight through destruction, a disclosure of hidden knowledge, which is why it is linked so strongly with religiosity—it is a reality hidden behind the social world made visible through ruination.

So, in our era of normalized end-time politics, what would transform the catastrophic into a form of revelation, a mode of social critique that could register more than just damage? What would denaturalize existing catastrophic practices and blunt simple fear-based emotional management campaigns, to make contemplating the end an opportunity for critical insight and self-understanding? In what follows, I explore catastrophe's apocalypse in two major visions of the end: in U.S. nuclear war plans from the height of the Cold War, and in the projections of contemporary climate science, exploring not only the futurities but also the revelatory potentials embedded in assessing life as permanent catastrophe. In particular, I wish to consider the historical conditions of possibility for assessing catastrophic potentials, as well as interrogate the slippages or disconnects between agency and imagination (as Anders would phrase it) for those living in a highly mass mediated, and technologically infused, universe.

Nuclear End-Times

In the U.S., nuclear fear colonized the very idea of the catastrophic in the twentieth century. It was officially deployed to create a new kind of national security state, and with it, a new citizen-state relationship mediated by images of absolute destruction. During the Cold War, the nuclear state not only built a meticulous global machinery for nuclear war, it also taught Americans to think and feel as nuclear subjects, to contemplate a sudden end of the U.S. and transform that cataclysmic vision into a perverse new form of nation-building. What we remember today as Civil Defense, the duck and cover drills and national nuclear attack exercises of the first decades of the Cold War were the means of installing specific ideas about nuclear crisis within American society, and then mobilizing that imagined crisis as a means of militarizing the public. The cataclysmic became a formal basis for political life in this moment, making claims on the imminent death of the nation a powerful new form of state- and nation-building. The nuclear revolution was thus both technological and psycho-social, simultaneously material, cultural, and emotional.

We forget today that the nuclear crisis has not always been with us, that before 1945 the future had many worries but not one overpowering, totalizing one. In the U.S., the atomic bomb has always been a double-edged revolution, simultaneously installing a new domestic vulnerability (in the form of surprise nuclear attack) as well as an absolute offensive power (in the form of the U.S. nuclear arsenal). The bomb becomes the basis for U.S. "superpower" standing but also reorganizes collective death as imminence, a pure potential loaded into every second of everyday life. Thus, it sutures the ability to destroy and be destroyed in a new machine form, one that folds official terrors and hegemonic desires together in a novel configuration. Beginning in the early 1950s, the public project of Civil Defense was to teach Americans to respond to nuclear danger productively as Cold Warriors, to train the public to psychologically engage nuclear crisis as the basis of American power and international order.[14] Civil Defense constituted (that is, both invented and installed) a new register of threat in everyday American life, the surprise nuclear attack that would decimate urban America and leave the rest of the country a radioactive ruin in a matter of minutes. Civil Defense was rehearsed for generations in public schools and through national mass media campaigns, and informs official disaster planning to this day. Its extraordinarily achievement was to turn contemplating the end of the nation-state into a form of national building, constituting an affective relation to destruction as the terms of a new collective beginning.[15]

This image of catastrophe, constituting the public side of nuclear war planning, was extraordinarily influential, enabling a new kind of Cold War consensus of anti-communism and global capitalism through mass psycho-social domestic regulation. In other words, by deploying the imminence of ultimate danger and using official secrecy to carefully calibrate the depiction of nuclear threat, the Cold War nuclear state transformed catastrophe itself into a politicized and instrumental vision, a core tool of domestic governance. Evoking the sudden end of American civilization has since become a basic tool in governance, a reliable means of blocking domestic debate as well as taking extraordinary international actions—most recently, invading other states (such as, Iraq in 2003) and conducting deadly drone strikes around the world.

But if the public side of Cold War nuclear crisis was civil defense, with its commitment to emotional management via images of the end of the nation-state,

---

14 See Guy Oakes, *The Imaginary War: Civil Defense and American Cold War Culture* (New York: Oxford University Press, 1994); and Jackie Orr, *Panic Diaries: A Genealogy of Panic Disorder* (Durham: Duke University Press 2006).

15 Joseph Masco, *The Theater of Operations: National Security Affect from the Cold War to the War on Terror* (Durham: Duke University Press, 2014).

what about official logics and registers; that is, what of the actual governance of nuclear war? With that question in mind let's consider the U.S. nuclear war plan of the early Cold War, the first formally coded U.S. nuclear war strategy, an official program for planetary destruction.[16] Conceived during a period of hyperactive U.S. and Soviet thermonuclear testing in the late 1950s, the official U.S. nuclear war program was breathtakingly simple and unprecedentedly violent.[17] The U.S. nuclear war plan consisted of two versions of the same option: a pre-emptory strike against global communism, and a retaliatory strike against global communism.[18] Both plans involved using the entire U.S. nuclear arsenal to eliminate communism worldwide (from the Soviet Union to North Korea to China) within a few hours of nuclear warfare. Thus, it inscribed as U.S. policy a commitment to maximal violence as "defense." This program was depicted in a U.S. Air Force film, *The Power of Decision*, commissioned in 1958 strictly for internal military use.[19] It was declassified, and provided to the openness activists at the National Security Archive by the U.S. National Archives and Records Administration in 2010, having not likely been watched in decades.[20] This is a rare record of how those in control of the nuclear arsenal first imagined and internally discussed fighting a global nuclear war. It was made for restricted internal Air Force use and thus was not trying to minimize the consequences of nuclear war for a public audience along the lines of Civil Defense, but rather sought to shape ideas about the rationality and reliability of the nuclear system itself for war fighters. As the American public was learning to duck and cover in the event of nuclear war, the command and control officers were learning how to push the buttons to launch a new kind of totalizing violence.

16 See Scott D. Sagan, "SIOP-62: The Nuclear War Plan Briefing to President Kennedy" *International Security* 12 no. 1 (1987): 22–51; and Desmond Ball and Robert C. Toth, "Revising the SIOP: Taking War-Fighting to Dangerous Extremes" *International Security* 14, no. 4 (1990): 65–92.

17 See L. Douglas Keeney, *15 Minutes: General Curtis LeMay and the Countdown to Nuclear Annihilation* (New York: St. Martin's Press, 2012); and L. Douglas Keeney, *The Doomsday Scenario* (St. Paul: MBI Publishing Company, 2002).

18 David Alan Rosenberg and W. B. Moor, "Smoking Radiating Ruin at the End of Two Hours: Documents on American Plans for Nuclear War with the Soviet Union, 1954–55" *International Security* 6, no. 3(1981–2): 3–38; and David Alan Rosenberg, "The Origins of Overkill; Nuclear Weapons and American Strategy, 1945–1960" *International Security* 7, no. 4(1983): 3–71.

19 U.S. Air Force, *The Power of Decision*. 47-minute documentary film (U.S. Air Force, 1958). Available at:

https://archive.org/details/AirForceSpecialFilmProject416powerOfDecision, accessed December 1, 2014.

20 William Burr (ed), "Nobody Wins in a Nuclear War but Success is Possible" *National Security Archive Electronic Briefing Book No. 336*, 2011. Available at: http://www2.gwu.edu/%7Ensarchiv/nukevault/ebb336/index.htm, accessed December 1, 2014.

Walking viewers through the command and control logics of nuclear weapons and war, the film offers a factual, and remarkably affectless, depiction of how the U.S. and the Soviet Union would consume each other under mushroom clouds. The film constitutes the ability of U.S. command and control to survive a nuclear attack and successfully retaliate as a "victory," regardless of the subsequent global nuclear cataclysm. Viewers are told early on that the U.S. has the power to "strike anywhere in the world" and, in a few hours of nuclear war, deliver "more explosive power than has been used that in all the previous wars in human history combined." Thus, this film is also about American self-fashioning as a reluctant but supremely powerful warrior-state, articulating the imaginary terms for righteous revenge against a surprise Soviet attack. *Power of Decision* depicts a psychosocial field of projection and fantasy, but one mediated by a global technological infrastructure of mass destruction.

Film has always been a key means of establishing—giving both form and image—to the nuclear danger in the U.S. Nuclear fear had to be learned before it could be felt. The nuclear security state created films for every audience—military personnel, civilians, scientists, and politicians—each crafted to bring them into a specific relationship to the bomb.[21] The vibrant production of public films for civil defense was only exceeded by the production of classified films for use within the weapons laboratories, military branches, and for policy makers. *The Power of Decision* establishes the serious authority and closed world system of early nuclear war plans within the classified networks of the time but also, in detailing how the U.S. would fight a nuclear war, demonstrates the paradox of that authority.[22] Here security and insecurity meet under the sign of the mushroom cloud, and nuclear governance—despite an all-out effort to make it logical and proportional—is rendered absurd as it contemplates generating hundreds of millions of deaths worldwide in a few minutes of nuclear warfare.

In the opening frame of *The Power of Decision*, viewers meet an Air Force officer, who stares directly at the camera and introduces the film. The style of his presentation is that of a military briefing, blunt but with certain flourishes: declaring that he is standing hundreds of feet underground in a blast and radiation proof bunker, our narrator theatrically walks through layer upon layer of internal security to the command center itself, stating that: "From this room, the [Air] Force throughout the world is controlled and monitored twenty-four hours a day—in peace as it would be in war." Rendering the distinction between war and peace suddenly murky, our narrator quickly introduces viewers to the "Big Board"—an analog map of all the various strike routes aimed at the Soviet Union, as well as the exercises that are currently taking place. A tangled web of multicolored lines, the diagram obliterates the USSR under the weight of Air Force bomber

21 See Joseph Masco, "Target Audience" *The Bulletin of the Atomic Scientists* 64, no.3 (2008): 23–31.

22 See Paul Edwards, *The Closed World: Computers and the Politics of Discourse in Cold War America* (Cambridge: MIT Press, 2006).

vectors, actual planes in the air, potential exercises, feints, and alerts. We are told that attack vectors are being flown every minute of every day and, to keep "the enemy" from being able to predict American routes and strategies, that there are fake exercises mixed into the planned assault strategy. Viewers are introduced to the "red phone," which over-rides all other communications in an alert, as well as the multiple systems for gaining information about the global fleet of American planes and the military actions of enemy states. This depiction of a global early warning and command and control system is the formal project of the film, but steely determination to fight a nuclear war is the fetish. Defense and deterrence are collapsed into nuclear war fighting ability in this presentation, which depicts nuclear war as an affectless circuit of human-machine interfaces and expertise. The will to fight is portrayed as equally crucial to the technological infrastructure of nuclear war as the bomb itself.

The film is organized in two parts, the first a briefing of Air Force nuclear logistics focused on "Operation Quickstart" (the ongoing training for nuclear attack), while the second, "Operation War Dance" offers a live action illustration of the process of recognizing a Soviet attack, pursuing an American counter-strike, and then conducting a post-nuclear war damage assessment. In the first part, an animation of the globe demonstrates how U.S. and Soviet aircraft can now fly over the polar north to attack one another, underscored by a second animation of a globe covered in mushroom clouds (see Figure 1.1). This animation is the precursor to dramatizing the global sequence of nuclear war, this time structured around actual U.S. nuclear test footage of thermonuclear detonations, as well as blast and destruction sequences from the nuclear test program, all intercut with staged command and control decision-making. The largely analog universe of American command control and information systems is presented as cutting edge technology, allowing near instantaneous global communications, a 24/7 monitoring of Soviet activities, and an always on alert nuclear Air Force that has at least 15 percent of its fleet in the air at all times. This is a system claiming the highest level of rationality: technological precision is combined with exacting timetables, sequential assessments, and escalating actions, but inevitably this techno-scientific system results in the end of the known world. Thus, the hyper-rationality of the nuclear system is mobilized in an attempt to over-ride the inevitable reality of its use, showing how security and defense have paradoxically merged with mass violence on a new kind of planetary scale in Cold War nuclear logics.

As reports come into the command center of a Soviet first use of nuclear weapons in Europe and Japan, a general intones: "By giving up the initiative, the West must expect to take the first blow." This is a coded reference to pre-emption, as nuclear debates in the 1950s focused on the illogic of allowing a nuclear strike on the U.S. if it could be pre-empted by a surprise U.S. nuclear attack on the Soviet Union. The head of the Strategic Air Command, Curtis LeMay, advocated striking the Soviet Union before their nuclear forces reached parity with the U.S..[23] But a U.S. military culture founded on the Japanese "sneak attack" at Pearl Harbor resisted the logics of nuclear pre-emption, arguing that such an assault would be against American values. Moreover, in the age of thermonuclear weapons, a pre-emptory attack would not eliminate the possibility of a nuclear counter-attack (precisely what is documented in *The Power of Decision*). As the film theatrically presents, no matter who starts a nuclear conflict, massive destruction occurs all around the world: there is no place of safety on planet Earth during a nuclear war. *The Power of Decision* is ultimately a documentary about a "defense system" that is also a planetary mechanism of collective suicide.

The Air Force soon unleashes its nuclear bombers, staging sequential and incremental runs across Soviet territories to close in on "Target M", presumably Moscow, which is soon reported destroyed. After less than a day of nuclear warfare, the U.S. has eliminated the Soviet Union, as one U.S. General puts it: "They must quit: We have the air and the power and they know it." But what does such a victory look like? The after assessment, also a briefing on the big board, reveals a stark reality: while the U.S. nuclear system worked perfectly in terms of command and control, over 60 million Americans are dead or injured. The industrial core of the U.S.—Detroit, Chicago, Pittsburgh, as well as New York—is destroyed. Similarly, major cities in Europe, Japan, as well as much of the Soviet Union and China are radioactive ruins. Viewers do not get an assessment of the total global dead. But in addition to the urban destruction, radioactive fallout would travel globally bringing a second wave of death in the form of radiation injury. In 1958, a "nuclear winter"—produced by the combined atmospheric effects of the particulate matter elevated into the stratosphere by destroying cities on this scale—was not yet an operative concept.[24] Thus, weather is only discussed as a problem for managing planes in flight and is not yet part of the post-nuclear world assessment, which we now know would likely include a massively destabilized climate. But, even on its own terms, *The Power of Decision* documents the nuclear cataclysm as a techno-rational system, one in which the ability to exert American "will" on the Soviet Union is constituted as a victory despite the hundreds of millions of deaths worldwide, leaving an image of victory at the end that is apocalyptic at its core. The insight that war is now too deadly to actually fight is a repeated refrain in the film. But this refrain is undermined by the obvious pleasure in detailing exactly how the nuclear war machine would function in a matter of minutes to bring about an unprecedented, and perhaps the very last, global calamity.

---

23 L. Douglas Keeney, *15 Minutes: General Curtis LeMay and the Countdown to Nuclear Annihilation* (New York: St. Martin's Press, 2012).

24 See Paul R. Ehrlich, Carl Sagan, Donald Kennedy and Walter Orr Roberts *The Cold and the Dark: The World After Nuclear War* (New York: W.W. Norton, 1984); and Lynn Eden, *Whole World on Fire: Organization, Knowledge, & Nuclear Weapons Devastation* (Ithaca: Cornell University Press, 2004).

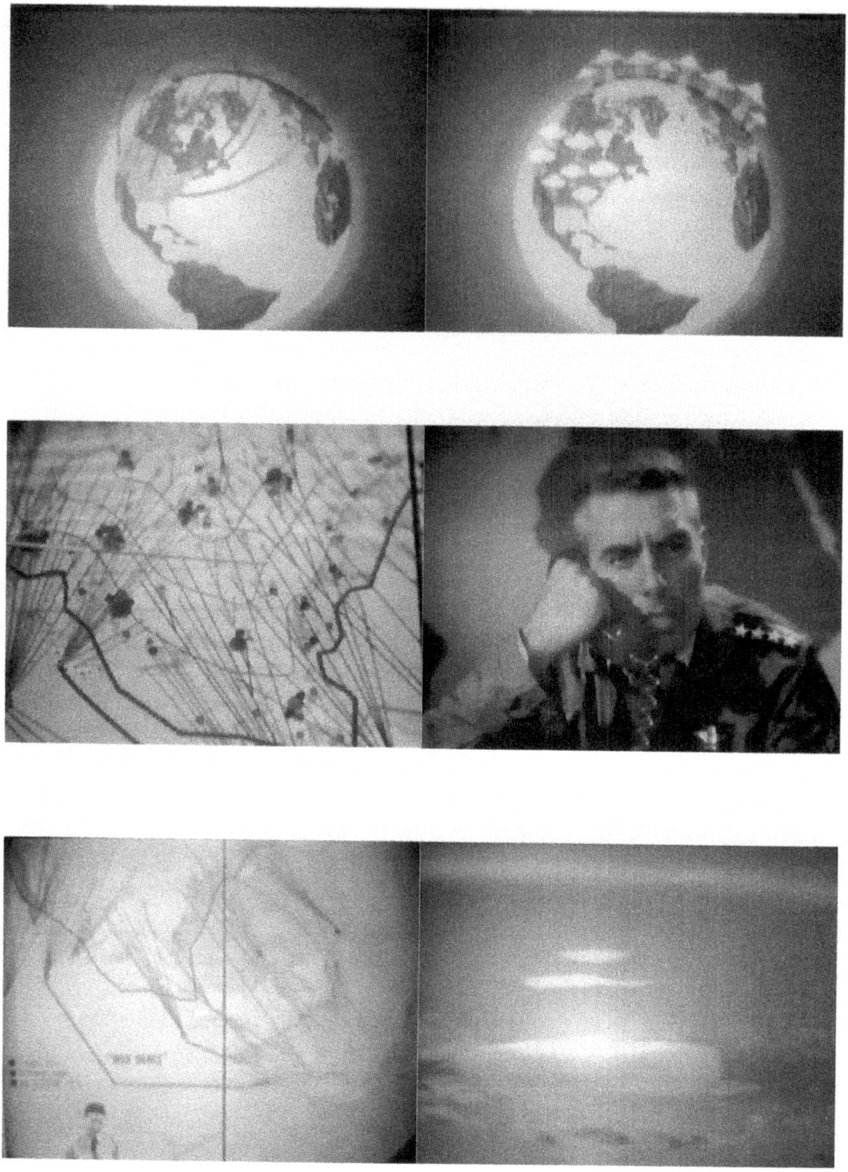

Figure 1.1 **Stills from *Power of Decision* (1958, U.S. Air Force, courtesy of the National Security Archive)**

This ever-expanding technical capacity to fight a global nuclear war constitutes the first human generated and controlled planetary crisis. In the first decade of the Cold War, people faced the possibility of an absolute ending of their own making for the first time, a political deployment of a global infrastructure of mass destruction in which there might not be a human left to tell the story of what happened and why. In this regard, *The Power of Decision* does not contemplate what the world would be like for the nuclear war fighting team as they leave the bunker, return to the surface, and enter the post-nuclear ruins. The new American empire would be highly radioactive, subject to a radically destabilized climate, and structured by unprecedented levels of material damage and psychological trauma. It might be a technical victory for the U.S. within the logics of the Cold War system as the film claims, but a planetary cataclysm nonetheless, all achieved in less than a day of warfare. *The Power of Decision* offers no insight into the cause or logic of the Soviet attack or considers the existence of the nuclear war machine itself, opting for a factual treatment of machines, vectors, targets, and casualties. There is no room for diplomacy in this vision—only military action. What is also lost in the description of closed world machines and nuclear delivery systems is the extraordinary amount of work that it took to build a global doomsday system. With each frame the nuclear fetish is ever more naturalized in this filmic production, making catastrophe the basis for state power rather than a feat of human engineering that could simply be dismantled or not extended in the name of collective security. Indeed, after 1958, the U.S. nuclear arsenal only grows in both numbers and explosive power, reaching a peak of over 35,000 nuclear weapons by the end of the 1960s, enough to destroy every major city on the planet many times over. U.S. "defense" remains to this day founded on the ability to strike anywhere on planet earth, and to destroy all major population centers outside the U.S., within a few minutes of nuclear warfare.

Culturally, this notion of the end—of a nuclear strike that obliterates totally and almost instantaneously—has come to define American notions of the cataclysmic. From nuclear war to the war on terror, U.S. security logics are structured by fear of the surprise attack that is constituted as both imminent and complete. To a remarkable degree, nuclear fear has been coded into the idea of disaster itself in American culture, allowing counter-formations that attempt to be equally total, equally surprising, equally violent. In this way, building a counter-communist state during the Cold War (and, a counter-terror state today) has relied on certain images of the end, promoted and magnified via official state systems as a means of affectively mobilizing diverse publics and experts. With constant technological improvements in missiles and warhead design, speed soon became a particular problem in the nuclear age. By the 1960s, the technological terms of nuclear war had advanced to such an extent that the entire system had to be slowed down to allow human decision-making in the midst of crisis. Everything from the telephone hot line between U.S. and Soviet leaders (established after the Cuban Missile Crisis) to nuclear war plans themselves were structured around the realization that a nuclear war could start before there was time for a political debate or alternative action to launching a full counter-strike.[25] The

25 William Burr (ed.), "The Creation of SIOP-62: More Evidence on the Origins of Overkill" *National Security Archive Electronic Briefing Book No. 130*, 2004. Available at: http://www.gwu.edu/~nsarchiv/NSAEBB/NSAEBB130/index.htm, accessed December 1,

always-on-alert system of missiles-bombers-submarines armed with thermonuclear weapons made *not* launching a nuclear war a minute-to-minute calculus, and then naturalized that restraint as the basis of "defense".

In psycho-social terms, this means that Americans have lived for more than half a century in the temporal space in which the missiles may have always already been launched—that is, within the 15-minute window offered by early warning systems. The nuclear cataclysm thus may have always already happened, with simply the global fallout to be negotiated. Nuclear crisis has in this way come to structure our very idea of crisis, where the sudden shock of a total ending becomes the basis for thinking large-scale threat. The slow and slower violences of capital, energy, health, and environment become difficult to see as forms of cataclysmic violence precisely because nuclear war offers Americans so perfect and speedy an image of the end.[26] Our notions of catastrophe today have been crafted by the nuclear system, which invented a machinery and imaginary of ultimate endings. This concept of danger—totalizing and short—is forever at odds with non-totalizing violences, cataclysms of slower duration, and particularly threats that exceed the power of the nation-state itself.

Atmospheres of Destruction

> Warming of the climate system is unequivocal.
>
> Human influence on the climate system is clear.
>
> It is very likely that the Arctic sea ice cover will continue to shrink and thin…
>
> Continued emissions of greenhouse gases will cause further warming and changes in all components of the climate system.
>
> IPCC, *Climate Change 2013*

The latest projections of the Intergovernmental Panel on Climate Change (IPCC) are startlingly depicting a new kind of collective violence that is escalating and will play out over the coming centuries in every ecosystem on Earth (see

2014; and "To Have the Only Option That of Killing 80 Million People is the Height of Immorality: The Nixon Administration, the SIOP, and the Search for Limited Nuclear Options, 1969–1974" *National Security Archive Electronic Briefing Book No. 173*, 2005. Available at: http://www.gwu.edu/~nsarchiv/NSAEBB/NSAEBB173/index.htm, accessed December 1, 2014.

26 Rob Nixon, *Slow Violence and the Environmentalism of the Poor* (Cambridge: Harvard University Press, 2011).

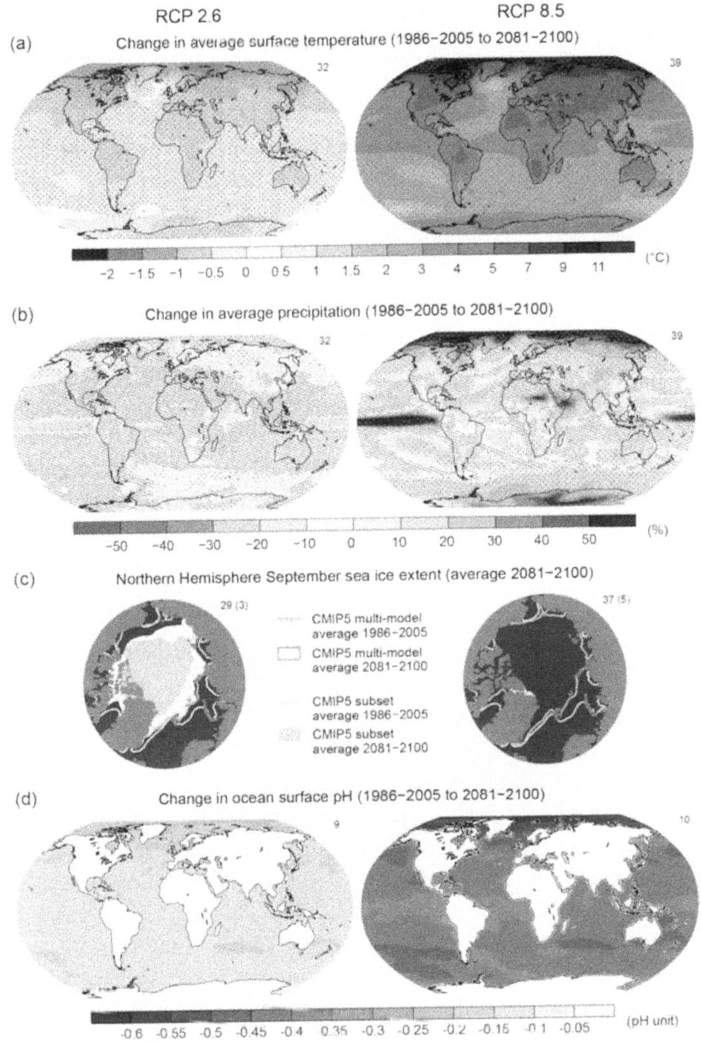

Figure 1.2 IPCC chart on climate change in the twenty-first century

Figure 1.2).[27] The extraordinary achievement of the IPCC is its radical interdisciplinary and multi-national cooperation, allowing teams of scientists across a vast range of fields to integrate huge data sets, and via computer

27 Intergovernmental Panel on Climate Change (IPCC), *Climate Change 2013: The Physical Science Basis, Summary for Policymakers*. Available at: http://www.ipcc.ch/repor/ar5/wg1/, accessed December 1, 2014.

simulations, project atmospheric effects out into the coming decades.[28] The portrait of the coming century that the IPCC presents, however, is not pretty and asks us to seriously rethink industrial age understandings of both progress and catastrophe. The predicted elevation of the global temperature by between two and six degrees by mid-century, the IPCC argues, will create increasingly volatile conditions. The reduction in polar ice will lead to rising ocean levels, which will flood islands and coastal cities worldwide. It will also produce a more acidic ocean leading to vast oceanic dead zones. Similarly, extreme weather patterns (producing regional droughts and flooding) will challenge food production worldwide, while changing habitat zones on a massive scale and enabling new emerging diseases. Moreover, human population growth, potentially rising from 7 to 9 billion people by 2050, will create more consumers, and only increase pressure on the global environment. The resulting ecological stress could exceed what ecologists calculate is the "carrying capacity" of the global biosphere, leading to widespread scarcity or even more shocking ecological destabilizations. The worst-case vision is of future where the food chain collapses, leading to mass starvation and pushing species of all kinds towards extinction.

Earth Scientists note that over 99 percent of the life forms that have ever lived on our planet have gone extinct. Extinction is thus not the exception but rather the rule over the long, *longue duree* of life on planet Earth. The best estimates today are that some four billion species have evolved over the past 3.5 billion years on this planet, almost all to die out. In addition to the process of natural selection in eliminating and promoting particular species, there have been five mass extinction events, periods where due to asteroid collisions or planetary-scale climatic changes, two-thirds or more of all the organisms on Earth have disappeared. In light of the IPCC assessments, there is much discussion today of a sixth mass extinction event—an ongoing shift in the terms of living on our planet drawn from the combined impacts of habitat destruction, pollution, overharvesting, invasive species, and human population growth. This sixth mass extinction will be unique in our planet's history as it does not arrive in the form of an asteroid collision or volcanic eruption, but rather through the hyperactive work on one indigenous species: people. The industrial age human has become an ecological, even a geological force, constituting a future of fewer species, less biodiversity, and potentially catastrophic disruptions in the food chain.[29]

Climate change thus now posits a vision of end-times that rivals that of the nuclear danger, as the incremental and cumulative effects of human industry have foundationally shifted the atmospheric chemistry on our planet, setting off a reverberating chain of effects throughout the biosphere. But if the global nuclear danger is characterized by its shocking immediacy, climate danger works on an

28 Paul Edwards, *The World In A Machine: Computer Models, Data Networks, and Global Atmospheric Politics* (Cambridge: MIT Press, 2010).

29 See Elizabeth Kolbert, *The Sixth Extinction: An Unnatural History* (New York: Henry Holt and Company, 2014).

opposite temporality, constituting a slower violence that is treacherous precisely because it is so incremental that it is difficult in any given moment to sense a change in the environment or to connect discreet issues (such as, sea level or drought or violent weather) to industrially generated greenhouse gas emissions. It is a cumulative and momentum driven process, operating on so vast a scale that it raises basic questions about human perception, memory, and the terms of visualization appropriate for a planetary problem. In light of climate change, geologists are now debating how to sequence planetary time to recognize the effects of human industry. The professional geological societies are formally contemplating the adoption of the term "anthropocene" to designate the era of human impacts on the planet, a startling recognition of a new agentive force on Earth; as leading advocates of the concept put it:

> The advent of the Anthropocene, the time interval in which human activities now rival global geophysical processes, suggests that we need to fundamentally alter our relationship with the planet we inhabit. Many approaches could be adopted, ranging from geoengineering solutions that purposefully manipulate parts of the Earth System to becoming active stewards of our own life support system. The Anthropocene is a reminder that the Holocene, during which complex human societies have developed, has been a stable, accommodating environment and is the only state of the Earth System that we know for sure can support contemporary society. The need to achieve effective planetary stewardship is urgent. As we go further into the Anthropocene, we risk driving the Earth System into a trajectory toward more hostile states from which we cannot easily return.[30]

Geoengineering, life support systems, planetary stewardship—these are the terms of a new kind of emergency, one that operates on a total environmental scale. The 10,000-plus years of the Holocene emerges as a temporary atmospheric condition on planet Earth, one particularly beneficial to humans, who, living in that special air, rose to become the dominant species, inventing agriculture, writing, cars, computers, and atomic bombs in the process. Our concept of the planet is now fundamentally shifting, from literally the stable ground under our feet, unchangeable in its nature, to a "lifeboat" in hostile waters, underscoring that the fragile environmental envelope on which we depend is changing under accumulated industrial stresses.

Historian Dipesh Chakrabarty has pointed out how climate change merges human history with natural history, creating a new kind of temporality that radically undercuts longstanding logics of economic progress and development.[31]

---

30 Will Steffen et al., "The Anthropocene: From Global Change to Planetary Stewardship" *Ambio* 40 (2011): 739–61.

31 Dipesh Chakrabarty, "The Climate of History: Four Theses" *Critical Inquiry* 35 (2009): 197–222.

This collapsing of human time into geological time forces us to think on unfamiliar scales—such as, the planet—and to think not of populations and nation-states but species level human impacts (earth systems of air, ice, water, and geology). Thus, climate change as a collective problem challenges our political, economic and industrial orders, requiring not only a reverse engineering of global infrastructure to prevent a deepening ecological crisis, but also new conceptual structures. Here, the built universe of things and the desires that organize our consumption patterns are revealed to be literally catastrophic. The petrochemical economy that has revolutionized human society has unintentionally generated an unprecedented global environmental crisis, one that transforms the smallest of everyday activities—driving in a car or eating a hamburger—into a new kind of end-times. Hamburgers, the quintessential American fast food, are ruinous for the planet. In fact, geologists now use the global proliferation of McDonald's restaurants as an index of *anthropocenic* environmental change.[32] Every aspect of the mass-produced burger—from the management of cattle to the global supply chains to the plastic containers—is now a planetary force. Here, the catastrophic is revealed to be not just an external threat—an asteroid or foreign attack—it is now coded into tastes, desires, and naturalized modes of consumption. The everyday consumption patterns of each person on the planet, unremarkable in their singularity, have become cumulatively destructive in their species totality. This makes the basic requirements for human life (including food, transportation, heating, clothing) fundamentally dangerous to the future stability of the climate as they are embedded in a petrochemical economy. The virtues of modernization, globalization, and technology have thus been turned upside down by climate change: rather than extending equality, security, and comfort, these practices are a negative form of geoengineering, putting ever more pressure on the atmospheric "lifeboat" on which we depend. McDonald's Big Mac now joins the atomic bomb as an existential threat to the collective future.

How could such a calamity—with so many vectors of change—appear so suddenly in American life, challenging twenty-first century society simultaneously to reinvent economy, consumption, and governance? Climate change has, of course, been a scientific concern for decades, emerging from the data sets and theories of Cold War earth sciences.[33] Indeed, one can find speculations about radical climate change from the mid-twentieth century that are eerie from a contemporary point

32 Will Steffen et al., "The Anthropocene: From Global Change to Planetary Stewardship" *Ambio* 40 (2011), 742.

33 Dale Jamison, *Reason in a Dark Time: Why the Struggle Against Climate Change Failed and what it Means for our Future* (New York: Oxford University Press, 2014); Spencer Weart, *The Discovery of Global Warming* (Cambridge: Harvard University Press, 2008); Joseph Masco, "Terraforming Planet Earth" in Elizabeth Deloughrey, Jill Didur, and Anthony Carrigan (eds) *Global Ecologies and the Environmental Humanities: Postcolonial Approaches* (New York: Routledge, 2015), pp. 309–32.

of view.[34] Consider Frank Capra's 1958 educational film, *Unchained Goddess*, part of The Bell Laboratory Science Series, a post-Sputnik campaign to interest Americans in scientific careers hosted by literary professor Frank Baxter.[35] The film, which merges cartoon characters, experts, actors, and documentary footage, presents an overview of meteorology but ends with a disturbing hypothesis about the future (see Figure 1.3). After a discussion of the possibility of weather modification and control, Baxter cautions:

> Extremely dangerous questions, because with our present knowledge we have no idea what would happen. Even now Man may be unwittingly changing the world's climate through the waste products of his civilization. Due to our release through our factories and automobiles every year of more than six billion tons of carbon dioxide, which helps air absorb heat from the sun, our atmosphere seems to be getting warmer … It's been calculated that a few degrees rise in the earth's temperature would melt the polar ice caps. And if this happens, an inland sea would fill a good portion of the Mississippi Valley. Tourists in glass bottom boats would be viewing the grand towers of Miami through 150-feet of tropical water. For in weather we are not only dealing with forces of a far greater variety than even the atomic physicists encounters but with life itself. Without air and water, which are weather, Man would never have appeared on this small planet earth. There would be no sky, no ocean, no fields, no forests, nothing but a barren rock rotating in an airless void.

Tourists in glass bottom boats over Miami. So what was part of a basic public survey of climatology in 1958 has suddenly become a collective emergency in the twenty-first century. The privileging of economy and nuclear threat over all other concerns in the second half of the twentieth century required a subsuming of climate danger, with mounting consequences. Thus, the environment emerges here as a problem not just of knowledge but also of perception, not just of understanding but also of collective memory. Catastrophe's apocalypse is to recognize the human agency not only in producing anthropogenic changes in the environment but also in mystifying and occluding those understandings while the problem intensifies.

Given the scale of environmental crisis, one of the immediate problems concerns its visualization and narration—of how to make hyper-complex, planetary dangers intelligible to nonexperts. We do not yet have a popular culture of climate change to match that of the nuclear danger, but it is emerging. J.C. Chandor's 2013 film, *All Is Lost*, offers a disciplined start to such an endeavor.[36] The plot is simple:

34 See, for example, Libby Robin, Sverker Sorlin, and Paul Warde (eds), *The Future of Nature* (New Haven: Yale University Press, 2013).

35 Richard Carlson, *The Unchained Goddess* 57-minute film (Bell Telephone Series, 1958)

36 J.C. Chandor (director), *All Is Lost* 106-minute feature film (Liongate, 2013).

a seventy-something white American male (played by Robert Redford) is alone, "somewhere in the Indian Ocean," sleeping comfortably in his sailboat when an errant shipping container afloat in the open ocean ruptures the hull. After attempting to patch the hole, he endures a massive storm and is forced onto an inflatable lifeboat when the sailboat sinks. Drifting into shipping lanes, he repeatedly tries to signal gigantic freighters (stacked with the kind of containers that damaged his ship) for help, but they pass him by unnoticed, completely indifferent to his plight. Eight traumatic days later, out of supplies and hope, he sees a light on the nighttime horizon that might be a small boat, he accidently ignites his lifeboat in hopes of drawing attention to his plight and watches from underneath the water as his sole means of shelter goes up in flames. The last frames of the film are of a hand from a small rescue boat reaching down into the ocean offering our protagonist one last chance for survival, which he swims towards.

A story with one character, known simply as "Our Man," and only two real words of dialog—"help" (thrown in vain at shipping vessels) and a singular "fuck" (when the situation turns irrevocable)—the story is ultimately about the fragility of all lifeboats. Our Man is the quintessential master of industry. He is likely retired and wealthy enough to own the boat. He is also a man of action, both able and strong. When problems appear he does not complain or hesitate but responds with a learned confidence (even taking time to shave before the giant storm hits). He does not make any real mistakes. The weather and ocean are simply too strong for his technology, which continually breaks down, but it is more than bad luck. It is as if his vision of danger is out of synch with the universe he now inhabits and despite his best efforts and seriousness, his world falls apart. The story can also be read as an illustration of the indifference of global capital to individual suffering: the shipping container that strikes his boat is carrying children's sneakers, a marker of the global industrial trade and not unlike the shoes Our Man is also wearing. His boat is filled with consumer products promising comfort and safety that ultimately prove insufficient. He is the big man rendered small in the face of linked planetary forces—capitalism and climate.

The film begins almost at the end of his story, with a voice over reading of a note Our Man puts in a jar and tosses into the ocean, a last message to his family and friends, set adrift in hopes of finding a reader:

> 13th of July, 4:50pm. I'm sorry … I know that means little at this point, but I am. I tried. I think you all agree that I tried: to be true, to be strong, to be kind, to love, to be right. But I wasn't. And I know you knew this, in each of your ways. And I am sorry. All is lost here … except for soul and body … that is what's left of them … and a half-day's ration. It's inexcusable really. I know that now. How it could have taken this long to admit that I'm not sure, but it did. I fought until the end, I'm not sure what that is worth, but know that I did. I have always hoped for more for you all. I will miss you. I'm sorry.

The embarrassment in the face of calamity here is the high note of the film. A man who is in control—and might well be part of the American elite that built the global infrastructure of neoliberal capitalism and petrochemical industry—loses that control when his technology fails in the face of global and planetary forces. He should have known better (given the obvious violence of global capital) but instead trusted his abilities and technology and resourcefulness. The global market is weaponized here in the form of the shipping container and the uncaring transport ships. A powerful storm—potentially amplified by climate change, a side effect of the petrochemical economy—merely finishes the job, leaving Our Man sinking in the open sea, to contemplate his decisions and fate. We do not know how far into the future the film is set—or if Our Man's boat is traveling over any flooded cities as predicted in the *Unchained Goddess*—but the fragility of the environment that supports human life on planet Earth is underscored in every frame. Our Man's message in a bottle is thus a profound projection of what we all might say in a few decades. It is an insufficient, if heartfelt, apology for embracing an economic form that offered short-term comfort in exchange for amplifying future dangers, and that abandons individuals increasingly to the uncontrollable and violent forces of capital/climate.

Figure 1.3 Effect of carbon emissions on future sea levels, *Unchained Goddess* (1958)

When is the Catastrophic?

> Think about the strangeness of today's situation. Thirty, forty years ago, we were still debating about what the future will be: communist, fascist, capitalist, whatever. Today, nobody even debates these issues. We all silently accept global capitalism is here to stay. On the other hand, we are obsessed with cosmic catastrophes: the whole life on earth disintegrating, because of some virus, because of an asteroid hitting the earth, and so on. So the paradox is, that it's much easier to imagine the end of all life on earth than a much more modest radical change in capitalism.
>
> Žižek, *Žižek!* 71-minute documentary film, directed by Astra Taylor. (Zeitgeist Films, 2005).

> "In relation to the history of organic life on earth," writes a modern biologist, "the paltry fifty millennia of *homo sapiens* constitutes something like two seconds at the close of a twenty-four hour day. On this scale, the history of civilized mankind would fill one-fifth of the last second of the last hour." The present, which, as the model of Messianic time comprises the entire history of mankind in a enormous abridgement, coincides exactly with the stature which the history of mankind has in the universe.
>
> Walter Benjamin, "Theses on the Philosophy of History" in *Illuminations* (New York: Harcourt, Brace, and World, 1969, 265).

In the early twenty-first century, narratives of end times proliferate—terrorism, peak oil, emerging disease, boom and bust capitalism, and a destabilized biosphere compete with each other for public attention. The difficulty of prioritizing which catastrophe should take precedence over all the others has created a curious new kind of psychosocial fatigue, where claims on imminent destruction are met with a retreat inward or simply a shrug. How is it that Americans, residents of the most powerful country in human history (unchallenged across military, economic, and political domains) have come to feel so precarious and vulnerable? It is important to note that our politics of catastrophe involve cultural formations as well as material assessments; they are historical projections that articulate fear but can also work to block both thought and action. Žižek (building on similar comments by Jameson about capitalism now seeming more permanent than the world) helps us see one dimension of this problem by underscoring the current lack of alternative ideologies to constitute the future today.[37] The demise of the large social engineering projects of the twentieth century, and the rise of an unrestrained neoliberalism in their wake, combine to create a vision of a market driven future that can only produce

37 See, Žižek, *Žižek!* 71-minute documentary film, directed by Astra Taylor. (Zeitgeist Films, 2005); and Fredric Jameson, "The Antinomies of Postmodernity" in *The Cultural Turn: Selected Writing on the Postmodern 1983–1998*) New York: Verso, 1998), 50; as well as, "Future City" *New Left Review* 21 (2003): 76.

profit by generating boom and bust cycles and extraction regimes that leave ruin in their wake.[38] Disaster has actually become a kind of industry in recent years, revealing an unplanned obsolescence for urban infrastructure breaking down under shifting environmental condition and lack of maintenance. This has enabled radical new kinds of corporate experimentation and profit-making, making disaster highly lucrative.[39] The formal end of the welfare state project (largely coterminous with the end of the Cold War, if not the nuclear danger) has also diminished the public space devoted to positive visions of a collective future in American life. It is difficult to find official commitments to a steady improvement in the qualities of collective life of the kind once used to balance images of nuclear catastrophe. Today, we are more than a generation removed from the kind of social contract that engineered most American institutions, and are instead increasingly reliant on market logics to design the collective future.[40] Thus, we have inherited from the twentieth-century's contest of utopian visions a world still organized by nuclear weapons but subject to the radical destabilizing effects of a boom and bust global capitalism that operates on ever-shorter windows of profitability and with fewer restraints and responsibilities. The reluctance of our systems of governance to imagine different futures, let alone to organize society on behalf of them, leaves crisis the predominant mode for political expression, as imminent danger becomes the primary motivating force outside of capital. Consequently, competing domains and scales of endangerment now seem to buffet U.S. citizens without respite, as the bursting of bubble economies resides alongside the minute-to-minute danger of a nuclear blast within the century-long sequence of anthropogenic environmental change.

In a striking passage from his "Theses on the Philosophy of History," Walter Benjamin evokes geological time as a way to shift the story of human beings on planet earth.[41] All human history becomes a brief moment of planetary time from this perspective, which raises the important question how temporality itself informs the cataclysmic and whether human beings have the right senses to understand collective danger at all. Pre-figuring the language of the anthropocene, Benjamin uses geological time to disrupt the time of capital and to reposition humanity as merely one kind of life on planet Earth, a species which may or may not be able to avoid the cataclysmic end most creatures meet. But if danger

38 Joseph Masco, "Terraforming Planet Earth" in Elizabeth Deloughrey, Jill Didur, and Anthony Carrigan (eds) *Global Ecologies and the Environmental Humanities: Postcolonial Approaches* (New York: Routledge, 2015), 309–32.

39 See Naomi Klein, *The Shock Doctrine: The Rise of Disaster Capitalism* (New York: Metropolitan Books, 2006); and, McKenzie Funk, *Windfall: The Booming Business of Global Warming* (New York: Penguin, 2014).

40 Susan Buck-Morss, *Dreamworld and Catastrophe: The Passing of Mass Utopia in East and West* (Cambridge: MIT Press, 2000).

41 Walter Benjamin, "Theses on the Philosophy of History" in *Illuminations* (New York: Harcourt, Brace, and World, 1969), 255–67.

incubates in the present, revealing itself in the catastrophic act, how can we see through a normative everyday to assess accruing danger operating on all possible temporal scales—particularly the forms that people generate and thus collectively control? Benjamin suggests that a radical emancipatory insight is also incubating in the present, a Messianic potential that could shift perception itself allowing a different kind of time to emerge, one that is not coded as "progress" (tied to homogenous empty time) and that is outside of capitalism. For Benjamin, just as the cataclysmic is coded into everyday life, so is the possibility for a radical shift in perception and with it an emancipatory politics. That this "potential" has not been activated is, for him, the ongoing state of emergency that he critiques so forcefully. In this way, he shifts the "emergency" from the narratives of violence that can function as heroic vehicles for self-sacrifice and warfare in the moment, to a more structural assessment of how social institutions normalize and render invisible the violence of capitalism itself. What Benjamin asks us to consider is how social institutions function as an expression and achievement of human engineering, and thus how the human-made can be remade under different concepts of value and with different futures in mind. Catastrophe's apocalypse would, in this case, be to see the agentive behind the everyday crisis, to see the possibility of a social order not yet conceived as forestalled in the name of history, class, or the status quo. Catastrophe's apocalypse would be to enter into a radically different temporality, a perspectival space for Benjamin in which structural violence is revealed as manufactured, enabling the current moment to be opened as a space of revolutionary critical potential. From this perspective, perhaps the proliferation of catastrophic images and narratives today has less to say about new objective degrees of endangerment than a shift in the psychosocial mechanisms of normalization and absorption. And here we might focus on a temporal paradox of our security culture today concerning the relation of nuclear danger to climate crisis.

The nuclear danger of Cold War—the fears of a nuclear war that would consume global civilization in an instant—seems distant to many American in the twenty-first century but the technological systems built to enable it are still present and active. The global nuclear infrastructure remains on high alert and nuclear war could still be launched at a moment's notice and between ever more nuclear powers. The Presidents of the U.S. and of Russia still carry launch codes with them every second of the day, and weapons scientists and defense personnel maintain a state of the art global nuclear system of war fighting. Americans tend to see global nuclear crisis now as an issue of the past, a matter for the last century (replaced by a wide range of terrorist threats). But today there are many more nuclear weapons on the planet than in 1958 when *The Power of Decision* was made, and the U.S. has committed to maintaining a state of the art arsenal for the indefinite future. Indeed, the nuclear fetish, despite the end of underground nuclear testing in 1992, remains firmly in place: In 2013, the U.S. Department of Energy asked Congress for funds to build a new nuclear complex for the twenty-first century, involving new weapons designs and production facilities—amounting to a $1 trillion expenditure over the next three decades.[42] Thus, while perceptions of nuclear danger have changed markedly since 1958, the technological possibility of a total ending has only increased: we live today on the edge of nuclear war and just don't seem to notice it anymore.[43] So what was once a national fixation on nuclear crisis no longer mobilizes in the same way, attaining an embedded-ness in everyday life that can be ignored by most citizens in favor of other concerns.

Similarly, the climate crisis of the twenty-first century was already present in 1958, when *The Power of Decision* articulated the terms of national crisis and *Unchained Goddess* warned viewers of a destabilized future environment. In the first decade of the Cold War, earth scientists publicized disturbing trends in their data sets, documenting shifts in air, water, and land quality via industrial pollutants. The debates about radioactive fallout from nuclear testing led to the Partial Test Ban treaty in 1963, which moved U.S. nuclear testing underground, eliminating the production of new radioactive fallout from the U.S. test program. However, the larger lesson of how industrial activity was harming the biosphere was left unaddressed as a security problem for decades. Had climate change risen to the level of a nation crisis in the 1950s the world would have been spared the coming destabilization of ecosystems, species die-offs, flooding, illness, and drought projected in the IPCC reports. Indeed, climate scientists now identify 1950 as the beginning of the "great acceleration"—a period of startling changes in human consumption patterns linked to the advance of the middle class and escalating carbon emissions.[44]

In other words, the inauguration of the global nuclear danger was also *the* inflection point for climate change, simultaneously installing two catastrophic potentials into everyday life that operate on vastly different time scales. Americans focused on the crisis of nuclear war in the twentieth century while missing the other incremental crisis of their own making, the expansion of a consumer economy that has become a highly destructive force on planet earth. Thus, nuclear and climate dangers are human-made crises decades in the making, and are deeply embedded within a petroleum-based capitalist-militarist-industrial system. After World War II, the security state embraced nuclear danger as its coordinating principle while rejecting the environment as a major security concern. Partly this is explained by the radically different temporalities evoked by each kind of danger: nuclear crisis playing out in minutes and hours while climate crisis plays out over decades

42 U.S. Department of Energy, *Fiscal-Year 2014: Stockpile Stewardship and Management Plan.* Washington: Government Printing Office, 2013); and Jon B. Wolfsthal, Jeffrey Lewis, and Marc Quint, *The Trillion Dollar Nuclear Triad* (Monterey: James Martin Center for Nonproliferation Studies, 2014).

43 Matthew G. McKinzie, Thomas B. Cochran, Robert S. Norris and William M Arkin, *The U.S. Nuclear War Plan: A Time For Change* (Washington DC: National Resources Defense Council, 2001).

44 See Will Steffen et al., "The Anthropocene: From Global Change to Planetary Stewardship" *Ambio* 40 (2011): 739–61.

and centuries. However, each crisis also evokes a different kind of sovereignty and requires very different kinds of governance. A global denuclearization project could substantially reduce the nuclear danger in a few years, but global warming is a planetary phenomenon that requires vast international cooperation—indeed, it now demands a post-national security logic of planetary defense. Perhaps this is also why so many images of climate change in the U.S. rely on tropes developed to communicate the danger of nuclear weapons, a way of acknowledging a collective danger without forcing a change in existing conceptual structures or modes of response.

In U.S. public discourse, nuclear and climate dangers are both grounded in images of a world that is no longer capable of supporting human society, a time when as nuclear strategist Herman Kahn, once put it, the "survivors would envy the dead."[45] This kind of catastrophic narrative, in its depiction of a perfect and total loss, however, requires an apocalyptic rendering precisely because it is an historical and highly politicized artifact. What is required now is a critical engagement that assesses not only the possibility of total endings but also the instrumentalities, ideologies, and practices that inform them. Perhaps today this could take the form of a reassessment of industrial reasoning itself and an effort to "cancel the apocalypse" not by a heroic suicide bombing (as in *Pacific Rim* or *The Power of Decision*) but rather by attending to local infrastructure itself as a social project that needs constant critical reassessment and reinvention to acknowledge radically changing environmental conditions. This would mean embracing both middle and deep futures as a collective security project, and thinking through multigenerational toxic legacies as well as imminent dangers (see Orff and Misrash 2012).[46] Above all, it would mean focusing expert and public energies not on rehearsing the perfect catastrophes of total endings but rather on the qualities, consequences, and insights of living in messy aftermaths.

45 Hermann Kahn, *On Thermonuclear War* (Princeton: Princeton University Press, 1960).

46 See Kate Orff and Richard Misrach, *Petrochemical America* (New York: Aperture, 2012).

Chapter 2
Law and Community in Fritz Lang's *M.*, BBC's *Luther*: Permanent Catastrophe?

Elizabeth Stewart

No-one has embodied the nodal point of where political and legal theory, philosophy, and ethics intersect in order to conceptualize what he and others have termed "bare life"—the catastrophic production of biological life devoid of politico-symbolic cover—more dramatically and more provocatively than Giorgio Agamben when he represents it by way of the figure of the *homo sacer.*[1] *Homo sacer,* the "sacred man," a person who is banned, who may be killed by anybody, but may not be sacrificed in a religious ritual: that is, a person who has no legal or social meaning, is reduced to bare biological life, and who does not even control whether or not he lives. The emergence of "bare life," creaturely human beings no longer framed by legal and formal protection, is, in Giorgio Agamben's words, produced by the world of "the camps," referring obviously to Auschwitz as well as to more recent reincarnations of such social, humanitarian, and legal catastrophes; a world in which the state, which in liberal democracies provides the legal definition, categorization, and protection of individuals, can metamorphose into a "killing machine" that can enable "life" and take it away to produce a population that has in some way been purified. "Bare life," for Agamben, is a universal, ahistorical category produced by a sovereign who under certain circumstances has the power to decide who (or what) should become an exception to the social community, who should become a "little piece of the real," to use a Lacanian concept of which I will make use a little later in order to inflect Agamben's thought with Lacan's.

Agamben seems to regard Western democracy as always already haunted by its own constitution which necessarily came into being by way of an act of anomie in which it was founded.[2] Agamben asks the question "why Western politics constitutes itself through an exclusion (that is simultaneously an inclusion) of bare life. What is the relation between politics and life, if life presents itself as what is included by means of an exclusion?" (Agamben 1998, 7) This included exclusion, this production of an exception in every person's socialized life, linked by Agamben to a defused death drive (hence the description of his theory as a "thanatology") makes bare life absolutely vulnerable to death and exiled from the protections of

1 Agamben, Giorgio. (1998). *Homo Sacer*. Stanford University Press.

2 Agamben, Giorgio. (2005). *State of Exception*. Translated by Kevin Attell. University of Chicago Press.

the symbolic order: *homo sacer* is *vogelfrei*, that is, outlawed and fair game, and absolutely divorced from ownership of his own body. For Agamben, what Lacan calls the Symbolic (*logos* and *bios*), the realm of language and law, is (it is not clear whether Agamben's argument is historical or ontological, one of the reasons he is often criticized), always already inhabited by the Real (*zoë*). In this chapter, I wish to offer some thoughts on the ways in which our era, our *zeitgeist*, ruminates on its own modernity in catastrophic, perhaps even permanently catastrophic terms. This will require an analysis of how psychoanalysis (as a viable theory of subjectivity) and political theory intersect, of how the two disciplines can together re-imagine whether the modern individual must give up on the possibility of living an ethical as well as political life within a community in which both the individual's *bios* and *zoë* can unfold and flourish simultaneously. Agamben describes a catastrophic legal, political, and humanitarian landscape in which "the camps" are destined to raise their heads again and again. It is the collapse of the political into biopolitics that motivates his thought. In order to respond to some of these questions, I wish to examine the ways in which aspects of Agamben's thought, brought into relation with his strong reader Roberto Esposito's thought on *Communitas*, *Immunitas*, and *Bios* can be developed and then bring both back together into a dialogue with one of their influences—the early Walter Benjamin—as well as the late Lacan.

Biopolitics/Thanatopolitics: Agamben

In his introduction to *Homo Sacer*, Agamben writes:

> The question "In what way does the living being have language?" corresponds exactly to the question "In what way does bare life dwell in the polis?" The living being has logos by taking away and conserving its own voice in it, even as it dwells in the polis by letting its own bare life be excluded, as an exception, within it. Politics therefore appears as the truly fundamental structure of Western metaphysics insofar as it occupies the threshold on which the relation between the living being and the logos is realized. In the "politicization" of bare life —the metaphysical task par excellence —the humanity of living man is decided. In assuming this task, modernity does nothing other than declare its own faithfulness to the essential structure of the metaphysical tradition. The fundamental categorical pair of Western politics is not that of friend/enemy but that of bare life/political existence, zoē/bios, exclusion/inclusion. There is politics because man is the living being who, in language, separates and opposes himself to his own bare life and, at the same time, maintains himself in relation to that bare life in an inclusive exclusion. (12)

In modernity a decisive change occurs:

> together with the process by which the exception everywhere becomes the rule, the realm of bare life —which is originally situated at the margins of the political order—gradually begins to coincide with the political realm, and exclusion and inclusion, outside and inside, bios and zoē, right and fact, enter into a zone of irreducible indistinction. At once excluding bare life from and capturing it within the political order, the state of exception actually constituted, in its very separateness, the hidden foundation on which the entire political system rested. (12)

At stake here is an understanding of the nature of power as it is enacted, in Agamben's opinion thanatically, on human life; that is, of biopower that is terroristic, traumatic, and catastrophic on both an individual and a communal level. Agamben suggests that *homo sacer* is a "catastrophized" person whose social, political, and symbolic identity have been removed in a way that is similar, both structurally and in terms of effect, to an individual who is traumatized by the bursting by an excessive stimulus of what Freud called the "protective shield" enveloping the "living vesicle"[3] which had categorized and therefore shielded in multiple ways what is practically unspeakable: bare life. Modernity, in which law becomes increasingly fused with absolute sovereignty, according to Agamben, encroaches catastrophically on individual life. It is a thanatopolitics.

Biopower and biopolitics take place in the sphere of life in which legal/political power intersects with biological life (*zoë*). According to Foucault, biopolitics regulates "the body-machine through an anatomo-politics of the human body and the species-body through a biopolitics of population."[4] The approach to biopolitics most relevant to us here is what Morar and Koopman refer to as the "naturalist" school.[5] This model of biopolitics "takes life as the basis of politics" and ultimately explains the social and political status quo as the result of evolutionary history. This naturalist theory[6] was most active in the early part of the twentieth century for thinkers for whom "social and political problems become the function of biological causes" and who were persuaded that social problems are manageable through active control, more specifically, to build "a politics with biological exigencies" (Morar and Koopman 17). I will go further into detail regarding the second, the "politicist," model, below when I discuss the crime drama *Luther*. Agamben claims that contemporary politics have become

3 Freud, Sigmund. (1920). Beyond the Pleasure Principle. *SE*,18,1–64, 27.

4 Morar, N. and Koopman, C. (2012). The Birth of the Concept of Biopolitics—A Critical Notice of Lemke's *Biopolitics. Theory and Event* 15 (4), The Johns Hopkins University Press. Project MUSE database: http://muse.jhu/journals/theory_and_event/v015/15.4.morar.html, accessed June 12, 2014.

5 The other two schools are the "politicist" and the "interactionist." See Maror and Koopman (2012) par. 1.

6 Names associated with it are Jakob Johann von Uexkuell and the Hertwig brothers, for example.

inundated by a biopolitical sovereignty, where law acts immediately on bodies (*zoë*) that are absolutely unprotected by a sheath, as it were, of *bios*. Sovereign power, exceptional law, and *zoë*: this is what the contemporary world has become, embodied in the "camps" and twentieth century fascism. This history, according to Agamben, allowed law and the sphere in which it is practiced under unexceptional circumstances, a society's Symbolic Order, to act directly upon biological life, setting in motion an exceptional and traumatic structure where the state, in liberal philosophy thought of as the protector of individual life, transforms exceptionally into a potential "killing machine": "The camp is the space that is opened when the state of exception begins to become the rule" (Agamben 168). Agamben has been criticized for his ahistoricism, since he names the catastrophe of the "state of exception" both "the camps" and "*homo sacer*," an obscure figure in classical Roman law, thus complicating the historicization of his argument. Agamben suggests that the figure of *homo sacer* as the exception underlies Western political theory, classical and modern, on the whole and that "democracy ... has proved itself incapable of saving zoë" (13). It seems that this state of affairs, together with the consequential erosion of the political sphere, leads Agamben to regard the realm of Western politics as being in a state of permanent catastrophe because of this constant danger within the law where the sovereign has the power to suspend and re-make law when he deems it necessary. September 11, 2001 is Agamben's privileged date for the contemporary return of the state of exception becoming the rule. With the reality of global terrorism, deemed by G.W. Bush to have become a permanent threat demanding a "War on Terror" that is equally permanent, declaring a state of emergency becomes, so to speak, a permanent every day possibility. Given these conditions, "permanent catastrophe" is the constant threat of a further erosion of *bios* and of a political community. Once again I wish to use Lacanian terminology here given that psychoanalysis may have something to offer political theory regarding the possibility of imagining non-fascist communities that interact in a *living* fashion with its own *zoë* and *bios* and with those of other communities. It is the meaning of the term "living"—rather than "vitalist"—on which my chapter hopes to shed some light, even if it is just a flicker: "permanent catastrophe" is the status quo of a symbolic order that, as an increasingly biopolitical order, is constantly under threat of being eradicated, inundated by a flooding real. "Permanent catastrophe" is also the increasingly more totally managed life that affects all citizens. On the one hand we have the production of a bare life that has been suddenly and radically desubjectified, such as that of refugees in detention centers around the world who have been reduced to the status of a number and lacking all social, political, and national identity. On the other, we have the everyday lives of citizens whose bodies are increasingly desubjectivized and managed by the various biopowers (control of health, populations, heredity, and so on) in operation.[7]

7 See Foucault, Michel. (2009). *Security, Territory, Population: Lectures at the Collège de France 1977–1978*. Palgrave Macmillan; Foucault. (2004). *Society Must Be*

I focus on law here because ultimately communities and societies are regulated by law, as are individuals' psyches which, by way of accessing a society's governing institutions and master narratives, become subjects within a society. Lacan links socialization and sexuation to the individual accessing the realm of language and law. The subject's psyche is a sort of microcosm for the symbolic order, the society in which the individual unfolds and acts. Both an individual's and a community's or society's psyche can become ill, schizoid, paranoid, or psychopathic; anomic and emergency moments in a society's relationship to the law have intense psychic and sociopolitical ramifications. Therefore, my chapter begins with Agamben's political theory of states of exception which he presents as "catastrophes" and "permanent catastrophes" (which I link to the emergence of biopolitics), and it fluctuates back and forth between stances toward the law and sociopolitical institutions that present as symptoms both on the level of individual and collective experience, both subjective and objective. My theoretical lens in looking at individual experiences of modern and contemporary biopolitical realities is mainly Lacanian; I hope to show that this same theoretical lens can also be fruitfully applied to Agamben's and Esposito's political theories in such a way that it may be possible to conceptualize an affirmative biopolitics. As my conclusions in what is essentially a search for at least a general framework in which an affirmative biopolitics, a coming community, might be able to take shape, emerge in part from late Lacanian theory, I suggest that it may be helpful to place an imagining of a "coming community" in a wider understanding of individual psychological, affective, and sensorial faculties. Theories about the coming community must be based on expanded theories of subjectivity. Early writings of Walter Benjamin combined with the late theory of subjectivity of Jacques Lacan—the theories that recognize within the subject the ways in which the utterly unintegratable otherness of human life must be hosted by what is recognizable within him- or herself—make such thinking possible. These are Lacan's theories of *extimacy* and the *sinthome*. Lacan's expanded, nearly destituting recognitions about subjectivity can—and should—be integrated by various conceptualizations of biopolitics.

Roberto Esposito's Critique of Agamben

Despite Agamben's references to contemporary global conditions, he is still accused of ahistoricism in his theorization of the *homo sacer*, and one may indeed argue that this figure is more of a literary figure, a trope, than a historically useful entity or concept. *Homo sacer* is a modernist trope, the centerpiece of a melancholy and abject representation of modernity, an image that despairs over the possibility of politics and seems to turn to aesthetics instead, thereby reversing what Walter Benjamin, Agamben's great precursor in the Bloomian sense, claimed is the

Defended. Penguin; Foucault. (2010). *The Birth of Biopolitics. Lectures at the Collège de France, 1978–1979.* Palgrave Macmillan.

definition of the anti-fascist thinker: "[Mankind's] self-alienation has reached such a degree that it can experience its own destruction as an aesthetic pleasure of the first order. This is the situation of politics which Fascism is rendering aesthetic. Communism responds by politicizing art. "[8]

Agamben's contemporary Roberto Esposito, however, arguably Agamben's "strong reader," does at the very least a couple of things: first,

> by focusing on the ways in which bíos becomes a juridical category and nómos (law) a biologized one, Esposito doesn't directly challenge Agamben's reading of the state of exception as an aporia of Western politics, one the Nazis intensified enormously so that the state of exception becomes the norm. Rather he privileges the figure of immunization as the ultimate horizon within which to understand Nazi political, social, juridical, and medical policies. In a sense he folds the state of exception in the more global reading of modern immunity dispositifs.[9]

Esposito offers, by way of his historically nuanced concept of "immunization" (*immunitas*), not only greater historical specificity but also insight into how Agamben's reading of contemporary politics, which is thanatopolitical as opposed to biopolitical, may itself open the door to new affirmative conceptions of community and politics. Esposito leaves no doubt as to whether he views contemporary sociopolitical, but also individually experiential, conditions as catastrophic (he does); he argues that contemporary societies unfold within an "immunitary *dispositif*":

> … the category of immunity and immunization. What do they mean? We all know that in bio-medical language one understands by immunity a form of exemption or protection with regard to an infection; while in the juridical lexicon it represents a sort of safeguard that makes one untouchable with respect to common law. In both cases, therefore, immunization alludes to a particular situation that keeps someone safe from the risks to which he or she is exposed (and to which the entire community is exposed). Here is delineated beforehand that underlying opposition between community and immunity from which my recent reflections are born. … [I]mmunity … is … the reverse of communitas. Both words derive from the term munus that signifies "gift," "office," and "obligation," but one, the communitas has a affirmative meaning while the other, immunitas, is negative. Thus, if the members of a community are characterized by this donative obligation, by this law of care with regard to the other, immunity implies an exemption or repeals such a condition: immune is he who is sheltered

8 Benjamin, Walter. (1968). *Illuminations*. Edited by Hannah Arendt. Schocken, 242.

9 Campbell, Timothy. (2008). "Bíos, Immunity, Life: The Thought of Roberto Esposito." In Roberto Esposito. *Bios: Biopolitics and Philosophy*. University of Minnesota Press.

> from obligations and dangers that concern everyone else. Immune is he who breaks the circuit of social circulation placing himself outside of it.[10]

Immunization distances, dissociates, and demands sacrifice, says Esposito: "To use Benjamin's language, we could say that immunization at high doses entails the sacrifice of the living, that is, of every qualified form of life, motivated by simple survival: the reduction of life to its simple biological layer."[11] Immunization is another word for the psychic mechanism of protecting life that in the Freudian schema is sacrificial as well and ultimately a variation on the theme of the Oedipus. In *Beyond the Pleasure Principle* the "protective shield" covering the "living vesicle" comes into being by the latter killing off a part of itself in order to protect itself against being killed off by the external world. The organism immunizes itself against external irruptions.

The "immunitary *dispositif*," Esposito goes on to argue, has become "the coagulating point, both real and symbolic, of contemporary experience ... the rotating axis around which is constructed both the practices and the imaginary of an entire civilization" (Immunization 4). Immunization, consisting of various acts of various sorts of self-protection, has itself become the fundamental problem:

> It is as if that fear which Elias Canetti singled out as the origin of our modernity in a perverse short-circuit between touch [tatto], contact [contatto], and contagion has grown more acute. The contact, the relation, the being in common, immediately appears as crushed by the risk of contamination. (5)

As with Agamben, Nazism is Esposito's prototype and extreme form of immunization:

> Nazism constitutes an irreducible protrusion for the history that precedes it because it introduces an antinomy that went unrecognized until then in its figure and in its effects. It is summarized in the principle that life defends itself and develops only through the progressive enlargement of the circle of death. Thus the paradigms of sovereignty and biopolitics, which seemed at a certain point to diverge, now experience a singular form of indistinction that makes one both the reverse and the complement of the other.[12]
>
> (110)

10 Esposito, Roberto. Immunization and Violence. http://www.biopolitica.cl/docs/Esposito_Immunization_Violence.pdf, accessed June 18, 2014, 3.

11 Campbell, Timothy and Roberto Esposito. (2006) "An Interview with Roberto Esposito—12.28.08." *diacritics* 36.2 (2006) 49–56, 51.

12 Esposito, Roberto. (2008) *Bios: Biopolitics and Philosophy (Posthumanities)*. Univ of Minnesota Press.

Decisionism, the extra-legal exertion of sovereign power in the political realm, is a form of immunization. As is the case with dissociation in the psychiatric realm, the immunity mechanism must always repeat itself and heighten the stakes. Once immunization has been put into practice, the same mechanism will be called upon with every successive fear of contagion. *Immunitas* can and does become compulsive, self-perpetuating, and exponential. Immunity is the opposite of community. It develops—on the individual as well as collective level—a cutting away from communal bonds, a numbing toward others; because immunization is self-perpetuating, increasing and solidifying through time, it may indeed be called dissociative and may indeed flip over into an auto-immune disease in which the social body, the immunized individuals who as a community that in reality no longer is one, attacks itself. How does immunization eventually lead to violence? Esposito imagines geopolitical immunity stances as capable of unleashing "convulsion[s] that ha[ve] the characteristics of the most devastating kind of auto-immune disease: an excess of defense with respect to the elements outside the organism is directed towards the organism itself with potentially lethal effects" (*Immunization* 9).[13] This would be a society that is geared toward a radicalization of violence within itself and that consists of atomized individuals who also alternate between emotional numbness and physical psychopathic violence. In an increasingly immunized society (which, according to Esposito, can no longer

13 The context here is Esposito's analysis of the effects of 9/11: it unleashed a violent "immunitary crisis": "In order to see non-metaphorically what I mean, consider what happens in so-called auto-immune diseases, when the immunitarian system is so powerful that it turns against itself, against the same mechanism that should defend it, and so doing destroying it. Certainly, immunitary systems are necessary. No individual or social body can do without them, but when they grow without limit they wind up pushing the entire organism towards an explosion or an implosion.

This is exactly the threat that took place after the tragic events of September 11, 2001 because I believe the war currently underway is doubly linked with the immunitary paradigm: that it is both the aggravated form and its moving beyond control [impazzimento]; the tragic epilogue of what we can call this "immunitarian crises," in the same sense that René Girard uses the expression of "sacrificial crises," when the logic of sacrifice sweeps past the banks that circumscribe the sacrificial victim, pushing as a result the entire society towards violence. It is then that blood spurts out everywhere and that men literally are torn to pieces. I want to say that the current conflict appears as originating in the combined pressure of two contrasting and mirror-like immunitarian obsessions, that of Islamic fundamentalism, determined to protect to the death its own presumed religious, ethnic, and cultural purity from contamination by Western secularization; and that of a West set on excluding the rest of the planet from sharing its own excessive amount of goods. When these two conflicting impulses [spinte] are brought together without any way of separating them, the entire world is shaken by a convulsion that has the characteristics of the most devastating kind of auto- immune disease: an excess of defense with respect to the elements outside the organism is directed towards the organism itself with potentially lethal effects. What exploded, along with the Twin Towers, was the double system of immunity that until then had held the world together."

function as a community) it is not only the case that Judaeo-Christian morality is severely endangered, but also that our very sensorium, our experience of being in the world, has been transformed. Within the context of Western ethics, understood in their widest scope, this is not only catastrophic, but also indicates that we are in a situation of "permanent catastrophe," given that the cycle of immunization and auto-immunity is self-perpetuating and will continue to increase with time if it is not in some way interrupted.

Esposito's main aim is to theorize a realm of thought and practice in which *bios*, politics, and community may be revived; reading Agamben not only with Esposito, but also with Walter Benjamin and Jacques Lacan can throw more light on how Agamben's thought can be developed in a more affirmative way by imagining to what extent "the political" is still possible, how it may need to be transformed, and what a "coming" philosophy might be. As we will see, such a transformation depends not only on derailing the immunitarian Impazzimento (its "going mad"), as Esposito calls it, but also on analysis and deflation of the cross-civilizational inclination to sacrifice, to sacrificial logic, and sacrificial intoxication.

Nazism: Immunization

Nazism plays a basic role both in *M.* and in *Luther*. Thinking of Agamben's and Esposito's theories of Nazism, we can make some sense of references to Nazism in some contemporary crime dramas and of the detectives invariably experiencing and acting out the loss of community, which is also the central theme of Lang's *M.*. The spectre of Nazism hangs over all of them. Late in the last season of *Prime Suspect*, in an episode about the killing, in London, of a Bosnian witness to a genocidal massacre in Bosnia by a former Serbian militia leader, Jane Tennyson visits her father in a nursing home. The episode in some way comes to a head with Tennyson's father's story about his participation in the liberation of Belsen. The suggestion is that "the camps" have not gone away, that they are a permanent fixture of our times. They multiply. The Gulf War dominates an entire episode in *Luther*. What is the significance of this persistence, this seemingly permanent fixture of Nazism in the Western psyche?

One might say that the *muselman* that Agamben claims is the embodiment of the twentieth-century *homo sacer*, and the Nazi politicization of medicine cannot be fully understood apart from the concepts of biopower and immunization. Rudolf Hess wrote, "National Socialism is nothing but applied biology." [14] "The entire Nazi regime was built," Lifton writes, "on a biomedical vision that required the kind of racial purification that would progress from sterilization to extensive killing." As early as the publication of *Mein Kampf* (1924–26), Lifton indicates:

14 Rudolf Hess, quoted in Lifton, Robert Jay. (2000) *The Nazi Doctors: Medical Killing and the Psychology of Genocide*. (Basic Books), 31

> Hitler had declared the sacred racial mission of the German people to be 'assembling and preserving the most valuable stocks of basic racial elements [and] ... slowly and severely raising them to a dominant position'[15]

In Nazism immunization and sacrifice come to a head, and killing, sacrificing, that part of the population that prevents the rest of the population from achieving genetic purity and thus perfection becomes the very reason for living. Cleansing and sacrificing spells life. Such a society, which heralds biopolitical sovereignty, an identification of absolute sovereignty in the shape of biopower, becomes a society in which potentially everyone can kill everyone, according to Esposito:

> Nazism constitutes an irreducible protrusion for the history that precedes it because it introduces an antinomy that went unrecognized until then in its figure and in its effects. It is summarized in the principle that life defends itself and develops only through the progressive enlargement of the circle of death. Thus the paradigms sovereignty and biopolitics, which seemed at a certain point to diverge, now experience a singular form of indistinction that makes one both the reverse and the complement of the other. Foucault locates the instrument of this process of super-imposition in racism. Once racism has been inscribed in the practices of biopolitics, it performs a double function: that of producing a separation within the biological continuum between those that need to remain alive and those, conversely, who are to be killed; and that more essential function of establishing a direct relation between the two conditions, in the sense that it is precisely the deaths of the latter that enable and authorize the survival of the former. But that isn't all. In order to get to the bottom of the constitutively lethal logic of the Nazi conception [of life], we need to take a final step. Contrary to much of what we have been led to believe, such a conception doesn't concentrate the supreme power of killing only in the hands of the leader [capo] as happens in classical dictatorships but rather distributes it in equal parts to the entire social body. Its absolute newness lies in the fact that everyone, directly or indirectly, can legitimately kill everyone else. (Esposito 2008, 110)

Nazism: Sacrifice

Esposito's concept of immunization is based on a Freudian understanding of the mechanism of sacrifice in combination with the Kantian categorical imperative, a move that introduces Lacan into the equation. The categorical imperative, as a "pure desire," demands the sacrifice of the "pathological object":

> In "Kant with Sade" [Lacan] says that Kant's desire is that of sacrifice. That is, to desire is to sacrifice what Kant called "the pathological object." In Kant's

15 Lifton, 24

> vocabulary, "pathological" means the object of particular interest, tenderness, and jouissance as well, that is, the object to which one is attached. Thus Kant's moral law consists in sacrificing every particular interest, everything pathological; it requires the subject to do without the pathological object. It is what Lacan calls a "pure desire," that is, a desire without a particular object.[16]

Sacrifice of part of one's living substance is demanded by the immunity compulsion in order to cut off from what is other, corrupt, and impure. Sacrifice of the "pathological" is needed in that process of cutting and anesthetizing that immunization involves. It is the real—or rather, the real remnant, the *objet petit a*, that little piece of the Thing, the mother-remnant, the cause of desire, in short: that which enables us to be interested in and to love objects in the world—that is sacrificed. Sophocles's *Theban Trilogy* can certainly be read as a drama about immunization: immunization, Esposito says, like Agamben's bare life,[17] involves the inclusion of what is excluded: the abject leftover is cast out even as it is first included. The image of Polyneices's corpse lying outside the walls of Thebes can be read as an emblem for immunization—the construction of ever more powerful defenses against what is perceived as corruption stemming from the outside—and in the end also auto-immunization: the excess of defense and exclusion comes to turn against the organism itself: immunization, defensiveness, and the casting out of the abject (Polyneices's corpse) leads to an internal lesion: Antigone's hanging corpse underground. In the immunity paradigm, law and sovereignty are repeatedly conflated; repeated emergencies and exceptions undermine the functioning of constitutional law where the space between sovereign and the subject is mediated by constitutional structures. In *Antigone*, Creon identifies himself entirely with the force of law, and in his process of immunizing the community against "corruption," he demands the sacrifice of anything that could modify the force of his orders by forbidding access to the body. Immunization tips over into auto-immune disorder and entropy, and sacrifice, according to Esposito, becomes rampant:

> what safeguards the individual and political body is also what impedes its development, and beyond a certain point risks destroying it. To use Benjamin's language, we could say that immunization at high doses entails the sacrifice of the living, that is, of every qualified form of life, motivated by simple survival: the reduction of life to its simple biological layer. (Campbell/Esposito 2006, 51)

The categorical imperative, which demands the sacrifice of the pathological object, is superegoic in essence, and the superego enjoys the subject's pangs of guilt, mortification, and self-flagellation in its attempts to fulfill an impossible

16 Feldstein, Richard, Bruce Fink, Maire Jaanus (eds) (1996) *Reading Seminars I and II: Lacan's Return to Freud*. SUNY Press, 281.

17 "We must ... ask why Western politics first constitutes itself through an exclusion (which is simultaneously an inclusion) of bare life" (Agamben 1998, 11).

law ("Love Thy Neighbor"); the vicious cycle of command, striving, destructive attack and suffering generated both by the impossibility of fulfilling the law *and* by the immunity compulsion tipping over into auto-immune disease, generates untold aggressiveness, defusing the death drive, and this destructive energy is channeled into sacrificing the pathological object with ever-increasing force and destructiveness, culminating in the obscene *jouissance* of sacrificing what is closest and dearest, in Lacanian terms, the *object a*. Lacan's most poetic conceptualization of the sacrifice of the pathological object occurs at the end of *Seminar XI* (and here I must quote at length):

> There is something profoundly masked in the critique of the history that we have experienced. This, re-enacting the most monstrous and supposedly superseded forms of the holocaust, is the drama of Nazism.
>
> I would hold that no meaning given to history, based on Hegeliano-Marxist premises, is capable of accounting for this resurgence—which only goes to show that the offering to obscure gods of an object of sacrifice is something to which few subjects can resist succumbing, as if under some monstrous spell.
>
> Ignorance, indifference, an averting of the eyes may explain beneath what veil this mystery still remains hidden. But for whoever is capable of turning a courageous gaze towards this phenomenon—and, once again, there are certainly few who do not succumb to the fascination of the sacrifice in itself—the sacrifice signifies that, in the object of our desires, we try to find evidence for the presence of the desire of this Other that I call here the dark God.
>
> It is the eternal meaning of the sacrifice, to which no one can resist, unless animated by that faith, so difficult to sustain, which, perhaps, one man alone has been able to formulate in a plausible way—namely, Spinoza, with his *Amor intellectualis Dei*.
>
> What, quite wrongly, has been thought of in Spinoza as pantheism is simply the reduction of the field of God to the universality of the signifier, which produces a serene,exceptional detachment from human desire. In so far as Spinoza says—desire is the essence of man, and in so far as he institutes this desire in the radical dependence of the universality of the divine attributes, which is possible only through the function of the signifier, in so far as he does this, he obtains that unique position by which the philosopher—and it is no accident that it is a Jew detached from his tradition who embodies it—may be confused with a transcendent love.
>
> This position is not tenable for us. Experience shows us that Kant is more true, and I have proved that his theory of consciousness, when he writes of practical reason, is sustained only by giving a specification of the moral law which, looked at more closely, is simply desire in its pure state, that very desire that culminates in the sacrifice, strictly speaking, of everything that is the object of love in one's human tenderness—I would say, not only in the rejection of the pathological object, but also in its sacrifice and murder. That is why I wrote Kant avec Sade.

> This is the prime example of the eye-opening effect ... that analysis makes possible in relation to the many efforts, even the most noble ones, of traditional ethics.
>
> This is an extreme position, but one that enables us to grasp that man can adumbrate his situation in a field made up of rediscovered knowledge only if he has previously experienced the limit within which, like desire, he is bound. Love, which, it seems to some, I have down-graded, can be posited only in that beyond, where, at first, it renounces its object. This also enables us to understand that any shelter in which may be established a viable, temperate relation of one sex to the other necessitates the intervention—this is what psychoanalysis teaches us—of that medium known as the paternalist metaphor.
>
> The analyst's desire is not a pure desire. It is a desire to obtain absolute difference, a desire which intervenes when, confronted with the primary signifier, the subject is, for the first time, in a position to subject himself to it. There only may the signification of a limitless love emerge, because it is outside the limits of the law, where alone it may live.[18]

Sacrifice, then, killing a part of oneself in order to defend against being killed, is the mechanism of immunization. Esposito writes in *Immunitas*:

> ... the deadly semantics of sacrifice ... [show] ... that religion saves—or heals—life through the absorption of something that binds it to its opposite, that draws life from death or includes death in life: Why is it, he wonders, that sacrifice, 'although it properly means 'to make sacred,' ... actually means 'to put to death'? Why does sacrifice necessarily involve a death sentence?[19]

Lacan's reference to "the offering to obscure gods of an object of sacrifice" occurs in (Schmittian) exceptionalist biopolitics in the form of those populations that in and immediately following a state of emergency are first denuded of their constitutional rights and then marked potentially as "enemies," thereby being excluded from not only a nation but even from humanity itself. The "dark god" to whom Lacan believes such a sacrifice has historically been made refers not only to any historical instance of sacrifice, but in particular points to what in Schmitt's writing was a "dark god," a Führer, who would take that position in a "re-theologized" German society. This is the figure of the sovereign or of sovereign power which has infiltrated the realm of the law, obliterating the realm of politics. Lacan invokes Spinoza as a defense against such "re-theologizing," the "universality of the signifier" corresponding to the legal cover pertaining to all

18 Lacan, Jacques. (1981). *The Four Fundamental Concepts of Psychoanalysis. The Seminar of Jacques Lacan. Book XI.* ed. by Jacques-Alain Miller. Trans. by Alan Sheridan. W.W. Norton & Company, 274–76.

19 Esposito, Roberto. (2011). *Immunitas: The Protection and Negation of Life*. Polity Press, 57.

citizens in a constitutional democracy. Lacan's reading of Kant, that the demands of the superego stem from desire, but a "*pure*" desire which demands the production of the enjoyment of prohibition itself, that is, the production of the superego which sadistically enjoys itself and demands the sacrifice, this is the deconstruction that psychoanalysis performs on the categorical imperative, on the law of the father, and on love, the love that makes that impossible demand to love thy neighbor as thyself. Kant's absolutism, like all absolutism and all demands for purity, produces the presence of sadism in the heart of the law even as its operations are initially operations of a self-protective immunization, though these operations go hand in hand with the loss of community, as Esposito claims. This "permanent catastrophe" at the heart of the intersection of immunizing numbing of experience, auto-immune attack, superegoic self- and other-directed sadism, immunizing morality and law may be, following Lacan, intimately tied to efforts at "re-theologizing" society, at de-symbolizing, de-formalizing symbolic structures, that is, reversing what Lacan describes as Spinoza's philosophical project of establishing the "universality of the signifier." Instead there are efforts to re-theocratize society, to involve it in a purifying "impazzimento," and to revert to those sacrifices to the dark god to which such processes invariably lead. There is an intimate connection between the human aggressive drive, says Lacan, absolute submission to law, and the outbreak of genocide that easily congeals unless the psychoanalytic impulse (by which we do not necessarily mean actual psychoanalytic treatment, but any instantiation of the distancing effects of the rule of the signifier) intervenes.

By reading a prototypical serial murder film made at a moment of great social and political crisis in 1931, as Weimar Germany faced the prospect of Nazism, together with a contemporary primarily British genre of TV crime drama from the point of view of my understanding of "permanent catastrophe" but with an Espositan/Lacanian inflection, I wish to show these interrelations at work.

Fritz Lang's *M.* and BBC's *Luther*

In what follows I wish to analyze, through the theoretical lens of Agamben and Esposito, on the one hand, and Benjamin and Lacan on the other, two crime dramas that concern themselves with the problems of biopolitics and genocidal individual and collective psychology and conditions, and how these relate to the possibility for politics and community, one directly so and the other far more indirectly. The first is Fritz Lang's 1931 film *M.*, often referred to as the first serial murderer movie, and the second is the BBC series *Luther*. The works address these issues in the key of crime and law. Why crime and law? Crime shows are essentially dramas that invite analysis of a particular society's symbolic order and analyze and expose various processes of subjectification that society makes use of. They do so mainly through privileging the realm of language: after all, the best crime dramas develop mainly in speech acts: interrogations, analysis of clues and motives, court scenes. They take place in relation to the law and examine individual subjects' relations to the law: both their transgressions of it and sometimes also the law's own transgressions as well as its failures, its neuroses, even its psychoses. Language is the privileged realm of inquiry for both Lacan and Walter Benjamin; through it we reach a society's and a culture's unconscious. But language is not only the medium of the symbolic; it also carries with it remnants of what language must exclude, punch a hole into: the body and its vital energy.

The relationship between the symbolic and the real takes center stage in crime drama: on the one hand, the operations of language and language analysis; on the other the dead body and the silent crime scene. Here we are reminded again of Agamben's vision of the camps, including Guantanamo, where language and symbolic cover have been traumatically separated from body. Criminals (in our case the psychotic serial child murderer Beckert in *M.* and the psychopathic parent-killer Alice in *Luther*) are symptoms of a society fallen ill with auto-immune disease that attacks its own; like all crime dramas, these two works then formulate a possible response to the social crises they depict. Usually, within the genre, the detectives are the nodal points who in part act out the malaise of the community but also try to work through the disease; in the detectives, symbolic and real intersect. John Luther, in BBC's *Luther*, like the detectives in most other contemporary, especially British, crime dramas, leads a life that is marked by profound alienation and, more importantly, immunization. The detectives seem to want to exorcise their private demons, whatever they might be, via their jobs (finding the culprit and exploiting their own failings) while, conversely, they can also be read as wanting to sacrifice their own private lives to the impossible job of improving a predatory, sadomasochistic and psychopathic society. Immunization (an insurmountable defensiveness, isolation, and impersonal violence that characterizes the societies represented) and sacrifice are the centerpieces of crime drama. Jane Tennyson in *Prime Suspect*, Fitz in *Cracker*, and John Luther, self-destruct in their personal relationships, they drink and smoke too much, and Luther in particular tends to act as if he were sovereign: at the very beginning of the series he decides to let the accused child killer Madsen fall to his death. Increasingly, the realm of language and law, the Symbolic, fails, and the violence and trauma of the Real emerge, uncovered and unshielded.

It is a feature of the serial crime drama, as it is also of *M.*, which ends pretty much with where it began, that the detectives are never successful. Though he usually (though not always—the case of Alice being the glaring example of his failure) nails his criminal, with each single success, John Luther is more drained, his engagement with any community whatsoever increasingly more limited (until in the end he walks off with Alice, the one criminal he never could, nor wanted to, capture), and the society, completely oblivious to itself, continues on its psychopathic path. The criminals, on the other hand, in these two works are more ambiguous and more diffuse; moreover, they really problematize the designation of "criminal." In *M.*, the child murderer Beckert and the genocidal Schränker act out what the vigilante Marwood, who is convinced that he is pursuing true justice, the vindication of life, acts out in *Luther*: both, implicitly and unconsciously, make a point about immunization and sacrifice. In *Luther,* Alice, the self-proclaimed psychopath who has killed her parents and others without blinking an eye and who offers cutting commentary on Judaeo-Christian morality and its applications to the law, is John Luther's joke: she represents his (unspoken) insight into the law and its tendency toward auto-immune attack. As I will show, both film and TV series open up an aporia regarding the law, show us a society in which the only communities are fascist mobs, but also keep open the question of any possible non-murderous coming community, though both are deeply pessimistic. I will suggest that both are nevertheless readable in terms of the questions they implicitly ask about the possibility of an affirmative biopolitics; they do provide an opportunity to imagine an individual and maybe even a community that would attempt to free itself from the tyranny of hyper-immunization. I will turn to Benjamin and Lacan—Benjamin in his philosophy of experience, of body-image, of language; Lacan in his late work in which he turns to the emergence of the real within the symbolic—to build on the questions that both works open up.

Fritz Lang's *M.*

Fritz Lang's 1931 film *M.* was inspired by the serial killer of children Peter Kürten, active in Düsseldorf between the years 1913 and 1929. The film is both a thriller about a serial child murderer terrorizing the city of Berlin in the early 1930s and a police procedural and drama about law, biopolitics, immunization, and social anomie. It puts on display all of these phenomena and dramatizes the concomitant loss of community. But it is not only community that is lost: the film also shows, in horrible detail, another loss, that of a symbolic and representational politics, a politics of "multiplicity of 'the flesh of the world,'"[20] to the catastrophe of Nazi biopower.

The film is not a mystery, as we know who the killer is almost from the start. In one memorable scene in *M.,* Peter Lorre who plays the killer Hans Beckert, as Roger Ebert put it, "at the time was 26, plump, baby-faced, clean-shaven, and as he [as Hans Beckert] looks at his reflected image he pulls down the corners of his mouth and tries to make hideous faces, to see in himself the monster others see in him."[21] The murders divide the city's population into four categories: the ineffective and borderline obsessive compulsive police, the city's criminal world, the population which, though controlled by the police, tends to favor the criminals as they are far more efficient in getting things done, and that alternates between its victim and perpetrator status, and Beckert, who becomes increasingly isolated and is also depicted as both perpetrator and victim. Ebert writes, "The city is in

20 Esposito, Roberto. (2012). *Terms of the Political:Community, Immunity, Biopolitics.* Fordham University Press

21 Ebert, Roger. (1997). http://www.rogerebert.com/reviews/great-movie-m-1931. Accessed March 1, 2014.

turmoil: The killer must be caught. The police put all their men on the case, making life unbearable for the criminal element ("There are more cops on the streets than girls," a pimp complains). To reduce the heat, the city's criminals team up to find the killer, and as Lang intercuts between two summit conferences—the cops and the criminals—we are struck by how similar the two groups are, visually. Both sit around tables in gloomy rooms, smoking so voluminously that at times their very faces are invisible. In their fat fingers their cigars look fecal." The criminals, filled with revulsion against a child killer and exasperated by the increased police surveillance, are determined to root out the killer. They trap him and drag him to a dungeon where, in a kangaroo court, with the vicious participation of "the public," Schränker, the leader of the criminals, sentences him to death in a process that is filled with contempt toward due process and human rights. Ebert writes, "One of the film's most spectacular shots is utterly silent, as the captured killer is dragged into a basement to be confronted by the city's assembled criminals, and the camera shows their faces: hard, cold, closed, implacable." Terrified and distraught, Becker then makes an impassioned speech in which he describes the mental illness that drives his actions, his own suffering. Even some elements in the public, who minutes ago had shouted for his immediate death, seem to react empathically, together, no doubt, with some of us viewers. Biopolitically inclined, Schränker, whose criminal personality transforms here into a heavily personalized presiding judge, and wearing his Goebbels-like leather coat, makes a counter-speech to Beckert's. He wants to do away with the murderer on the spot in order to save the lives of, and cleanse and purify, the rest of the community. He ridicules the idea of due process and the very notion of the accused's right to a defense, and sentences him to death on the spot. The mob rushes at him, but then, at the last moment, the police and the constitutional protections intervene—in the form of a disembodied pacifying hand—to save Beckert from a lynching and to re-subjectify him by allowing him due process, which, in his case, will include an insanity defense (the Weimar Republic's Paragraph 51).

M. is to a large extent a representation of Nazi biopower, and it is also a film about the miserably encroached status of the modern urban individual.[22] One of the film's iconic images occurs when Beckert stands in front of a shop window and we see his reflection in it encroached upon by knives. Beckert eats an apple while visually fenced in by knives, the fallen modern individual. Following this image, Beckert walks on to the next shop window that frames him as well. There he stands in front of a gyrating hypnotic circle while a large arrow moves up and down in the window, pointing down on Beckert's oblivious head. Hypnosis and entrancement too point to the *anomie*-producing duo encroachment/immunization.

M. (1931) was co-written by Lang and his wife Thea von Harbou—who was later to become a member of the Nazi party. The city of Berlin, in turmoil over the series of murders, is in a state of emergency; the criminals decide to catch the

22 See Stewart, Elizabeth. (2010) *Catastrophe and Survival: Walter Benjamin and Psychoanalysis*. Continuum Press.

killer themselves not only because child murder violates their code (thus they are trying to “protect life,” the essence of immunization, according to Esposito), as they say, but also because the pervasive police presence—raids and surveillance—is suffocating their far more direct means of staying alive. Police and criminals are therefore rivals, representing rival models of community life. Throughout much of the film, we watch the narrative unfold in form of parallels such as this. For example, Lohmann, the chief detective, and Beckert, the murderer, are associated in that they both whistle; their paralleling sets up the parallel between police and underworld. The other obvious parallels are police and criminal methods of detection and procedure, culminating in the famous “trial” scene in the criminals' kangaroo court in which Hans Beckert gives his impassioned speech and Schränker sentences him to death after explicitly denying him due process and declaring that vermin like him does not deserve to live. In this critical scene, as Horst Lange writes,[23]

> Schränker (the boss of bosses) raises his voice and, while the others nod in assent, bursts out: “Diese Bestie hat kein Recht zu existieren, die muß weg, die muß ausgerottet werden, vertilgt. Ohne Gnade, ohne Barrnherzigkeit!” (“This animal has no right to stay alive; it must be eliminated, it must be exterminated, extirpated. No mercy, no clemency!”) What seems to be at work here is not financial self-interest or a sense of honor, but rather an emotionally charged, deep-seated conviction about who counts as human and who does not, and—more importantly—what should happen to the subhuman. Only this reason explains why the possibility of turning the murderer in is so quickly dismissed: since the police can hardly be expected to be involved in a campaign of Ausrottung and Austilgung, the criminals have to do the job themselves. If that is true, the degree of risk they are willing to take on is the proper measure of the depth of their eliminationist convictions. (174)

Even Roger Ebert almost automatically and probably unwittingly falls into a biopolitical vocabulary:

> When you watch “M,” you see a hatred for the Germany of the early 1930s that is visible and palpable. Apart from a few perfunctory shots of everyday bourgeoisie life (such as the pathetic scene of the mother waiting for her little girl to return from school), the entire movie consists of men seen in shadows, in smokefilled dens, in disgusting dives, in conspiratorial conferences. And the faces of these men are cruel caricatures: Fleshy, twisted, beetle-browed, dark-jowled, out of proportion. ... Certainly “M” is a portrait of a diseased society ...

23 Lange, Horst. 2009. Nazis vs. the Rule of Law: Allegory and Narrative Structure in Fritz Lang's *M. Monatshefte,* Vol. 101, No. 2: 170–85.

M.'s central preoccupation is with the state of a community which seems to have been dragged into a deep depression characterized by malaise and ennui in which time is measured serially, punctuated by serial killings. Seriality and repetition are symptoms of immunization and what Benjamin called "mythical law"; both are reaction formations and immunity acts of self-protection against unpredictable as well as against the exceptionality of sovereign power, just like repetition is a reaction formation against trauma. The need for self-protection has turned into auto-immune disease in *M.*. Beckert's murders mirror microcosmically the emergence of death and anxious defense against death that biopower engages in its quest for total *immunitas*. This occurs by way of the identification of Beckert, first by way of the actual marked "M" on Beckert's coat and then by way of a second actual touch, a touch that leaves no doubt in the blind beggar (and thus in the "court"), engaged by the criminals, who is asked to *identify* Beckert: "Oh, nein. Kein Irrtum. Ausgeschlossen (meaning both "impossible" and "excluded"). Das ist kein Irrtum. (Oh, no. No mistake. Impossible/out of the question/excluded. There is no mistake.)" Defensive immunization and auto-immune outbreaks—the use Esposito makes of these metaphor-concepts ultimately have their source in Carl Schmitt's friend-foe determination[24]—as theme begin early in the film. Crisis and state of emergency, a "society in the grip of self-destructive urges," as Kaes writes [25] immediately pit citizen against citizen as friends accuse one another: "*Mörder unter uns*. (Murderers among us.)" According to Kaes, "the war experience was re-enacted (in *M.*) in a repetition compulsion which, for Freud, was a symptom of trauma" (43). The various forms of identifications and markings—the most famous one, of course, being the marking of Beckert with the letter "M" in chalk based on the loosest imaginable association between him and the murderer, as well as the fact that the blind beggar's touching Beckert's coat in the court room actually has the status of evidence—that are represented in the film, aside from determining who is friend, who foe, recreate, in a wish fulfillment, a sense of truth and authenticity, as well as a quest for purity. In this manner the sociopolitical function of the markings seems to be to counteract seriality, anonymity, and empty chatter with clear definition, markings—and elimination, echoing the children's endless game of serial identification and elimination at the opening of the film where we see and hear them play an elimination game in which one of them is tagged as being "it" and is eliminated. Eventually, as we saw, Beckert is "framed" and caged by the knives in the shop window.

Thanatopolitics in *M.*

M.'s Berlin is the Berlin of the Weimar Republic: dead in crucial ways, and frighteningly threatened by what comes across in the film as an oppressed vitality

24 Schmitt, Carl. (2007). *The Concept of the Political*. University of Chicago Press.
25 Kaes, Anton (2000). *M.* BFI Publishing.

that could well, if properly manipulated, burst into these ossified and deadened social bonds to "revitalize" them—by way of *anomic* pure energy. How can the catastrophic loss of vitality, of a "multiple flesh" community, of hospitable, other-directed politics be countered? It is this latter rumination, this questioning about what twentieth and twenty-first century Western communities and individuals need in order to break down the *impazziti* walls and aggressions of auto-immune disease that I will attempt to address in my conclusions. Nazism, as we know, presented itself as just this kind of savior, the savior of Aryan life: it would resurrect a deadened German Reich. The very last line of the film is spoken by Elsie's mother, in mourning, sitting listlessly and weeping, flanked by two additional mourning mothers, on what might be a bench in the court room where Beckert is ultimately judged as a protected citizen. The next to the last sentence of the film is: "*Davon werden unsere Kinder auch nicht wieder lebendig* (this won't bring our children back to life either)" "*wieder lebendig* (again alive)" expressing the key element of vitalism. Vitalism would wish to order social life according to "living laws," an extension of the "living authority" that, in Schmitt's thought, is *impersonated* by a specific person, the person and body of the sovereign. Nazi biopolitics would be the source of new life. In *M.* the vitalistic infusion, the *anomic* subversion of normative law and the regeneration/resurrection of a Germanic *Volk* defined as friend against its foe, life against death,—individuals excluded from the *Volk* by way of confining/concentrating and then killing him/her, that is, the creation of a fascist community—fails, though only for the moment.

Luther

While *M.* is preoccupied with Nazi biopolitics—thanatopolitics—embodied in the child killer Beckert and the lynch-happy mob during the kangaroo court, and with a boundlessly fanatic and murderous community that hopes, by killing Beckert, to immunize the entire community against "corruption," in *Luther* we are confronted not only with sadism, child killing, psychosis and corrupt as well as weak law-enforcement in its individual episodes, but also with a "criminal" whose function in the drama is similar to Beckert's, which is to mimic on the micro-level the society's pathology, except that this criminal embodies a society in a state of advanced immunization in the sense in which Esposito understands it: this criminal is incapable of empathy—she cannot attach emotionally at all (except to John Luther himself who does *not* represent normative law-enforcement) and has absolutely no desire to do so, whereas Beckert still wishes to be accepted by a biopolitically regulated society. Beckert still wants to fit in. Alice Morgan moves back and forth between clinical detachment from the individuals, the society, and their respective psychic structures that she is capable of brilliantly and amusingly analyzing—and killing. Arguably, her only crime of passion was killing her parents whom she hated. Alice embodies and parodies a pathologically non-empathic—that is, a psychopathic—and bloody social order that wallows in its own bloodthirstiness, its own narcissistic and borderline self-indulgence. Luther's and Alice's strange relationship creates an aporia in Luther's life. From now on he stands with one foot in the world of mundane everyday life in his "Serious and Serial" homicide division where the police is often mocked by extraordinarily horrific and traumatizing crimes, in particular serial murders that are, as in *M.*, also symptomatic of the exceedingly dreary dehumanized parts of London in which Luther operates; and with the other he is placed outside of it, in a morally disorienting space, with Alice Morgan. In between the two positions lies the abyss … and this is also how the series opens: Luther climbing and running up a flimsy scaffolding in pursuit of a suspect who suddenly trips, falls, and hangs over the abyss, barely holding on, his hands slowly slipping, as Luther stands over him and watches him fall after getting the necessary information from this man sentenced to death by John Luther himself. While Alice will clearly never be a part of a larger community, she acts as a humorous, yet scathing critic of a society that is incapable of recognizing its own bloodthirsty sacrificial logic and its immunized state, its auto-immune self-destructiveness, and its utterly deluded sense of morality. While she does not pretend to have knowledge about other ways of living, she is nevertheless the one who seeks out Luther who, she knows, shares her insights. It seems that at the end of the series, when the two of them walk off together after their customary meeting on the bridge, that what they can be walking toward could only be a way of living that is no longer connected to the catastrophic sacrificial messes and auto-destructions which are impossible to disentangle. Throughout the series Alice's project, it seems, is to teach Luther that the enforcement of a codified normative and constitutional law, equal for all, cannot coexist with love of the pathological object, that neither love nor the coded constitutional law are possible as such. This is, of course, the secret Luther seems to share with Alice and that she endlessly taunts him with: his role in Henry Madsen's fall. While Luther has destroyed his personal life beyond repair, it seems that when he walks off with Alice that their companionship has a future. Of course, one may say that in walking away from the social order Luther had been acting within, they choose to immunize themselves. One may may also say, however, that they intend to improvise a different way of living, a different morality, one that needs neither an enemy nor an outlet for aggression. Both characters, individually and in relation to one another, experiment with an altogether different modality of attachment.

When Alice reappears in Season 3 of *Luther*, she hijacks him out of the deadly realm of an auto-immune-diseased society in the grip of sacrificing Luther himself. From that moment on the two characters are associated with other, literally higher, spaces. Alice as someone who is "above" marks her as a pervert in the Lacanian sense insofar as she knows of the Law-of-the-Father and its sacrificial logic, but *consciously* disavows it. Alice tells Luther: "I've come to help the people you love. You used to have a fabulous moral conscience, John. Adherence to ... and yet, time and again it devastates the people you claim to hold dear, yet you don't stop. Seems to me your conscience has killed more people than I have" (Season 3, Ep. 4, 14:18).

She is referring to the death of Luther's wife, the appropriately named Zoë, at the hands of Ian Reed, the dirty cop trying to get Luther off his back by framing him for his wife's murder, and others; she is also referring to his passive killing of Henry Madsen at the very beginning of the series. In the sequence of events in this last episode, when the soft-spoken, "kind," vigilante Marwood, who claims to be taking the moral high ground by killing killers, torturing torturers, psychopaths, and pedophiles, becomes, like Luther himself at times, caught in the contradictions of an auto-immune disorder-driven society and the permanent and self-perpetuating catastrophe of the obliteration of a functioning community, Alice becomes in a way Luther's analyst. With her interventions, Luther becomes capable of understanding the workings of signifiers and the dangers of conventionally understood "truth", "justice," "love," and "good" as mirages that are always fueled by a superego enacted by loss and sacrifice and invariably making itself, or the organisms that it is to protect, increasingly more vulnerable to its own rage. Marwood, she suggests, is trapped in his need for approval by an alienated, sadistic status quo, a sacrifice-obsessed culture. As Luther and Alice watch Marwood prepare a public execution to be shown on TV (this is how he imagines himself to be helping the public good, providing enjoyment for a sadistic Law) in a forlorn abandoned warehouse, Alice comments: "Goodness Gracious, what a needy little fishy":[26] Marwood has fallen victim to his fantasy of his own goodness; his own tyranny of the Other as the "better" superego is unleashed by way of his fantasy. The self-perpetuating nature of his psychic structure, nurtured by his culture, his society, is thereby laid bare: "The superego steals the *jouissance* of whoever seeks to be moral."[27] In discussing with Alice plans for capturing Marwood, Luther describes his intention as wanting to rob Marwood of the *meaning* he imagines he is creating, and thus destroying his fantasy (his "hero complex"), which is to make his wife's death (killed by a murderer released only a few years later) "mean something" through his vigilantism. Alice comments on Luther's deflationary plans by saying, "That's cruel," thus confirming Luther's insights about the nature of sacrificial and immunitary fantasies. Luther has become able to see through the Symbolic order, its legal system and its morality as *semblants*, as violent master signifiers to be renounced as fantasies: commenting on Marwood's acting out, he says, "there's nothing more potent than private pain made public." Together with Alice, Luther

26 In this scene, clearly meant to be understood as the realization of Marwood's fantasy by the writers because of its staging for the camera in a room without (receptive) audience, by being a performance, an inscenation that harks back to the trial scene in *M.*, Marwood "speaks to" his unconscious victim whom he is, in his mind, about publicly to execute: "This isn't about Mr. Clark's rights, this is about our responsibility, this is about us doing for ourselves what the state refuses to do for us."" Hiding, Alice comments: "Oh boy. He really does need the world to love him, doesn't he?"

27 Voruz, Veronique. (2009). 'That which in life might prefer death…': From the Death Drive to the Desire of the Analyst. In *Law and Evil: Philosophy, Politics, Psychoanalysis*. Edited by Ari Hirvonen and Janne Porttikivi. Routledge Press.

seems to have transcended his own master signifiers and unbound himself from that potent social bond constituted by law-making and law-preserving violence, sacrifice, love, and fantasy of purification. Together, one could say, Alice and Luther perform the analytic act.

A New Community?

Who or what is Alice Morgan and how are we to read her close to angelic protection of John Luther? How are we to understand his decision to follow her? Does Alice practice a Benjaminian divine violence,[28] a non-violent force that, whatever its means may be, makes possible a disengagement from sovereignty, an opting out from the authority of idolatrous truths. Divine violence shatters mythic, law-preserving violence by way of a different kind of force. It aims at justice, not the preservation of the law with its ever increasing obscene violence and its growing fusion with corruption and violence. (By the end of Season 3 of *Luther*, the police force has become so corrupt, operating so heavily through extra-legal means, so vulnerable to internal decay, that it is rent to pieces from the inside.) Throughout the series Alice and Luther meet halfway across the same bridge, the two of them arriving from opposite sides, he from the left, she from the right, until at the very end of the last episode, they walk off together.

The entire series ruminates on Luther's conception of law. Ultimately, Luther's desire, which he seems to accomplish precisely by way of Alice's desire, the desire of the analyst, is to find "the 'universal' law of one's singularity" (Voruz 261); this means "separating the subject from the master-signifiers which collectivize him, to isolate his or her absolute difference, to circumscribe subjective solitude" (Voruz 275). This is the positive outcome of Luther's forays into what one might call personal states of exception as he gradually disengages from the auto-immune-diseased community which he officially endorses and whose laws he enforces. In Season 3, Luther, not having been visited by Alice in a significant amount of time, begins a relationship with a woman by the name of Mary, who is earnest, vulnerable, and absolutely innocent of the sort of psychoanalysis that Luther and Alice are capable of performing on the world of crime, detection, punishment and processes of forging individual and collective identities of the world in which they live. When Alice reappears she asks Luther about the state of this relationship, the first one he has had since losing his wife Zoë. Alice has an *anomic* understanding of love: love is not what the sadistic superego allows and orders—in this case, the publicly sanctioned Mary. Alice ridicules this possibility by calling Mary a "Zoë surrogate": "You've got enough self-knowledge to avoid that trap. She's not what you want. She's what you want to want" (3/4, 18:40), she says, indicating that

28 Benjamin, Walter. (1996) Critique of Violence. *Walter Benjamin. Selected Writings*, Harvard University Press. While Benjamin's essay is absolutely basic to the work of Agamben and Esposito, I cannot go any further into his argument here.

Luther, too, has seen through this Oedipally centered conception of love which, Lacan never tired of saying, is imaginary. In the last episode of Season 3, Alice verbally offers Luther a self-sacrifice in which he would choose Mary's life (Mary being so fittingly named) over Alice's. He seems to do so; he seems actually to choose to sacrifice Alice. It is only at the very end that we realize that Luther and Alice had both understood that sacrifice to have been a ruse, that they are in fact not in the least bound by a sacrificial understanding of the law—or love. Through parody, Alice enables Luther to escape the world in which he had remained stuck. They have both left it behind. They do not sacrifice their *object a*, it survives—as do they—, though they will do so only by *absenting* themselves from this particular social order. As they walk off together in the last scene, Luther throws into the river the coat that had marked him throughout the series as "Luther, Detective."[29]

Conclusion: Affirmative Biopolitics?

Esposito seeks to salvage an affirmative appropriation of biopolitics that might facilitate a new way of conceiving of *Communitas*. Making attempts at the former are very necessary in my opinion, but I wonder whether Derrida's notion of "friendship," might not be a safer aim than the forging of a new community, given the tendencies of communities to organize themselves around the idea of sovereignty. Focus on singularity and on the individual from within late Lacanian theory may serve us better in the aim of undoing the effects of hyper-immunity. Late Lacanian theory takes us into the realm of "bare life"; Lacan refers to the encounter with bare life *extimacy* and *identification with the symptom—the sinthome*. Some of the thinking of the early Benjamin also takes us into the realm of bare life or of realms associated with it. I will indicate only in cursory fashion where one might look for guidance regarding the conceptualization of an affirmative biopolitics.

1. *Lacan: Extimacy,* Sinthome

According to Esposito, an affirmative biopolitics would have to put an end to sacrifice. Via our reading of Lang's *M.*, we can understand better what Lacan means by "the fascination of sacrifice," the "*dark god*," and a "monstrous spell" at the end of his Seminar XI. The main thrust of Lacanian ethics has to do with overcoming this "monstrous spell," this fascination. This thing that must be "traversed" determines the end—that is, the ethics—of psychoanalysis: the rather modest-sounding aim of being a good person. How does this traversal occur in psychoanalysis? According to Lacanian theory, the lost object and its remainder—the *object a*, the cause of desire, that "thing" that forever reminds us of our loss,

---

29 Interestingly, from the very beginning of the entire series, Alice had "presented" herself as *absence*. As Luther catches on to her having killed her parents in the very first episode, he realizes that her m.o. is quite simply absence: "Absence is the point," he says.

that fuels desire and can therefore be maddening, hated, that object of envy—also fuels our aggression. We love and hate it and love and hate to sacrifice it; it causes desire, but, because it is unrecoverable, it also causes the death drive to emerge. In analysis, the analyst is to take the place of the analysand's *object a* of *jouissance*. When the analysand is able to make that transference, the analyst ceases to support the *semblant*, the analysand's unquestioned beliefs, his or her "master signifier," the signifier that stops the slippage of the signified under the signifier and that establishes itself rather than other signifiers as the guarantor of the symbolic structure. A subject's truth, in other words. It pretends (hence the word *semblant*) not to be a signifier like other, "ordinary" ones that associate with other "ordinary" signifiers, but presents itself as the final and authoritative signifier that provides stable meaning and control. It functions as a quilting point around which other signifiers can stabilize. Žižek writes, "The elementary operation of the *point de capiton* should be sought in this 'miraculous' turn, in this quid pro quo by means of which what was previously the very source of disarray becomes proof and testimony of a triumph."[30] The establishment of a master signifier is the product of an (unwarranted) totalization, a sleight of hand, a semblance of truth. The use of the word "miraculous" links this operation—here an intra-psychic operation—to the "miracle" that Schmitt describes the sovereign's "decision" as being. It is the "miracle" of law-making violence. In a successful analysis, the analyst's role is not to support the master narrative that the analysand had wished, miraculously, to enable him to provide firm anchored meaning of his or her world; rather, the analyst comes to stand in for the analysand's *object a*, thus treating the analysand via his or her drives. The *object a* is to be extracted (and not sacrificed), thereby "destituting" the analysand who must now confront the absence of guarantee. Destitution by a loss of guarantee for truth and meaning is to be accompanied by the survival of *jouissance* by way of identification with one's symptom, the *sinthome*: the survival of *jouissance* so that the patient gains a sense of, as Lacan puts it, "deserving" to live:

> Lacan's notion of the *sinthome*[31] describes what is left to the subject after the end of analysis, after the deflation of the Father-image, the Oedipus, the law, and after the existence of the Other of the Other and even the blinding misrecognitions of the ego have evaporated. The question the *sinthome* answers to is, "How does the subject live after analysis and the demise of master signifiers? What supports her to live?"The *sinthome* understood as phenomenology and experience is the subject's identification with and immersion into the symptom (which rarely makes a total retreat), the corporeal remnant and side-product of the inscriptions of symbolic signifiers. After the superego of the Law has been deflated and

30 Žižek, Slavoj. (2006). *Interrogating the Real*. 2006. Edited by Rex Butler and Scott Stephens. Continuum, 116

31 Lacan, Jacques. 1975–76/1999. *Le Séminaire livre XXIII. Le sinthome*. Texte établi par Jacques-Alain Miller. Paris: Seuil.

> the symptom has been "read" in analysis—that is, interpreted, its meaning retrieved, leaving the material shell—the subject must find a way to *be* or, more hauntingly, a way for "deserving to live". It is tempting to read Oedipus leaning on his daughter Antigone in *Oedipus at Colonus* as leaning on his *sinthome*. She remains to him after he has seen—so much that he is blinded—through all else.[32]

When the analyst takes the position of *object a* he causes desire; he is the "little piece of the original object" to which enjoyment clings. He provides love, because he makes *jouissance* safe when the analysand comes to find *jouissance* in the identification with his or her symptom. The *sinthome* is the "symptom after the fall of the *object a*, a symptom reduced to its core, ciphering a singular mode of enjoyment" (Voruz 278).

What does it mean that *object a* survives in the analyst and that the analysand finds *jouissance* in the *sinthome*? It means, for one, that *object a* is not sacrificed, that that absolutely unique object is found not in someone or something or some group that is to be marked with it and then done away with, but rather that the analysand learns to experience it as love—the love of words and symbolization, and the love of the signfying non-sense of his or her own meaning. This means that ultimately, at the end of analysis, understanding involves the deflation of master signifiers which can be upheld, in the end, only by way of belief, belief in what is known to be a *semblant*. "Analytic knowledge is insight into the experience of this meaning-seeking-in-the-Other as the ultimate support for this Other that supposedly holds ultimate meanings for us."[33] Master signifiers and universal categories implode in on themselves, leaving the analysand at the end with what Lacan claimed in the 1950s to be the end of analysis: namely, the "being-for-death,"[34] the acceptance of one's own mortality, of one's flesh and of the other's flesh, the analyst's love, and identification with one's unique modality of *jouissance*, that is, one's own *sinthome*. Public meaning, universal categories deflate, and the subject retreats into contingent signification and attachment.

Throughout the *Luther* series Alice has called attention to the ways in which Luther has thought erroneously about love and justice both. She suggests repeatedly that non-sacrificial love and mythical law, which is also sacrificial, cannot coexist. From the very beginning, with her murder of her parents, she has made it clear that she rejects—and utterly obliterates in her own life, the love-and-law paradigm of the Oedipal configuration. Instead, she treasures—and teaches Luther to treasure—the "pathological object." Any new paradigm for community, friendship, or love, her behavior and her utterances express, must explode sacrifice,

---

32 Stewart, Elizabeth. (2010) *Catastrophe and Survival: Walter Benjamin and Psychoanalysis*. Continuum Press.

33 http://battleofthegiants.wordpress.com/2009/01/11/signifying-non-sense-according-to-lacan/ accessed June 19, 2014.

34 Lacan, Jacques. (1977). *Écrits: A Selection.* Translated from the French by Alan Sheridan. New York/London: W.W. Norton & Company, 104–105.

immunity, and all subjugation to the biopowers ruling the contemporary world. What is to be treasured is the world of affect, singular embodiment, parody and humor. And whereas the overwhelming affect in *M.* is disgust, disgust with the modern world, the ending of *Luther* is light, humorous, producing relief upon exiting the inextricably self-entangled and chaotic world of auto-immune attacks and bloodletting.

2. Benjamin

The very last words in *M.* are spoken by Elsie's mother. She says, "*man muss eben noch besser auf die Kinder achtgeben*" ("I guess we must just pay better attention to our children"). "Achtgeben," I would suggest here, has the same meaning it has in the phrase Benjamin uses in his essay on Kafka, when he praises Kafka for his "attentiveness to the creaturely"[35]: an attentiveness for forms of expression that encompass the body and materiality on the whole. This is a topic so large that I cannot possibly get into it here. Benjamin's thoughts on divine language, divine violence, his philosophy of experience on the whole, are all of relevance here. Suffice it let Esposito speak about what sorts of new attentiveness would, according to him, have to play a role in a future *Communitas*:

> The notion of flesh, first Christian and then phenomenological, when reread today against the backdrop of a twentieth-century artistic avant-garde (I'm thinking of Bacon and Cronenberg), can have a disruptive force. Flesh is the body that doesn't coincide completely with itself (as Nazism wanted, according as well to Levinas's interpretation), that isn't unified beforehand in an organic form, and that is not led by a head (which therefore is acephalous, as Bataille would say). No. Flesh is constitutively plural, multiple, and deformed. It is also from this point of view that one can begin to imagine an affirmative biopolitics. (Campbell/Esposito Interview, 52)

35 Benjamin (1968), 134.

Chapter 3

Photographs of Catastrophe and the Representation of Vulnerable Humanity

Carolyn J. Dean

As is now oft-noted, catastrophe conceived as the human-made possibility of species-destruction is a recent historical phenomenon that began with the Holocaust and the detonation of nuclear bombs over Hiroshima and Nagasaki. Jean-François Lyotard said that the Holocaust was equivalent to an earthquake that destroyed "the very instruments used to measure earthquakes" so that all efforts to measure its magnitude quantitatively are bound to fail.[1] Sociologist Ulrich Beck echoes this idea in reference to a "catastrophe society" in which disasters escape clear measures, uncertainty prevails, emergencies are the normal state of affairs, and all remedies create new risks.[2] According to Eric Santner and Moishe Postone, violence is the permanent condition of humanity in the twenty-first century, and catastrophe signifies "an ontological absence that would seem to escape the efficacy of social and psychic practices of integration, representation, ... any kind of repair … or 'redemption.'"[3] Once defined as "ontological absence" or immeasurable, catastrophe implies a permanent condition that is hard to conceive in historical terms.[4]

Technological improvement and innovation have obviously generated new kinds of disasters. Moreover, genocides, terrorist attacks, post-colonial massacres, "ethnic cleansing," and environmental degradation—human-made catastrophes on a dramatic scale—define a frail humanity now enjoying or suffering globalization, development, and their excesses, which include the possibility of human self-destruction.[5] Social scientists and legal scholars work on risk assessment

1 Jean-François Lyotard, *The Differend: Phrases in Dispute*, trans. Georges Van Den Abbeele (Minneapolis, 1989), 56–7.

2 Ulrich Beck, *Risk Society: Towards a New Modernity*, trans. Mark Ritter (London, 1992), 79, 156–57.

3 Introduction to Moishe Postone and Eric Santner (eds), *Catastrophe and Meaning: The Holocaust and the Twentieth Century* (Chicago, 2003), 13.

4 See also in this vein the work of Lecia Rosenthal, *Mourning Modernism: Literature, Catastrophe, and the Politics of Consolation* (New York, 2011), 12.

5 Steven Pinker has argued that modern Western institutions have reduced violence in the world, but his account arguably paints an excessively affirmative or anodyne picture of Western culture that barely touches on the excesses of colonialism and relies heavily on neuroscience. Regarding Nazi Germany, Pinker writes, referring to historian Christopher

and jurisprudence in this world where disasters are no longer simply natural occurrences.[6] But it is less clear how we can address the meaning of catastrophe historically, especially in the face of so many assertions by Lyotard, Santner, and others for whom in the end catastrophes defy assessment, measurement, and thus historical meaning. There are some precedents. Hannah Arendt asserted famously over half a century ago that the catastrophe wrought by the Holocaust of European Jewry destroyed the very concept of humanity. She argued that the Jewish refugee crisis revealed that human dignity in practice was a property of citizens and thus dependent on our contingent circumstances rather than intrinsic in our status as rights-bearing human beings.[7] She thus suggested that Nazism and its consequences destroyed the construction of human dignity as metaphorically whole and upright even in its vulnerability and nakedness, and constituted a new historical reality. Indeed, the refugee has become a figure for the "human waste" generated by catastrophe in the work of thinkers as diverse as sociologist Zygmunt Bauman and philosopher Giorgio Agamben.[8] Arendt moved on to discuss in philosophical terms how to create conditions for a political and emotional will to dignity normatively understood in her later work. But Agamben sustains Arendt's critique in other terms. In his writing on Auschwitz, he asserts "[Primo] Levi

Browning's work on German policemen: "During the Holocaust, soldiers and policemen rounded up unarmed civilians, lined them up in front of pits, and shot them to death, *not out of animus to the victims or a commitment to Nazi ideology* [my emphasis] but so that they would not shirk their responsibilities or let down their brothers-in-arms." This is one interpretation of the killers' behavior, but it is hardly the only one and particularly reductive even of Browning, whose conclusions derive from a limited set of postwar trials, presume a functionalist explanation of human behavior under pressure but also insist on the importance of anti-Semitic ideology and are hardly generalizable to the many varieties of such murderers. Pinker's effort to emphasize a trajectory of human self-improvement and the banality of lots of what passes for evil is admirable, but relies on a wholesale dismissal of a great deal of evidence to the contrary. Pinker, *The Better Angels of Our Nature: The Decline of Violence in History and Its Causes* (London, 2012), 559.

6 See, among others mentioned in this chapter, Austin Sarat, Lawrence Douglas, Merril Umphrey (eds), *Law and Catastrophe* (Stanford, 2009).

7 Hannah Arendt, *The Origins of Totalitarianism* (New York, 1974), 267–301. The idea that modernity and destruction are historical bedfellows is of course a preeminent theme in critical theory and some sociology in its wake. See Max Horkheimer and Theodor W. Adorno, *The Dialectic of Enlightenment*, trans. John Cumming (London, 1986); and Zygmunt Bauman, *Modernity and the Holocaust* (Ithaca, 2000). On history as "catastrophe" see Walter Benjamin, "Theses on History," in *Illuminations*, ed. Hannah Arendt, trans. Harry Zohn (New York, 1978), 257–8.

8 Zygmunt Bauman, *Wasted Lives: Modernity and Its Outcasts* (Oxford, 2004), 32–9, 66, 98; Giorgio Agamben, *Means Without Ends: Notes on Politics* [this section trans. by Vincenzo Binetti and Cesare Casarino] (Minneapolis, 2000), 13–28.

begins to bear witness only after dehumanization has been achieved, only once it no longer makes any sense to speak of dignity."[9]

There is not one way to assess the concept of "catastrophe" historically, but after Arendt and Agamben we might begin by addressing its relationship to the concept of "humanity" whose modern secular basis is the intrinsic dignity of all people no matter their contingent circumstances (though the relationship between dignity and rights, and rights and responsibilities is another matter and varies from culture to culture). This intrinsic quality is animated by an image of humanity as metaphorically resilient, radiant, upright and whole, an image of dignified comportment that arguably became central to the narration of all struggles for social justice. The "catastrophe" many scholars now describe refers to violence of extraordinary proportions, to a very broad temporal construction termed modernity or post-modernity, and to globalization and its impact on human suffering. But catastrophe also refers fundamentally to the violation or destruction of human dignity—hence Bauman's references to "wasted lives" and "human waste" generated by globalization and population "flows."[10] If this is true, then catastrophe's impact is not necessarily an ontological loss, but the loss of specific meaning attributed to being human since the Second World War.

The assertion that catastrophe generates wasted humanity obviously refers to the poor and disenfranchised victims of neo-liberalism and its global expansion. But the concept of "wasted humanity" also begs the question of what meaning attributed to being human has ended up in the refuse and what "catastrophe" has changed. Is human dignity no longer an anchor point of humanity, as Agamben suggests? At the same time, though arguments for the self-evidence of dignity have been problematized, much historical work still asserts that catastrophes from the Holocaust to Hurricane Katrina are ideally temporary episodes in the unraveling of a broader redemptive narrative about humanity. Eric Hobsbawm famously dubbed the years from the Great War to 1950 the "age of catastrophe."[11] He believed that catastrophe describes events that deviate from the standard course of things, and attributed the destruction wrought to specific causes, defined its limits, and did not question the historicist commitment to a model of autonomous, rational, and

9 Giorgio Agamben, *Remnants of Auschwitz: The Witness and the Archive*, trans. Daniel Heller-Roazen (New York, 2001), 59.

10 The term "Wasted Lives" also appears as the title of one part of an exhibit in the Rwandan Genocide Museum in Kigali. I thank Olivia Rosenthal, whose paper "A Memorial of Instability: The Kigali Memorial Center and RPF's Atttempt to Produce a Stable Narrative of Genocide," brought this to my attention. Her source is the pamphlet accompanying the exhibit by James M. Smith, Stephen D. Smith, Kigali Memorial Centre, and Aegis Organization, *Jenoside*. Kigali: Kigali Memorial Centre, 2004).

11 Eric Hobsbawm, *The Age of Extremes: The Short Twentieth Century 1914–1991* (New York, 1996), 6–7.

dignified humanity.[12] Such arguments cannot address the shifting meaning of humanity across cultures and certainly not in relation to catastrophic events

To address the historical meaning of catastrophe, I suggest we begin by asking how we define the humanity whose life is "wasted" by neo-liberal economic globalization. What is a wasted life? I take up the spectacle of suffering humanity in the contemporary period—this time of so-called catastrophe—in the form of what my title calls "photographs of catastrophe." In what follows I will also refer to "atrocity photographs" because that is the way in which these images are usually designated, though "catastrophe" describes their content and the problems they raise equally well. I explore how the critical narrative about these photographs suggests that such pictures may define varied fields of intelligibility within which the image of catastrophe as shattered human dignity or "wasted life" can be recognized, assessed, as well as disavowed.

Photographs of Catastrophe

The discussion of images and photographs of catastrophe repeats older anxieties—iconoclasts' anxieties about the representation of Christ's original "humiliation" and Platonic worries about the substitution of false idols for essences. [13] Photographic illusionism repeats these older anxieties, but also engenders new forms of objectification that reframes atrocity anew. As has been amply chronicled, photographic images heralded new forms of transformative realism, but they also generated mechanically reproducible images for passive consumption, advertising, technological surveillance, and political manipulation.[14] Thus photographs of dead soldiers in the American Civil War and the Great War objectified human beings, violated their privacy, and infringed upon "decency." But by 1918 and the end of

---

12 Though few historians subscribe to a Whiggish narrative of progress, the concept of rational and autonomous human beings remains the dominant ideology of professional historians regardless of challenges imported into the discipline from literary theory. That is why the invocation by literary theorists and social scientists of a language of catastrophe (to very different ends, of course) receives little attention from historians, most of whom analyze catastrophic events as discrete moments in time with particular causes and effects. Of course there are volumes of work that criticize human rights as the extension of neocolonial policies or exemplary of post-Foucauldian views of biopolitical power, but with some exceptions, they are not written by historians. Far more standard is Lynn Hunt, *Inventing Human Rights: A History* (New York: Norton, 2007). Once could devote a long essay to this particular phenomenon itself.

13 Arnold Hauser, *The Social History of Art, Volume 1: Prehistoric, Ancient, Oriental, Greece & Rome, Middle Ages* (New York, 1985 [1957]), 138. See also Alain Besançon, *The Forbidden Image: An Intellectual History of Iconoclasm*, trans. Jane Marie Todd (Chicago, 2000).

14 See the discussion in Martin Jay, *Downcast Eyes: The Denigration of Vision in Twentieth-Century French Thought* (Berkeley, 1994), 125–47.

the Great War, such photographs, by virtue of their ostensible evidentiary value, also played a critical moral role in rejecting redemptive narratives of war. Anti-war critics compiled books of such pictures meant to shock publics into grasping the human costs of war.

Discourses about photographs of catastrophe after the publication of images of Buchenwald and Bergen-Belsen appeared repeat all of these themes, including their moral outrage. When General Eisenhower called upon spectators to witness the horrors of the camp, he meant that we should testify to the unimaginable horrors they depicted. Though the call to "witness" was surely an effort to justify the war, it also became part of larger political and cultural efforts (the creation of supranational institutions like the United Nations; the emergence of international human rights as a global discourse in the 1948 UN Declaration of Human Rights) to prevent future conflicts. Photographs had become more than ever a means of constructing the humanity of others. To "witness" in its secular version simply meant "to testify" and thus to see. But by the time interest in the concentration camps and other Holocaust photography gave birth to an unofficial genre of atrocity photography as the consciousness of that event increased in the 1970s and 1980s, looking at such images had also become part of a more expansive secularized moral imperative "to bear witness." Thus Frances Guerin and Roger Hallas note recently that atrocity images should no longer be viewed as "the image's technological ability to furnish empirical evidence of the event, but [as] faith in the image's phenomenological capacity to bring the event into iconic presence and to mediate the inter-subjective relations that ground bearing witness."[15]

Though it is not clear exactly what this means, or how the recognition of others' suffering in this mediated context could ever be more than a metaphorical displacement, critics increasingly invoke the language of "bearing witness" in relationship to photographs, and that phrase can mean many things, from the literal act of "seeing" to Guerin and Hallas' suggestion: in so doing, as they note, photographs are no longer self-evident reproductions of reality, but might also test faith: we may believe what we see, but if we have to have "faith," is it possible they are illusions? What if we find them fascinating and unbearably tempting to look at—the opposite of the critical perspective "iconic presence" is supposed to generate? Could one really see what they revealed? In her discussion of Lee Miller's images of Dachau, Sharon Sliwinski writes: "The public bore witness in 1945, but they did not know what they had seen."[16] "Visible blindness"[17] appears elsewhere to describe this problem. In any case, the call to witness photographs underlines a moral imperative to look, in which looking redeems or makes

15 Frances Guerin and Roger Hallas, "Introduction," in *The Image and the Witness: Trauma, Memory and Visual Culture,* Frances Guerin and Roger Hallas (eds) (London, 2007), 12.

16 Sharon Sliwinski, *Human Rights in Camera* (Chicago, 2011), 83.

17 Cornelia Brink, "Secular Icons: Looking at Photographs of Nazi Concentration Camps," *History and Memory*, 12 (2000): 146.

meaning out of catastrophe rather than assumes wasted lives, much as the birth of global humanity through pictures was supposed to reflect the triumph of human solidarity in spite of catastrophe. But, as is implicit in the idea that spectators could not "know what they had seen," the relatively recent critical discourses on atrocity photography focus above all on the ethical and emotional difficulties as well as importance of looking that is part of a new historical landscape in which images not only construct collective memory (and hence are ideologically laden) but also generate traumatic effects whose impact is now discussed in terms far broader than their violation of "decency" and ability to shock. Already in 1960, Gerhard Schoenberner, who compiled a book of atrocity snapshots for West German consumption in 1960, wrote that they "put [the viewers] into the role of the murderers."[18] And Guerin and Hallas remind us that images of "historical trauma" require particular care because of the emotions they arouse.[19]

In line with these post-war developments, there have been two main, if often overlapping, lines of argument about photographs of suffering and persecution specific to twentieth-century and more recent catastrophes. Their central questions, perhaps not surprisingly, recognize the destabilizing and dislocating force of catastrophe itself: they ask how we might look, and whether we should or can "witness" catastrophe and its consequences. One line of argument emphasizes the various forms of spectators' complicity in the violence pictured. It is continuous with earlier, nineteenth century discourses condemning viewer's potential voyeurism, spectacle and the hyperstimulation created by urban spaces and the passivity of a new consumer culture. The second pervasive argument about atrocity photographs is that they can't be absorbed because traumatic events—catastrophes—cannot be represented as they are lived, and thus exceed our ability to grasp. This view is expressed by Sliwinski's comments about Lee Miller's photographs. In what follows I address two critical analyses about the limits of representation and how they combine the conceptual tensions and problems inherent in pervasive arguments about catastrophe photographs. They each focus on different kinds of spectators to demonstrate how they consciously or not fall into catastrophic time because they cannot control the excessive violence manifest in what critics conceive to be viewers' inevitable complicity with or disavowal of the photographs. I then address several efforts to envision moral responses to catastrophic violence now by defending against the dislocation of and violence toward human dignity they engender or by transforming catastrophe itself into a historical phenomenon that might be alterable or at least viewed critically. My immediate interest is not to analyze the images—though critical readings of the images is of course a crucial part of a larger project devoted to understanding how catastrophe is infused with meaning. Instead, by synthesizing disparate critical narratives about these images, I seek to define how critics interpret the

18 Gerhard Schoenberner, quoted in Robert Sachett, "Pictures of Atrocity: Public Reception of Der gelbe Stern in 1960s West Germany," *German History* 24 (2006), 529.

19 Guerin and Hallas, *The Image and the Witness*, 14.

rhetorical and affective dimensions of images of catastrophe (and are surrogates for contemporary viewers). The chapter is thus about how critical discourses about photographs of catastrophe reveal not only how catastrophe specifically impacts the meaning of being human—what is lost or laid to waste—but also whether it might be generative of other visions of humanity, how the violence it generates is imaginatively enabled and potentially constrained.[20]

Catastrophic Time

Most historical discussions of photographs of catastrophe are concerned almost exclusively with their evidentiary status, with what they show, or with the politics of why and how they are shown. Rarely do historians engage with the images themselves or critical discourses about them. Rather, they assess how they constitute, support, or defy dominant political and cultural narratives about certain kinds of catastrophes (the putative inevitability, for example, of famine in Ethiopia).[21] Moreover, most art theorists and scholars of media tend to focus on the condensed complexity of cultural icons rather than vernacular photographs, and shy away from images that make ethical as well as aesthetic demands (or assume the superiority of the aesthetic in generating a responsible "witness").[22] Still, the

20 For reasons of conceptual coherence I do not seek to expand the kinds of photographs these discourses address, which are almost exclusively those of suffering and persecuted humanity. Photographs of tormented animals (in war or in other contexts), as well as sites at which capital punishment is administered may be conceived as atrocity photographs, but tend not to be assimilated into these arguments. See Wendy Lesser, *Pictures at an Execution* (Cambridge, MA, 1993); Maria Pia di Bella, "Observing Executions: From Spectator to Witness," in Maria Pia di Bella and James Elkins (eds), *Representations of Pain in Art and Visual Culture* (New York, 2013), 170–85. Thanks to Austin Sarat for asking about the more capacious images implied by the term "atrocity photography."

21 Barbie Zelizer, *Remembering to Forget: Holocaust Memory Through the Camera's Eye* (Chicago 1998); David Shneer, *Through Soviet Jewish Eyes: Photography, War, and the Holocaust* (New Brunswick, 2011). Zelizer's pioneering work on how the Holocaust was shaped as an icon of evil is a crucial referent. But in that work she is focused on a history of the reception and institutionalization of atrocity images rather than on theoretical questions about the photographs.

22 See Frank Möller, "Rwanda Revisualized: Genocide, Photography, and the Era of the Witness," *Alternatives: Global, Local, Political*, 35 (2010): 113–36. This article articulates clearly why, in the author's views, photojournalism and other kinds of vernacular photographs cannot "bear witness" both because genocide cannot be represented and because the medium inevitably reproduces dominant forms of knowledge. Thus, art photography alone guarantees the critical reception of such events. This is indeed often the case, but it is worth examining non-art photography because, as he notes, images constitute political space and yet their meaning can't be grasped. The work on atrocity photography I address here tries hard to figure out how trauma gets in the way of representation but also how photographs nonetheless provide the space for some critical reflection.

ethical pressure of unmediated or often graphic, if professionally made, images by photojournalists, the demands that we "witness" what they have to show us even if we are also complicit when we look, are considerable. Struggles about how to "witness" if photographs reproduce dominant ideology, are no longer merely self-evident truths, and generate traumatic effects, are the issues with which most critical discourses about such photographs engage.

Documentary photographer Janina Struk's *Photographing the Holocaust* is a *tour de force* of detective work.[23] She seeks to find the proper locations of mostly anonymously taken snapshots of extreme forms of victimization and to warn about how their anonymity renders them easy to manipulate and thus liable to fit any particular agenda. She is also on guard against Holocaust deniers who exploit belief in the evidentiary status of photographs to use any errors of designation or editing to prove that the Holocaust has been exaggerated or did not really happen.[24] Hers is above all a work of painstaking contextualization. The book begins with a detailed discussion of the life of one horrific photo of Jewish men and a boy about to be executed on the Eastern Front. She expresses mixed feelings about the purpose of the picture and feels voyeuristic observing them. She also feels complicit in her own eyes with the photographer, whose angle of vision meant that he was among or known to the perpetrators. "But I was compelled to look," she states, "as if the more I looked, the more information I could gain."[25] As the book goes on and she gleans more information, she also grows wearier of the voyeurism, complicity, and potential malleability of the images. By the end of the book she makes an iconoclastic plea that victims be left alone by the camera, as if they were still alive: "Whoever they were, they have been condemned to tread the path [to Birkenau] forever. (...) They had no choice but to be photographed. Now they have no choice but to be viewed by posterity. Didn't they suffer enough the first time around?"[26] Of course the victims' suffering ceased long ago, but she repeats these assertions about the violence simply of taking pictures again and again by reference to a series of other images. For Struk, these pictures tell us that catastrophe is not merely the destruction of human beings, but also describes their mechanical reproduction. Thus, she argues, the pictures Nazis took of dead Jews in the Warsaw ghetto, their bodies in piles awaiting disposal, are no different from

23 Janina Struk, *Photographing the Holocaust: Interpretations of the Evidence* (London, 2004).

24 For a fairly recent example, see the Hamburger Institut für Sozialforschung, *Verbrechen der Wehrmacht: Dimensionen des Vernichtungskrieges 1941–1944, Austellungskatalog* (Hamburg, 2003). The exhibit, which sought to document the involvement of the German army (hence, "Crimes of the Wehrmacht" in the catalogue title) in war crimes against Jews and partisans, was closed because of two inaccurately designated photographs out of hundreds.

25 Struk, *Photographing the Holocaust*, 3.

26 Struk, *Photographing the Holocaust*, 216. Sybil Milton shares this view in "Documentary Photography and the Holocaust," *Simon Wiesenthal Center Annual*, 1 (1984): 49.

those taken by the Allied troops who liberated Buchenwald and Dachau. The photo albums surreptitiously kept by German soldiers and SS are in the end no different from those kept by tourists taking pictures at Auschwitz-Birkenau. Finally, there is no difference between photos of suffering taken for entertainment by Nazis and those provided for consumption on the internet, often accompanied by all sorts of ads. Images conjure up and become indistinguishable from the violence of others. "As visitors gasp with horror at the way victims were photographed, they photograph them again. Why photograph an atrocity photograph?"[27]

Struk notes, after Susan Sontag, that cameras may put distance between photographer and subject, and that taking pictures gives shape to the tourist's experience. Thus the camera's distance makes picture taking and thus witnessing bearable, but it might also—as critics of such photographs say often—be a form of entertainment. In an interesting way, Struk's argument for restricting photography to its purely evidentiary value ends up denouncing the instrument that provides evidence, however problematically, as itself catastrophic. As one image she evokes flows into another image taken at another time often far removed, the camera not only records the doomed, but is also a harbinger of more doom, as if picture taking by definition could only reiterate the catastrophe regardless of who takes the pictures and in what violent context. Struk tries hard to restrict meaning to context in order to supply adequate historical information to prevent the misuse of images, and yet she also brings the dead to life, ventriloquizing voices. Struk hears and conveys the photographed people's desires to be left alone, as if they still lived and spoke.

Why photograph an atrocity photograph? The relationship between cause and effect is a spiral of ever-intensifying voyeurism, complicity, and violence that shatters human integrity in an effort to preserve it. This spectacular, unremittingly violent view of the camera's potential leads to iconoclastic anger and imagined murmurings of the dead. If the author's tone is not apocalyptic, it is nonetheless dismissive of a way out of the abyss into which humanity presumably fell after the Holocaust. Struk never quite resolves the question: do we need the pictures? She implies that we do, but throughout the book she also makes clear that in the end the price for information is that the victims will be symbolically degraded again and again. In order to preserve the memory of the Holocaust we participate in a general repetition of violence against its subjects here and now, and provide fodder for new forms of violence so dramatically that is not clear why one need remember at all.

This spiral in which efforts to preserve something meaningful from catastrophe end in catastrophe is equally intense in discussions of catastrophic images that are far more self-conscious of the problems they pose as evidence because of their traumatic effects. Thus Cornelia Brink emphasizes the traumatic dimension of the

27 Struk, *Photographing the Holocaust*, 190. Other references are, in order, to pages 130, 199, 209–10.

photographs of concentration camps Americans forced Germans to watch after the war and concludes, "the visible makes us blind:"

> In the case of photographs of piles of corpses, the association that the photograph might hold a "trace" of those who were murdered must trigger terror and fear. The world that has been fixed photographically is not subject to transitoriness; something transcends death, the event has been preserved for eternity. This is the irrational power of photography, and it can create an eerie sense of a visual return of the dead. Because the dead themselves, so it seems, could demand settlement of the unsettled debt, the viewers tend to reject their images. The objects reproduced in the photographs are repressed and replaced by the photographs themselves. It is not the fact represented by the photographs that is rejected—the power of their authenticity has hardly ever been challenged—but their projective tendency, the moral appeal connected to them since their first publication in Germany.[28]

Here Germans reject the "moral appeal" because the pictures have been forced upon them. Brink attributes this response to the traumatic nature of the images—their "terror and fear" cannot be grasped by definition—and to the rejection of their moral appeal because the dead appear making impossible demands. In order to explain how photographs that usually serve an evidentiary purpose now function as an alibi for German bystanders, Brink identifies a resemblance between Orthodox religious icons and these now photographic icons. In the case of the Holocaust, these pictures are "sacred" because the Allies rendered them iconic of human evil, showing them in newsreels spliced together by none other than Alfred Hitchcock, putting them on display, and ordering, as did General Eisenhower, that Americans "see" them to understand what they were fighting against.[29] In so doing, the Allies not only used the images as part of so-called victor's justice, but also made fetishes of them, which stood in for human evil rather than the specific evil with which

---

28 Brink, "Secular Icons," 146. Brink draws the term "secular icon" from Patrick Maynard, cited in Brink, *Ikonen der Vernichtung: Öffentlichter Gebrauch von Fotografien aus nationalsozialistischen Konzentrationslagern nach 1945* (Berlin, 1998), 233n7. The book fleshes out the larger frameworks Brink addresses, both theoretical (on images) and historical. The English translation in *History and Memory*, "Secular Icons," [see n17] is a version of the epilogue, which is most consequential, even if it lacks historical and other information about various exhibits in Germany after the war. Brink expands on some of this material regarding the photo-exhibitions in Frankfurt at the time of the Frankfurt Auschwitz trials (1963–65) in her *'Auschwitz in der Paulskirche': Erinnerungspolitik in Fotoausstellungen der sechziger Jahre* (Marburg, 2000). She makes a similar argument about how the photographs universalized and thus dehistoricized Nazi crimes and were made familiar (pictures of the Warsaw Ghetto were arranged as stations on the cross). In both books she seeks to understand the role of the photographs in shaping Germans' responses to Nazi criminality in the post-war period.

29 See the discussion in Zelizer, *Remembering to Forget*, 86–140.

German bystanders were said to have been complicit. Such images thus acted as a "protective layer" between Germans and the photographs of victims of Nazism, "numbness" combining with "superior eloquence." Brink argues that such photos became memento mori—she refers in particular to Marguerite Bourke-White's image of liberated inmates in Buchenwald——but only insofar as they represented generalized human brutality rather than Nazi crimes. This effect, she suggests, was enabled by the symbolic familiarity of the images, specifically in Bourke-White's image of a man in a Christ-like loin-clothe.

Thus Brink summons visual traditions of expressive suffering (in an understatement she remarks that Jewish victims may not have perceived these images in such terms). Photographs are like religious icons, and photography transforms the dead into images that, spectral-like, haunt eternity. The images transcend time because they are sacred, and their sacredness allows Germans not to live in the time of the photographs and not to believe that these images have anything to do with them. The photographs represent the continuous time of human sinfulness, the anxiety-generating possibilities of divine wrath that the images both show and screen at once. Like all icons, they do not simply honor that which they represent but also screen, fetish-like, the object thus "beheld." This argument about the uselessness of Allied efforts to use photos and film footage, not to mention visits to the camps, as pedagogical tools is common: the historiographical consensus is now that the failure of de-Nazification in the long run led to the smoother incorporation of previously Nazified Germans into the Federal Republic and thus, in the midst of the Cold War, into a liberal democratic state.[30] Brink's admirable effort to historicize these photographs accords with the argument that political success went together with ethical failure. But she also argues that as the photographs stand in for the actual objects in the photographs—the Nazis' Jewish victims are effectively screened, though it is less clear how they become utterly impossible to take in at all—they also replace a narrative of what happened, and thus of who did what to whom, with the universal and infinite time of human evil. Of course, iconic images are condensations of complexity that capture a particular historical moment for all time. In so doing, they transcend the messiness of specific historical circumstances, and critics argue that their power is derived from their tacit consonance with specific cultural codes and normative frameworks.[31] Brink

30 For a synthesis over the long term, see Harold Marcuse, *Legacies of Dachau: The Uses and Abuses of a Concentration Camp, 1933–2001* (Cambridge, UK, 2001), 47–186. See especially 114–119 for a summary of this view, with which Brink is consistent. Margaret Bourke-White documented the failure of postwar Germans to acknowledge what had been done in their name in her *"Dear Fatherland, Rest Quietly": A Report on the Collapse of Hitler's "Thousand Years"* (New York, 1946), and there is a voluminous literature on the topic of German 'forgetting' after the war that I cannot possibly review here.

31 Zelizer argues powerfully that by becoming the icon of 'evil in our time,' Auschwitz and the Holocaust of European Jewry have been dehistoricized. As the story became increasingly about Jews in the 1980s and 1990s, it also became a purveyor of

argues that insofar as they became secular icons, the pictures allowed post-war Germans to *disavow* their meaning. People observed them as if the pictures were from another world.

In both Struk and Brink, the context that is supposed to be illuminated—the facts of genocide, the indifference of German civilians—is conflated with catastrophic time conceived as a fall into the abyss. Eternal mourning and eternal disavowal both see and hear lost objects everywhere. Struk hears the victims' asking to be left alone, and Brink imagines them demanding that their "debts be settled," since one is concerned with victims and the other with guilty bystanders (though it isn't entirely clear how hearing accusing voices can be reconciled with German bystanders' utter disavowal).[32] Struk moves from historical to catastrophic time, while Brink's account leaves us with a disavowed catastrophe as itself catastrophic, since there can be no accountability, no acknowledgment of crimes, no agency, only images that screen the crimes committed according to collective cultural demands, unconscious or not.

Both Struk and Brink thus leave us with a question of how, if at all, witnessing atrocity photographs can help us understand better the conditions of victimization and torture because they transform suffering merely into the evil that people do to others. In both, images' ability to transcend time limits their ability to tell us much about what they seek to represent. Moreover, humanity is irreparably lost or displaced in a timeless violence that exceeds the frame of the photograph and appears to be a permanent feature of a now traumatic history.

Catastrophe and Humanity

What both these accounts suggest is that humanity and the human dignity that forms its touchstone have themselves become catastrophic: loss is permanent and unredeemable and humanity is eternally wounded and without any foundation. Catastrophe, that is, cannot no longer escape its traumatic effects: it generates

---

universal truths about human history. Zelizer's focus is on how Auschwitz became such an icon from an American perspective, not on how the iconic photographs impacted Germans after the war. Zelizer, *Remembering to Forget.* The most positive views of the iconic quality of some Holocaust photography ("aesthetic effects deliver historical data" [205]) are offered for the most part by art historians. See essays by Janet Wolff, "The Iconic and the Allusive: The Case for Beauty in Holocaust Art," and Carol Zemel, "Emblems of Atrocity: Holocaust Liberation Photographs," in *Image and Remembrance: Representation and the Holocaust*, Shelley Hornstein and Florence Jacobowitz (eds) (Bloomington, 2001), 153–74, 201–19. These essays are extremely rare. Admittedly Zemel's defense of stylization in Holocaust images, while important, repeats arguments about how they "plunge" us into the abject and are "sublime" (205).

32 Brink, quoting Detlev Claussen in "Secular Icons," 144. She notes that "looking at these pictures paralyzes us … the result is often a remarkable 'inviolability' which seems to preclude a detailed pictorial analysis."

fragmented time in which effects have no clear relations to their causes, violence is thus doomed to repetition, and meaning remains fundamentally ungraspable. At least that is the implication of these failures to redeem the meaning of some normative precept of dignity and thus a foundation for humanity in the wake of catastrophe. In what remains, I want to discuss recent critical efforts to sustain some meaning of humanity in the face of catastrophe—to prevent its conflation with the insuperable loss catastrophe represents. And I want to conclude with Judith Butler's creative, if unsuccessful, effort to suggest that catastrophic destruction might be conceived as a moment in the transformation of our understanding of humanity. The latter is not a refusal of catastrophic time, but suggests that catastrophe constitutes and is constituted by historical transformations to which we must be attentive, as Hannah Arendt sought to argue some 60 years ago.

Media critic Barbie Zelizer refers to one photograph of the 2004 tsunami which wrought so much death and destruction in Southern India, Sri Lanka, and Indonesia. She includes natural calamities in her repertoire of images because she assumes their impact has intensified in the wake of environmental degradation, infrastructure failures, and human-made poverty:

> One frequently displayed image from Madras, India, powerful more for what it forced the public to imagine than for what it showed, displayed a beach that bore no visible resemblance to recognizable ground (…) What was significant was what was not shown—people struggling to survive or corpses which had failed to do so. Viewers thus needed to imagine what rested underneath the muddy water swirls, particularly the dead bodies that they knew to be there.[33]

The photograph in question affirms rules dictated by an ethics of representation of the dead and dying in which bodies are not exposed but must be imagined. Zelizer herself does not believe that such a photograph represents the most effective kind of atrocity photograph, a point to which we will return. Both art and photojournalism are accountable when they disturb an ethics of decency, and Zelizer takes up the challenge about how to provide ethical or digestible and thus critically salient or meaningful photographs of catastrophe. What she calls "about to die" photographs allow us to empathize with suffering others against the prevalent notion that catastrophe lays to waste not only all normative precepts about humanity, but also the human solidarity implied by the empathy a photograph might generate.[34] "About to die" pictures that are most effective do not show human beings expressing too much weakness or anxiety in the face of death in spite of the traumatic nature of their experience. The most horrific and often iconic photos become viewable, Zelizer argues, because of strategic decisions about their framing and presentation that emphasize even frontal shots of violence.

---

33 Barbie Zelizer, *About to Die: How News Images Move the Public* (Oxford, 2010), 252.

34 Zelizer, *About To Die*, 56, 223.

"About to die" photographs reject the conflation of humanity and catastrophe, the unremitting, unredeemable traumatic violence and destruction of the human neither Struk nor Brink could elude. Zelizer notes how the focus on an unfolding death whose finality must still be imagined is often combined with a tendency to select subjects who are "unflinching." In so doing, they make viewers complicit in suffering, but reduce rather than enhance the viewer's domination over the victim. The victims may be in the midst of a catastrophic event, but play central roles in the image of what is being done to them. The complicity the photographs evoke is thus not on the side of catastrophe—of an inevitable identification with or entrapment in the forces of destruction—but designed to make the viewer ashamed, exposed, and to reject the horror of the scene she witnesses.[35]

But "about to die" pictures also take on less direct forms. Zelizer claims that pictures of monks who set themselves on fire in protest of war or dictatorship in Southeast Asia (Vietnam and Myanmar) are powerful because there is no crying out and no death—these pictures unsettle because the viewer knows what is happening, but the flames spectacularly occlude the pain of the dying bodies they display. In her discussion of the media coverage of 9/11, Zelizer notes that networks and newspapers stopped showing pictures of bodies jumping from the Twin Towers because they were too disturbing. Photographers instead depicted victims whom viewers knew would have to jump or succumb to smoke and fire. Zelizer argues that images of those "about to die" need not be violations of victims because they do not show wounded bodies or atrocities. By showing impending death and yet leaving death itself to the imagination, the picture conveys and openly pictures the incommensurability of power and powerlessness that constitutes the brutality of the various scenes. The imagination cannot be contained by the frame because it is focused on an afterward that is forever deferred but whose weight crushes: in the 9/11 shots the buildings dwarf the victims, representing not death but the power that has so mercilessly condemned these people to die. The violence deferred does not affirm the unredeemable and uncontainable violence of catastrophe but allows for an intangible identification with the victim that condemns the power of catastrophe to destroy human lives. Zelizer's goal is to demonstrate empirically that these are the kinds of drawings and photographs that have long dominated the picturing of violent events because of their indirection, which renders identification with victims possible. She does not engage explicitly with theoretical questions about atrocity photos, and does not address the epistemological problem implicit in the identification with the victim—how do we conceive the relationship between affective response and the political recognition of and condemnation of powerlessness—except by overwhelming evidence that such images predominate in this genre of photojournalism.

"About to die" moments repress meaningless suffering so that photographs of catastrophe cannot reduce human beings to nothing. Photographs of these "about to die" moments are dramatic not because there is any reference to human freedom

35 Zelizer, *About to Die*, 56.

that might triumph to face the enemy against impossible odds, no tragic sense of inevitable failure. None of these human beings is reduced to nothing because they are powerless, even though the unflinching bodies are still swatted about like flies or tormented. Their refusal to flinch marks one way in which some victims display their humanity—resilient, resolute, and whole—against catastrophic destruction.

Zelizer argues that images of suffering and pain are either indecent or generate discomfort. In so doing, they violate a normative concept of decency and dignity (a view that implicitly characterizes Struk and Brink's essays as well) that the "about to die" moment strategically counters. By contrast, literary theorist Ulrich Baer calls this view of violated human integrity, rendered irrelevant by modern catastrophic loss, a form of "phobic repression."[36] His main goal is to expose the way historians use documentary photographs reductively, as if the fact that Holocaust photos were taken by Nazis ensures that they can only show degraded victims. He claims that in the hands of historians, photographs of Holocaust atrocities currently "block access to the event instead of facilitating a self-aware, rather than rote, commemoration and witnessing" (69); and he seeks to move beyond "the rush of moral indignation that often accompanies the encounter with graphic pictures of atrocities, [which] may be narcissistically satisfying, but it may also free us from the responsibility of placing our own experiences in relation to something that remains, finally, incomprehensible" (84). In order to propose this alternative reading, he suggests that the photograph has a "structural affinity" with trauma. The photographic flash replicates trauma—that is, in Cathy Caruth's terms, it is "unclaimed experience" because the experience cannot enter into the subject's lived time except as an empty signifier of something he or she cannot grasp.[37] After all, the "flash" of the camera is a moment of self-alienation, according to Baer, analogous with trauma to the extent its very capturing of the subject splits the self's lived reality from the camera's ability to reiterate a moment over and over. The question is how this reading of photography as an allegory for traumatic memory helps us to imagine the catastrophe of the Holocaust outside the frame of what he calls "rote commemoration," "cognitive numbing," or moral indignation.

Baer offers a sensitive discussion of landscape photographs of sites where death camps were once located to demonstrate that like trauma, the photographs refuse to fulfill the viewer's imagination—indeed they actively thwart it by inviting the spectator in only to make the same place inhospitable and uncontainable (the trees exceed the frame, the convention of the landscape painting is transformed into a scene of beauty that becomes increasingly abstract as the plants turn into figures and ground dissolves into mud). Like trauma, these images convey an experience that cannot be absorbed into narrative memory and leave the spectator haunted by something he or she can see and yet not know, divorcing the visual, documentary

36 Ulrich Baer, *Spectral Evidence: The Photography of Trauma* (Cambridge, MA, 2005), 12.

37 Cathy Caruth, *Unclaimed Experience: Trauma, Narrative, History* (Baltimore, 1996).

like pretense of the photograph from its status as evidence, and pointing, according to Baer, to a spectral beyond. Baer then discusses photographs of everyday life in the Lódź ghetto between 1941 and 1944 taken by its SS accountant, Walter Genewein, as well as a documentary film about these photos, *The Photographer*, by Polish filmmaker Dariusz Jablonski. These pictures in particular are the kind of evidence historians have dismissed as necessarily objectifying because taken from the perpetrators' view, and it is this perspective Baer wishes to challenge.

As in Zelizer's account, in Baer's too it is crucial that the photos taken are images of people "about to die" in the sense that death is outside of the frame: the victims are alive. But these photographs also militate against responses like moral indignation about the victims' violation: there is no room for empathic identification. Baer takes aim at once at the historians who presume that the images are evidence only of Nazi perspectives of Jews *and* at those who identify "narcissistically" with victims. Indeed, the empathy viewers might feel toward victims has an affinity, he claims, with the "Nazi gaze":

> If, however, that technical dimension records in these photographs something that might be saved from the Nazi gaze, it also undercuts our facile identification with the 'humanity' portrayed in them. Such an identification can be achieved only at the risk of hitching the photograph's visual field onto a single viewpoint drenched in empathy. As we have seen … the empathic, identificatory perspective favored by some critics remains tied to the seductive myth of a viewer's self-aware, unified, and all-encompassing nonalienated [meaning selfsame, nontraumatic] gaze. The notion of such a gaze is itself part of the legacy of the Nazi worldview.[38]

The assimilation of this gaze to Nazism is obviously hyperbolic unless one is prepared to associate all moral indignation with narcissistic identification and all contemporary humanitarianism with the legacy of Nazism. Nonetheless, what Baer means by the Nazi gaze is that the illusion proffered by the one-way gaze of the camera is confused with reality. If so, the illusion of transparency has triumphed and with it, so has the idea that we can feel our way into the suffering human being on the other side of the camera, denying all the difference between them and us. We believe we are part of the same humanity when in fact we are dispassionate observers who dominate the reality on the other side of the lens (a portrait of spectators gazing at atrocities that Zelizer too seeks to undermine). Baer insists instead on a division between seeing and knowing that mimics traumatic experience ("they did not know what they had seen," to repeat Sliwinski's comments about Lee Miller's Holocaust photographs). What emerges when we look is not understanding or empathy but the revelation of how little we know—a spectral and nontranscendental beyond. But does the incommensurability of seeing and knowing then merely reiterate the ever-destabilizing violence of catastrophic

38 Baer, *Spectral Trauma*, 177.

time, its haunting non-meaning, its description as "ontological loss?" When Baer claims that "we can see through these slides by viewing them critically instead of responding to them ritualistically with fear, outrage, or pity" (150), what is critical response except an assertion that catastrophe has compromised our ability to see or feel in humanistic terms?[39]

It turns out that, in two significant instances cited by Baer, the "beyond" we cannot know is the face of a human being who "accuses" his tormentors. Jabolinski's film focuses on a photograph of a Jewish man in a ghetto barber shop. In a gesture staged for the photograph, the man looks directly into the camera. In the photograph he is frozen, but the film zooms in so that he fills the screen in a close-up shot that is then dissolved. The image is dissolved because the face, Baer says, can't be made into a symbol but can only point to an unknowable beyond in which the viewer will not know who the man was but will be forced to reflect about him. And yet: "the film not does not invite viewers to identify with the Jew in the picture … Instead they are made to feel addressed, and the right to appeal, to look back, to accuse, or to denounce is restored to the Jew who was captured, framed, and labeled by the Nazi photographer" (156). And in another instance where a Jew appears almost invisible in a particular frame, the Jew "stares back" (169) and "deflects his objectification and implicit subordination … ." (166). In short, though the dissolution of the face is supposed to refuse symbolization, what is being done to him is captured by reference to the victim's refusal to comply with the state of things, the accusation, the refusal to submit to Nazi domination. Baer thus celebrates the refusal of identification by reference to the toughness and resilience of the victim rather than by his inability to be fully present to the camera (that the film is not a photograph but a medium that revitalizes photographs, and through the use of the close-up dissolves symbolic identification and empathy, is a problem Baer does not address.[40] The film can render the 'resistance' portrayed

39 This question formulated differently in regard to poststructuralist uses of traumatic memory has received an extraordinary response from Dominick LaCapra, who has noted how indebted such analyses are to the sublime—the "beyond," the overwhelming force of something that exceeds our reason and cannot, as Kant had suggested it might, be reconciled with a transcendent reason that allowed us to reflect upon our own limitations. LaCapra argues that some critical work transforms the Holocaust itself into a sublime object that confuses structural trauma (say, the Biblical "fall" of man into sin) with historical trauma. The allegory Baer proposes grafts structural trauma (the haunting and spectral beyond that cannot be identified) onto what is effectively a historical trauma (the Holocaust) with actual contexts, even if the experience itself cannot be reduced to contextualization. The Holocaust becomes a sublime object that cannot be apprehended historically or even rationally. Here I seek less to reiterate LaCapra's incisive critical readings than to demonstrate how, in Baer's case, this "sublime" rendering of Holocaust photographs is not sustained. LaCapra, *Writing History, Writing Trauma* (Baltimore, 2001), 82.

40 It is worth noting that the close up is often used as an image that cinema must and does seek to contain, but is characterized generally as that which always exceeds the screen and thus the film's effort to maintain the illusion of narrative control. Mary Ann

in the photograph invisible). In short, Baer, unlike Zelizer, rejects a foundational concept of humanity and yet the return of resolute and resilient "humanity" in relation to catastrophic destruction seems to function as a disavowed referent that returns again and again.

Catastrophe and Vulnerable Humanity

Judith Butler claims that atrocity photographs taken at Abu Ghraib offer an alternative framework to extant arguments within which the catastrophe represented by the war on Iraq might be interpreted. Her framework stresses our interconnection and commonality as human social animals prior to our formation as autonomous individuals and questions humanist norms of individualism and autonomy. Butler uses atrocity photography to address the question of when life is grievable, a question that assumes that some lives are deemed worthier than others even though all life is precarious. She refers in particular to the racism and colonialism that makes Western eyes respond more powerfully and empathically to the pain of people 'like them' than to the pain of those who are culturally foreign. These assumptions are hardly unusual. But Butler thinks through the larger question of how the media create hierarchies of recognition at great length and thoughtfully. She argues that normative frameworks of human worthiness based on others' likeness to us may be broken or altered. With permanent catastrophe—torture, after all, is renormalized even in a nation whose entire self-image is predicated on the condemnation of its practice—a new framework emerges in which human vulnerability to destruction replaces the tough and resilient meaning attributed to a construction of a humanity in thrall to itself and striving for self-betterment. She imagines a concept and picture of humanity that is entirely consistent with its vulnerability to suffering, dying, and death: all sentient being is subject to injury and thus intrinsically and equally worthy based on this vulnerability.[41]

This image of bare, even destroyed humanity, of course, is the one that Arendt argued was revealed to be intolerable by the refugee crisis of the Second World War, when it became clear that human dignity was not based on bare humanity but on the social status of the citizen. In Butler's reformulation, it becomes clear that in light of Arendt's critique, all of the critics we have discussed either cannot exit a discourse of catastrophic violence or do so by strategic or disavowed reference to the resolute image of humanity that emerged most forcefully in the eighteenth century and presumes its metaphorical wholeness. Struk and Brink's essays are in

Doane, "The Close Up: Scale and Detail in the Cinema," *differences: A Journal of Feminist Cultural Studies*, 14 (2003): 89–111.

41 This alternative understanding of human community not allegedly based on a universal concept of humanity but on differentiated perceptions of vulnerability shaped by norms of recognition is worked out in Judith Butler, *Precarious Life: The Powers of Mourning and Violence* (New York, 2003).

their own ways catastrophic because they conceive bare humanity as a symptom of catastrophe, a conceptual and emotional demotion from the integral humanity the images destroy. Zelizer and Baer, in radically different formulations, struggle against catastrophe by reference to images of integral humanity that catastrophe seems to have rendered outmoded. Instead, Butler (like Baer) begins within catastrophic time, but asks how to make its relentless violence meaningful, or whether we can.

The shock of atrocity photographs is their unbearable humanity, humanity that unsettles the frameworks of recognition:

> What we are left with are photos of people who are for the most part faceless and nameless. But can we nevertheless say that the obscured face and the absent name function as the visual trace—even if it is the lacuna within the visible field—of the very mark of humanity? This is a mark, in other words, not registered through a norm, but by the fragments that follow in the wake of an abrogation of the normatively human. In other words, the humans who were tortured do not readily conform to a visual, corporeal, or socially recognizable identity; their occlusion and erasure become the continuing sign of their suffering and of their humanity.[42]

The occlusion of humanity in the photographs paradoxically leaves traces of the human even in the absence of recognizable human identities. Looking at photographs unsettles, repairs connections, intensifies longings that this suffering not be. If we feel any kind of shock, it is similar to the inarticulate grief that undoes us in relation to the loss of another.[43]

The point is not, as Butler notes, to replace one norm with another but to try and see what the normative frame represses, which is a visual trace of another image of humanity. She also insists that the decision by U.S. media (in accord with the Geneva Conventions that were flouted) not to show the faces of those victims who might be identified is right because "the face and names are not ours to know, and affirming this cognitive limit is a way of affirming the humanity that has escaped the visual control of the photograph." But then we return to a familiar argument articulated most clearly by Struk: "to expose the victim further would be to reiterate the crime."[44]

There is no reason why there cannot be multiple frameworks within which humanity is made recognizable. Butler acknowledges that her reading is limited to contexts of first-world consumption of such images. She insists too that bodily autonomy has to be part of any "normative aspiration" of women and minorities and seeks elsewhere to ask if there is any way to transform the attachment to others that makes us vulnerable into a normative aspiration "within the field of

---

42 Judith Butler, *Frames of War: When is Life Grievable?* (London, 2010), 94.

43 Butler, *Precarious Life*, 30–39.

44 Butler, *Frames of War*, 95.

politics."[45] At the same time, Butler's emphasis on the unthought, the "cognitive limit," and the "mark of humanity" that undoes the viewer's autonomy makes it difficult to discern the relationship between norms of recognition and different affective responses attached to them. Here, as in traumatic disempowerment, the affective response is impossible to articulate except in terms of fragments, traces, and occlusions, or must be assimilated to narratives in which exposure marks the indecency of human vulnerability, or at least of showing it.

But if affective response to vulnerability based on connectedness rather than on autonomy is not articulated in the "field of politics," isn't the vulnerable body a symptom of catastrophic destruction rather than its meaningful reframing? Doesn't the body's exposure and the shame it provokes now mark the triumph of catastrophe rather than the underside of once-triumphant "humanity" modelled on the image of the metaphorically upright man? How are these multiple frames of reference that mobilize different affective responses related to historically and culturally constituted norms of recognition? The emphasis on grieving rather than mourning suggests an individualistic as opposed to collective response to the photographs, since grief is not a collective ritual but an individualized mode of mourning. Can human solidarity based on vulnerability be fashioned in the recognition of injury as disempowerment? And if so, why wouldn't so much atrocity "numb"—after all, that is a common response to witnessing traumatic disempowerment given its overwhelming assault on the senses—rather than generate outrage? Finally, why does Butler herself offer a far more conventional argument about humanity when she returns to the power of images? She asserts that "the task at hand is to create modes of public seeing and hearing" that might challenge the dehumanization of enemy combatants and the aestheticization of war, but the example she provides is how images of Vietnam in their "graphic effectivity" took viewers "beyond the frame" the state sought to regulate.[46] The assertions claim that showing what is usually unseen and rendered off-limits by the state can change public attitudes to war. The claim is indubitable. But not all photographs have this Vietnam effect: the discussion of atrocity photos, such that it is, asks how we should interpret "graphic effectivity." After all, the photos of Abu Ghraib did not prevent the re-election of George W. Bush in 2004.

We still have not resolved the fundamental questions encountered in discussions of atrocity photos about how, by witnessing an event, the spectator can make meaning out of the injury she witnesses. But Butler draws our attention to the necessity of analyzing the relationship between norms of recognition and affective response whose cultural and temporal stability Zelizer assumes rather than questions. Butler proposes another framework that conceptualizes human solidarity in terms of our surrender of sovereignty and in terms of our precariousness. She uses the more conventional language of "exposure" when she seeks a strategic political response because the traumatic undoing that alters the frame cannot be

45 Butler, *Precarious Life*, 26.

46 Butler, *Precarious Life*, 147–50.

articulated except in precognitive terms that preclude interpretation or critical reflection. Thus vulnerability could theoretically reframe the normatively human, but it cannot do so without simply mimicking the violent meaninglessness and loss to which catastrophe has condemned humanity.

Of course, injurability should not preclude autonomy—it merely presumes that the forcible denial of our autonomy is not a cause for shame. Similarly, captivity should not necessarily provoke tragic drama, since it can be represented simply as a quality of life denied rather than a potential proving ground of heroism against the odds. The difficulty Butler has articulating a means of recognizing the Abu Ghraib victims' frailty in terms other than the agreement not to expose them suggests the absence of a cultural form in which human vulnerability to political persecution shorn of shame, generative of aversion or dislocation, or evocative of a potentially condescending pity might be articulated.[47] Whatever is to be gained from "witnessing," it is indeed a fraught activity, perhaps less obviously ritualized and more complex than Baer suggests.

Richard Rorty addresses this problem when he claims that fellow feeling moves us to help others rather than any sort of argument about what we might have in common with them, for the "in common" argument begs the question of why having things in common with others should move us to act on their behalf. His position presumes that "we" recognize the pain of others like us and is not an opportunity for pity or prurience. Rorty anticipates objections to his use of the West as his frame of recognition and insists on the strategic revelation of our universal sameness: "We shall have to accept the fact that the fate of the woman in Bosnia depends on whether TV journalists manage to do for them what Harriet Beecher Stowe did for black slaves, whether these journalists can make us, the audience back in the safe countries, feel that these women are more like us … than we had realized."[48] This reliance on 'our' ability to recognize others is exactly what Butler rejects when she glimpses a different picture of humanity. And yet she does not offer a solution to the intractable problem of how human vulnerability can be witnessed from a perspective that is not wrenched by anxiety about the exposure of vulnerable bodies. She frames very clearly a central problem: how do we link the affect the photographs generate and their ability to confer historical meaning on catastrophe? In so doing she is implicitly critical of the view that catastrophe has created an image of humanity that is immediately identified as that

47 Wendy Brown and Lauren Berlant claim in different ways that images of suffering encourage audiences to feel better about themselves for enduring the spectacle rather than constitute calls to action or revelations of structural inequities. Berlant, "The Subject of True Pain, Privacy, and Politics," and Brown, "Suffering the Paradoxes of Rights" in *Left Legalism/Left Critique*, Wendy Brown and Janet Halley (eds) (Durham, 2002), 105–33; Wendy Brown, *States of Injury: Power and Freedom in Late Modernity* (Princeton, 1995).

48 Richard Rorty, "Human Rights, Rationality, and Sentimentality," in *On Human Rights: The Oxford Amnesty Lectures 1993*, Stephen Shute and Susan Hurley (eds) (New York, 1993), 133,129.

from which we must avert our eyes. But it is nonetheless hard to figure out how to look. And those images are used over and over to encourage people to donate to organizations that struggle to stop the suffering they portray, as if they were meaningful, paradoxically, only to the extent that they affirm the endlessness of catastrophe, its unremitting violence.

Conclusion

Thus far Butler provides us with material to speculate about whether or how permanent catastrophe alters and is altered by renewed constructions of humanity—that is to say, for our immediate purposes, the affective animation of human dignity. Assessing the meaning of global humanity in times of catastrophe also helps us define more clearly how we constitute human worth in conjunction with all the ideological prisms through which different kinds of human beings are perceived. We could suggest that hand-wringing about how to approach catastrophe photos defines human dignity within a specific frame of recognition that treats vulnerability and fragility as unsightly and abject or as incentives to reinvigorate human resilience and determination against oppression. What if the very problem defined by the critical reception of photographs of catastrophe—their ostensible reiteration of the victim's powerlessness, the aliveness of and hence violence done to their subjects that Struk found unbearable and Brink demonstrates was disavowed—revealed a representational process through which narratives of political persecution render images of disempowered people "indecent"? What if these images reveal how a glimmer of freedom on the horizon implicit in resistance, refusal, and stoicism becomes the necessary condition of our ability to look, and that that pressure to be human as such has been intensified with the kind of industrial destruction of human life catastrophe has wrought? What if our admiration for resilient victims obscures how our respect for victims might be accompanied by contempt for other, frail ones? Could this be one way of at least demonstrating that vulnerable people may well be forced beneath the level of common dignity through no fault of their own, a simple assertion about the mechanisms of persecution that images of vulnerability manifest, but which spectators have trouble seeing pictured; that catastrophe conceived as unremitting destruction often obscures the agency of persecution and celebrates the valiant struggles of victims?

This is not to say that contextualization cannot go far in counteracting recoil and paradox. It makes no sense to argue that texts that expose the usage, say, of lynching as "folk pornography" become part of that genre, but the anxiety about displaying such images and the inevitable failure to control all their effects suggests that anxiety is real.[49] I mean only to argue that context is an insufficient screen as

49 See Leon Litwack, "Hellhounds," in *Without Sanctuary: Lynching Photography in America*, James Allen, Hilton Als, Congressman John Lewis, and Leon F. Litwack (eds)

long as dignity imagined as resilience under pressure is still a powerful picture of idealized humanity that traverses all time. In the instances we have discussed, the incommensurability of power and powerlessness in extreme cases overwhelms the frame and provides an image of humanity in crisis, of disempowerment that is not a structural property of the image but a highly individualized and precognitive response. Thus catastrophe photographs do not provide an alternative to the idealized picture of human dignity as much as they begin to render human vulnerability seeable, reveal a rupture in the frame as itself a focus of critical reflection as well as affective response. Georges Didi-Huberman has called this rupture a "tear" in the image of horror that allows it to operate as both veil and rupture, what he calls "fetish and fact."[50] At the very least, vulnerability and frailty in this context may affirm that catastrophe has altered our image of idealized humanity, displacing it slowly but surely: dignity understood stubbornly as resilience and honor comes increasingly to appear as a defense against abjection—against powerlessness and injury—all that which threatens upright and whole subjects capable of using their last ounce of strength to fight oppression. This effort to uncouple dignity from honor is part of an effort to demonstrate the potential alteration in the meaning conferred on human agency under duress.

My aim here has not been to claim that abjection is now the appropriate description of the human condition under regimes of bio-power that control and constrain "bare life" and in which Auschwitz once and for all eliminated human dignity and that catastrophe, with its "wasted lives," has prevailed. Ultimately, Agamben equates all "morality and dignity" with the abject figure of the *Muselmann* in the concentration camps, who embodies death in life and is a figure for modernity itself.[51] As others have argued, this extreme reversal transforms human dignity into human abjection (and our time into catastrophic time), but never interrogates human dignity itself except as a condition that modernity has destroyed. Atrocity images can provide a historical forum for imagining the transformations catastrophe has wrought, for thinking through the claim that it has no end and cannot be measured except in terms of the waste it creates. If the catastrophes of the twentieth and twenty-first centuries reveal that dignity was always contingent on citizenship or other social privileges rather than intrinsic in bare humanity, they also call forth a new image of human dignity suited to a time of intensified catastrophe. That image restores dignity in revised terms rather than mourns its loss.

Zelizer and Baer suggest that catastrophe's impact on human dignity is still imagined by recourse to bearable images of resilience, however violent. But their work also suggests that this framework may be historicized. Zelizer documents to what extent this particular construction of unflinching humanity renders

(Hong Kong, 2000), 22.

50 Georges Didi-Huberman, *Images in Spite of All: Four Photographs from Auschwitz* (Chicago, 2007), 79–80.

51 Agamben, *Remnants of Auschwitz*, 59.

images bearable and defines their power over the long term, while Baer almost inadvertently (really in spite of himself) finds in the hard look "back" a sign of human dignity. Both arguments rely problematically on normative constructions of dignity elaborated since the eighteenth century, and sustain human dignity ideally as an image of wholeness, resoluteness already explicit in the ancient concept of dignified bearing that was originally limited to men of rank alone. The admiration for victims who resist humiliation should be balanced with some awareness that resistance itself is a mode of comportment that is historically associated with human dignity and a narrative of redemption linked to tragic drama.

Is it possible to conceptualize an alternative form of imagining human dignity under stress that could be articulated in the realm of politics—meaning one that had some cultural power that could not be reduced to pitying the vulnerable, a sentiment always laced with contempt? If we were able to alter our image of human dignity then we would alter the meaning of the impact of catastrophes: they might destroy human beings, but might also allow us to envision human dignity in Butler's terms, to render dignity now consistent with human vulnerability as well as or in place of, resilience.

Chapter 4
Catastrophe and Human Order: From Political Theology to Political Physiology

David W. Bates

"Disease is shock and danger for existence."

Kurt Goldstein, The Organism (1934)

If catastrophe is in its essence an unpredictable, devastating interruption of the normal rhythms of human community, it is, strictly speaking, impossible to speak of "permanent catastrophe." But the phrase alerts us to a new understanding of catastrophe, one that emphasizes not just the "act of God" (whether literal or figural) but also the myriad ways that normal human order itself can contribute to the violence and devastation.[1] Instead of focusing on the spectacular violence of the catastrophic event—the violence that seems to indicate a radical rupture, a cut into the continuity of normal existence—some contemporary thinkers seek to expose the often hidden links between catastrophic disorder and the supposedly regular forms of existence. In other words, catastrophe can be said to be permanent—it is a permanent possibility—once we understand how extreme threats to human community can come not just from "outside," but indeed from within the very normal modes of functioning; the catastrophe is itself a sign of an omnipresent fragility. Natural catastrophes might be the best example of this notion of permanent catastrophe. For instance, the terrible violence and destruction wrought by Hurricane Katrina might have been caused by the extreme force of nature, but its effects could be traced to the normal conditions of life in the region. In other words, Katrina as a catastrophic "event" was just a catalyst that exposed the more permanent failures and shortcomings tied to weak institutions, systemic economic inequality, large-scale urban organizations, and structures of political authority and responsibility. Failure to see the deep relations between catastrophe as event, and the pathologies of "normal" human order, can only perpetuate the regular appearance of the unpredictable. As Adi Ophir has written, "by focusing on catastrophes and their victims, contemporary humanitarianism dissociates the catastrophic event and the camp where its survivors live from a series of interrelated economic, political, and cultural processes that have made

1 Nick Bostrom and Milan M. Cirkovic, *Global Catastrophic Risks* (Oxford: Oxford University Press, 2008).

the catastrophe possible."[2] Here, we can discern a conception of catastrophe that is predicated on a deep relationship between permanent conditions of order and seemingly discrete eruptions of unexpected disaster.

Indeed, one could argue that it is the very spectacular forms of catastrophe that occlude the *permanent* catastrophic tendencies inherent in our current political, social, and economic order. At least this is what Naomi Klein has recently suggested, in a book that shows how the "disaster capitalism" characteristic of our contemporary era thrives in the midst of catastrophe, as it feeds off of the strange new hybrid political forms that have resulted from the fusion of neo-liberal economic principles and hyper-militarized state apparatuses.[3] In other words, it is now possible to see catastrophe as permanent, as an expected feature of modern existence, but only if we look beyond the most extreme occurrences of unexpected violence and focus attention on the less spectacular forms. As Slavoj Žižek has pointed out, the suddenness and intensity of an event like 9/11 can often serve to reinforce the very structural conditions that helped to prepare it—terrorist attacks appear as catastrophes for us in the West, because they take the form of rupture and discontinuity. However, as Žižek suggests, these ruptures can often blind us to the "dreary permanent catastrophe" of, say, the Palestinians under occupation, which can be structurally linked to the global infrastructure of terrorism.[4] Contemporary concepts of catastrophe are emphasizing the ways in which human forms of order harbor within themselves the permanent possibility of violence and disorder.

We can trace some of these ideas to Walter Benjamin, who claimed that history was not the narration of what is stable and continuous in the human past, much less a story of ongoing progressive movement. Instead, human history was just an endless series of catastrophic events, which piled up on each other with no logic other than that of violence itself. In a memorable image, Benjamin imagined that the angel of history "sees one single catastrophe which keeps piling wreckage upon wreckage and hurls it in front of his feet."[5] For Benjamin, catastrophe did not punctuate some normal form of human life. Catastrophe was a permanent condition of unredeemed violence that was itself punctuated by the merely apparent forms of stable order.

This notion that history is defined by the repetition of catastrophe—the perpetual undoing of order—was at once theological and political for Benjamin. In the modern era, we cannot understand history as somehow divinely ordered, Benjamin said, and nor should we think it had even a secularized eschatological

2 Adi Ophir, "The sovereign, the humanitarian, and the Terrorist." At: http://roundtable.kein.org/node/123, accessed April 28, 2015.

3 Naomi Klein, *The Shock Doctrine: The Rise of Disaster Capitalism* (New York: Henry Holt, 2007).

4 Slavoj Žižek, "Catastrophes real and imagined," (2003). At: http://www.lacan.com/zizekcatastrophes.htm, accessed April 28, 2015.

5 Walter Benjamin, "Theses on the philosophy of history," *Illuminations*, tr. Harry Zohn (New York: Schocken, 1968), 255.

structure. Human community had no sacred or privileged source. We therefore had no insight into the nature of divine order on earth. The "messianic" moment that Benjamin described was a negative experience. The messianic was something that *interrupted* historical continuity to remind us of the *permanence of discontinuity*. This messianic appearance was engendered by catastrophe itself, Benjamin thought, because only the "sudden turn" could expose clearly the underlying fragility and impermanence of human communal life on earth. The necessary presence of violence at the heart of human historical order explained both the permanence of the castastrophic possibility, and the *occlusion* of this possibility. Only what Benjamin called "divine" violence—meaningless, foreign, totally devastating, we might say truly catastrophic—was capable of reminding us that all of our human orders were founded on an inherently violent and oppressive logic of negation. Writing at a time in the 1930s and 1940s when European states were operating in a permanent "state of emergency" in order to counter the endless internal threats to its existence and to wage war, Benjamin undermined the legitimacy of this "law-preserving violence." He would argue that we ought "to bring about a real state of emergency" as a way of exposing the mythological origins of the state, to counter the conditions in which the exception had become the rule, and the temporary and improvised structure of crisis government had devolved into a permanent form of political rule.

Since 9/11, the apocalyptic tone of Benjamin's writings from the 1930s and 1940s has returned. And given the religious dimension of the new "clash of civilizations" that the wars in the Middle East have spawned, it is hardly surprising that interest in religion and in the theological *structures* of modernity has only surged since 2001. The complex intersection of political and theological concepts—what Carl Schmitt, drawing on Erik Peterson, called "political theology"—now shapes much of the contemporary theoretical debate on the nature of human political authority and its role in producing catastrophic violence, in both its spectacular and dreary instantiations. If the state as a theoretical problem had all but disappeared in political theory debates at the end of the twentieth century, it has now reemerged as a significant question. Is it the site of dangerous tendencies toward "emergency rule" or the protector of rights? Is it the bastion of human rationality against the excesses of religious radicalism, or does its very secular foundation support a globalized violence that rivals the most brutal theological conflicts in historical memory? Lurking behind these questions is a key issue raised by political theology: when Schmitt declared that all political concepts are secularized theological concepts (in their history and in their essential form) he challenged us to think metaphysically about the structures of political authority and the forms of legitimation.[6]

The complexities (and confusions) surrounding politics, religion, and theology in the present moment are many. I want to focus on one crucially important aspect

6 Carl Schmitt, *Political Theology: Four Chapters on the Concept of Sovereignty*, tr. George Schwab (Chicago: University of Chicago, 2006).

of political theology that is often glossed over, namely the claim that political concepts are *secularized* theological notions. Schmitt argued in the methodological third chapter of *Political Theology* that the way human beings understand political authority in any historical period must be substantially consistent with contemporary theological thinking, which was another way of saying that there is always a dominant metaphysical form of belief that grounds analogies across different conceptual spheres. The challenge of this analysis today is twofold: first, one must identify *what the dominant form of metaphysical belief* is, and second, track that form in the political concepts in order to draw out the potential challenges and possibilities inherent in that conceptual space.

My argument is that a political-theological perspective grounds Benjamin's influential idea of "permanent catastrophe" as well as many of the current ideas about catastrophe's inevitability. However, this perspective does, I think, fail to take into account that we have already come to the end of theology—metaphysically speaking, that is. New metaphysical categories, drawn largely from the sciences, have become dominant in contemporary intellectual life. While the end of theology (or even the "end" of metaphysics) can itself be the object of a certain apocalyptic framing of modern secularism, I want to argue that "political theology" as a category of analysis was already largely exhausted in Schmitt's own epoch, and that Schmitt himself clearly recognized this. Now, he did go on to elaborate a complex political and legal philosophy that was grounded in this *retreat* of theology, and our contemporary theorizations of political theology dwell on the implications of a radical secularization. Yet these perspectives are so often negative.

It seems to me that a new historical perspective on the twentieth-century problem of the political is possible if we understand that an original metaphysical orientation concerning unity and order was developing within the biological sciences. The questions concerning the nature of "life" were remarkably congruent with the pressing contemporary issues that were raised in thinking about the nature of political authority—especially the problem of maintaining and preserving human order in times of struggle, crisis, and even catastrophic violence and breakdown. The interwar period marks a transition, I will suggest, from political theology to what we might call *political physiology*. Within this framework of political physiology, catastrophe will appear in a new light. Catastrophic disorder was not simply the result of a singular external interruption of some normal internal functioning. But neither was it the sign of some foundational violence inherent in the appearance of any "order," as the theorists of permanent catastrophe maintain. Instead, the physiologically inspired sense of unitary life pointed to the catastrophe as something that illuminated both the fragility of these organismic unities and their vitality. Catastrophe was the constant risk of death, but it was also the opportunity for creativity and improvisation. Catastrophe was permanent in the sense that organisms (and by extension other vital unities) were always refounding their order, and not merely protecting it, in response to the perpetual threat of dissolution.

This dialectic of threat and refoundation will serve as a thread linking the discourse of political theology and its alternative, political physiology. I will begin with the "end" of political theology in the work of Carl Schmitt by focusing on his idea of the *kathechon*, developed during and after the Second World War. Appearing in Saint Paul's Second Letter to the Thessalonians, this figure "restrains" the *anomie* of the Anti-Christ, delaying the moment when Christ will appear and sweep away the chaos and violence of lawlessness by his own presence. The *katechon* is therefore not a positive incarnation of divine order, for Schmitt, but instead a negative (and therefore resolutely secular) instrument of what is always a historically contingent order. I will then track the evolution of political theology in our own era through this figure of the *katechon*, as it appears prominently in the current work of two theorists of permanent catastrophe, namely the Italian philosophers Giorgio Agamben and Roberto Esposito. In both cases, the reflection on the *katechon* helps to frame the relationship between sovereign political authority—so central to Schmitt's thinking about political theology—and an alternative form of political control that Michel Foucault called *biopower*, that is, the way political institutions manage populations by exercising pervasive control over bodies, producing and maintaining norms of behavior. On the one side Agamben privileges the concept of sovereignty and uses it to explain the emergence of a new biopolitical regularization of human life, predicting (and here he echoes Benjamin) that the continuation of a "permanent state of exception" in the forms of political life can only lead to a coming "biopolitical catastrophe." On the other, Esposito argues that sovereignty and the legal technologies of power are just two of the many tactics deployed by what he calls "immunitary" regimes, regimes that are designed to protect individuals from the ever-present threat of some catastrophic *collective* violence. Like Agamben, Esposito warns that this threat has reappeared in modern states, where biopolitical and sovereign powers that are meant to preserve life end up threatening it. In both cases, the example of the "thanatopolitics" of the Nazi regime inspires their analysis of contemporary developments. Both look to the figure of the *katechon* to untangle the relationship between violence and the logic of restraint, so as to prepare the way for a new understanding of political life in the twenty-first century.

However, if we can see that political theology was, by mid-century, already losing its efficacy as a viable category and ceding its position to what I am calling here political physiology, then the intersection of sovereignty and biopolitical forms of governmentality—along with the permanent threat of catastrophe that this intersection has supposedly engendered—must be completely rethought. As I will show, once we take seriously the structural analogies between physiological concepts and political concepts in the crisis-ridden twentieth century, the possibility that catastrophic disruption might be *integrated* into the sphere of politics, without permanently contaminating the genuine promise of human security and stability, can at least be entertained. In its physiological instantiation, it turns out that an unpredictable catastrophe could be a catalyst for a radical reorganization of order, and not the mere force of devastating destruction. This idea of reorganization will open up new ways of thinking about political organization and its legitimation. Catastrophe is a permanent threat, but it is also the site where what we might call the *life* of a particular collective emerges most clearly and powerfully.

The *Katechon* at the End of History

In 1997, Mark Lilla delivered what was intended to be a withering critique of Carl Schmitt's long career, perhaps to counter what was fast becoming a veritable Schmitt Renaissance, around the globe, but especially in the English-speaking world. Lilla's tactic was to expose the irrationality of Schmitt's intellectual orientation. Citing Heinrich Meier's *The Lesson of Carl Schmitt*, Lilla noted how important it was to hear, like Meier, the "deep religious chords" that lurked in all of Schmitt's text "beneath the surface of his seductive prose." Lilla went on to remind his readers that Schmitt, who could be celebrated by both conservatives and those on the left for his hard realism and an existential approach to political decisions, in fact believed that political enemies were really part of "a divine order, and that war has the character of a divine judgment." Not only that, Schmitt romanticized the Catholic Church, Lilla warned, and went so far as to describe himself after the Second World War as a *katechon*—the restrainer who holds off the Anti-Christ until the Second Coming. Pointing to Schmitt's lesser-known (at the time) work on the new "nomos" of the earth, published in 1950, Lilla dismissively characterized Schmitt's thinking as "the messianic longings of an aging apocalyptic thinker."[7]

Of course, only a few years later, in the wake of 9/11, Schmitt's ideas became increasingly relevant. First, after years of debate about "deliberative democracy," the public sphere, and the politics of performative identity, political theorists and other intellectuals were now scrambling to make sense of the return of such issues as emergency executive power, the sovereign exception, and the political and ethical significance of "just war." Second, translations of Schmitt's postwar works on international law and the emergence of asymmetric warfare in the Cold War (*Nomos of the Earth* and its short follow up *Theory of the Partisan*) found new audiences, alongside parallel efforts (for example, Michael Hardt and Antonio Negri's 2000 book *Empire*) to conceptualize new global structures of power and violence. Third, despite Lilla's rather shrill warning, Schmitt's deep commitment to political theology only added to the attraction and interest in his work, precisely because the post 9/11 world was saturated with religious and civilizational conflict. An earlier (perhaps prophetic) "messianic turn" within critical theory and political philosophy, partly inspired by readings of Benjamin's thought, took on new significance as well in this period, with the ideas of Jacques Derrida, Giorgio Agamben, and Jean-Luc Nancy, among others, sparking debates on the future of democratic and cosmopolitan principles in the era of "homeland security" and global networks of violence.

---

7 Mark Lilla, "The end of liberalism," *New York Review of Books*, May 17, 1997.

It is precisely in this new intellectual and political context that a central question concerning Schmitt's ideas and method has become more pressing. Was his theorization of the political as an autonomous category always determined (or better, contaminated) by his theological commitments, as Meier and others have argued? Or was Schmitt's political existentialism just a facet of his own political theology, that is, only a mark of an *analogy* between his own theological thinking and his political concepts? Many casual readers of Schmitt are struck by the various theological analogies he invokes in his infamous definition of sovereignty in his short 1922 book *Political Theology*: the juridical exception, he noted, is like the "miracle" in theology, the sovereign decision is like the intervention of the theistic god, and so on. But one of Schmitt's central concerns in that text was the question of what kind of theology could possibly work as an appropriate analogue (and support) for the modern parliamentary state, wracked as it was with dissension and conflict, and the disappearance of any claim that it could genuinely represent some unified "people." The problem, Schmitt saw, was that no serious intellectual—or even serious theologian for that matter—really believed that the theistic, deistic, or pantheistic visions of divine presence (these were the theological concepts that were successively dominant in the previous three centuries) were at all plausible. This rendered the analogous question of locating genuine forms of *political* presence highly problematic.

Schmitt's depiction of the sovereign in *Political Theology* as a purely juridical figure, one whose suspension of the law in the exception was legitimated only by his successful protection of the possibility of a future *legal* order, was, I would argue, an evacuation of any positive forms of identity or presence from the sphere of the political. The sovereign was never meant to "incarnate" or even represent any metaphysically stable political subject—whether that subject was understood to be a nation of citizens, an ethnic identity, or even an economic class. The metaphysics of the political was completely displaced. For Schmitt, the challenge of the exception pointed to the fact that the sovereign was bound to refound and maintain only the bare *unity* of a community in crisis. This existential unity was not invested with the kind of sacred aura that earlier sovereign figures (including democratic ones) had possessed. In a way, Schmitt's notion of sovereignty was fundamentally *a-theological*, as his quotation of Kierkegaard in the first chapter hinted: the exception is no longer an opportunity for "divine" presence, Schmitt implies, a genuine miracle; it is only a reminder that faith in any permanent regularity and normality is always misplaced (both theologically and politically).

Schmitt's concept of the political as the foundational decision on the friend and enemy distinction was similarly structured—the essence of the political and its foundational legitimation was not the incarnation of some given metaphysical identity but only the "neutral" effort to maintain the existence of any historically constituted, historically contingent community. The political "does not describe its own substance, but only the intensity of an association or dissociation of human beings whose motives can be religious, national ... , ethnic, or of another kind ... "[8] The political decision, in other words, was governed by the strict logic of preservation and should never be contaminated by the principles inherent in the community's own beliefs. Indeed, Schmitt often insisted in the interwar period even that the political was an essentially *pluralist* category. Here we might glimpse Schmitt's own political theology: the aim of the state is to preserve a "fragment" of order on earth, alongside other fragments.[9] The abstraction of order pointed to the ongoing aspiration to escape conflict and chaos on earth; in this form any political order was an echo of some otherworldly divine order; but it was never the instantiation of this order.

So Schmitt's own political theology, in Weimar and under the Nazi regime, sought to rigorously connect the stark politics of order less with theological musing than with the concrete, historical effort of the Catholic Church to build a legal and political institution that was the earthly *substitute* of divine presence. In both the political and theological spheres, Schmitt was suggesting, the constitution of human order was predicated on the *absence* of any given order; or, to be more precise, on the idea of the *loss* of any positive identity that could serve to legitimate a political order.[10]

Yet Schmitt began to think quite differently about the relationship between theology and the political during and after the Second World War. He now saw that the question of the political had migrated from the individual nation-state to the configuration of states in the "large spaces" of the world defined by colonial extensions of European power. His point was that the emergence of a European notion of international law after the wars of religion helped to bracket or neutralize the potentially catastrophic episodes of violence such as the Wars of Religion, by displacing the military "tests" of power to the free zones beyond Europe, in the outer regions of the globe. Schmitt was offering a new political theology appropriate to the Age of Empire. The figure of the *katechon* was invoked to show that human political and legal order did not represent positively some value or identity, but instead served to *prevent* the worst excesses of conflict and chaos.[11] In Paul's description, the *katechon* struggled with the "lawless one," the force of chaos (usually taken to be the anti-Christ) in order to delay the Second Coming of Christ. If at first Schmitt was critical of this idea (precisely because of this notion of a delay of the return), he quickly adopted it as the structural parallel of his

8 Carl Schmitt, *Concept of the Political*, tr. George Schwab (Chicago: University of Chicago Press, 1996), 38.

9 Carl Schmitt, "State ethics and the pluralist state," in *Weimar: A Jurisprudence of Crisis* (Berkeley: University of California Press, 2000), 300–12.

10 I have tracked this line of thought in David Bates, "Political theology and the Nazi state: Carl Schmitt's concept of the institution," *Modern Intellectual History* 3 (2006): 415–32.

11 Carl Schmitt, *The Nomos of the Earth in the International Law of Jus Publicum Europaeum* (New York: Telos, 2003).

new international, planetary view of political order.[12] The first *katechon* was the Roman Empire (according to Tertullian's interpretation of Paul), a structure that maintained order across disparate peoples and communities, thereby preventing the lawlessness of war and the terrors of civil war. Schmitt would suggest that the Holy Roman Empire and then the *jus publicum europaeum* of the modern age took on this role with the collapse of Imperial Rome. With this turn, there begins a blurring, perhaps even erasure, of the distinction between the political and the theological. Once Christ and the divine presence were thoroughly evacuated from human historical time, political action was secularized. Revelation would not occur in historical time. A strange inversion then takes place: the *theological* structure of the political is itself the ground for a thoroughly *secularized* notion of history.

Benjamin had already pointed this out in his late "Political-theological fragment": the Messiah only redeems history by consummating it, by completing it. "For this reason nothing historical can relate itself on its own account to anything Messianic. Therefore the Kingdom of God is not the *telos* of the historical dynamic; it cannot be set as a goal. From the standpoint of history it is not a goal, but an end."[13] Similarly, in Karl Barth's "crisis theology" the possibility of divine presence in human institutions (even the Church) is resolutely denied. Writing in the aftermath of the devastating and futile violence of the Great War, Barth pronounced the utter impermanence of all earthly institutions. One could return to God only by renouncing historical time altogether: "the possibility of religion must be dissolved catastrophically," he wrote.[14] A turn to the divine can take place only when "dissolution and catastrophe are encountered," because that shows how "useless and ineffective" purely human action is. God is "*beyond the catastrophe*."[15] So catastrophe reveals what is permanent about human existence, namely its impermanence.

Once Schmitt radically separated the first and second comings, human history became thoroughly secularized even as it was framed within Christian eschatology. He noted that the Christian era was not a "long march," but instead "a single long period of waiting, a long interim between the two simultaneities ... "[16] The *katechon* figure was wholly negative, in that the delay of the end was effected through human institutions with no inspired foundation. The *threat* of catastrophic disorder, the *anomie* of chaos, was therefore a permanent threat. And with the experience and memory of catastrophe came the legitimacy of human order—not any particular order, that is, but secure order in any substantial form. Hence Schmitt's repeated

---

12 See Julia Hell's excellent essay, "*Katechon*: Carl Schmitt's imperial theology and the ruins of the future," *Germanic Review* (2009): 283–326.

13 Walter Benjamin, "Theologico-Political fragment," in *Reflections*, tr. Edmund Jephcott (New York: Schocken, 1986), 312.

14 Karl Barth, *Epistle to the Romans* (Oxford: Oxford University Press, 1933), 186.

15 Ibid., 290; my emphasis.

16 Carl Schmitt, *Political Theology II: The Myth of the Closure of any Political Theology* (New York: Polity, 2008), 59.

celebration of the jurist as the one who finds order and elaborates it from within any institutional and political form. The main point was this: the history of the twentieth century was now opening up into an unknown future. With the emergence of new "large space" configurations in the Cold War, new opportunities for devastating conflict were prepared—indeed, the total destruction of humanity was at stake in this age of nuclear weaponry, making the appearance of a "restrainer" all the more urgent. In this context, whether the *katechon* was understood to be a purely theological notion, or alternatively as a structural concept with purely secular implications, there was no real difference—since human history was in both cases still abandoned to itself, seeking protection from often overwhelming forces of disorder.

Schmitt's postwar work therefore pushed political theology to its very limit. Ultimately, the *katechon* creates and preserves order only to resist the permanent threat of the evil that is disorder, chaos; this can occur whenever humanity is turned loose with no restrictions. In the secular space of politics, this katechontic role was legitimated only existentially, that is, by the anthropological claim that humans are both unpredictable (dangerous) *and* desiring of security and community (social animals). This a-theological perspective of course maintains the trace of its theological framework in that it resolutely excludes morality and redemption from the political sphere. But with this move, we are back to Schmitt's concept of the political as a sphere that is *independent* of all other concerns. The political is a purely existential concept even as it must derive its energy parasitically from particular forms of human community.

The conclusion we can draw from Schmitt's prolonged engagement with political theology and existential politics? That the theology appropriate to the postwar era was a Christian eschatological concept that implied human order was thoroughly historical, and therefore *always* temporary. The essence of human history is therefore its *discontinuity* and eternal rupturing. All secular philosophies of history that attributed order and direction to human life were in fact only weak theologies and hence dangerous because they moralized politics and created new opportunities for extreme violence. No doubt Schmitt would have approved of Benjamin's evacuation of the divine from history. But he would not have accepted Benjamin's conclusion, which was: "The concept of progress is to be grounded in the idea of catastrophe. That things 'just go on' *is* the catastrophe. It is not that which is approaching but that which is."[17] We know that Benjamin would look to the "fissures" in the "ongoing catastrophe" of history for some form of redemption, and he advocated actively interrupting human continuities to remind us all of this. Schmitt would resolutely condemn this blurring of political revolution and the "divine violence" outside of all human meaning. Schmitt believed profoundly that locating and supporting order wherever legal and political institutions provided protection was the only bulwark against the always looming catastrophic condition that was total lawlessness.

---

17 Walter Benjamin, "Central Park," tr. Lloyd Spencer and Mark Harrington, *New German Critique* 34 (1985) §35, 50.

A Biopolitical *Katechon* for the Modern Era

In his commentary on Romans, *The Time that Remains* (2000), Giorgio Agamben took up Schmitt's postwar concept of the *katechon*, but reinterpreted this figure in line with Schmitt's early, infamous definition of the sovereign as "he who decides on the exception." Agamben's own theoretical work on the nature of the political, *Homo Sacer: Sovereign Power and Bare Life* (1995), was prompted by what he called the "bloody mystification of a new planetary order."[18] In this book he argued, as Schmitt did in *Nomos of the Earth*, that with the current "dissolution" of the great state structures humanity was now confronted more clearly with the question of the political. For Agamben, the essence of the political was the "sovereign ban," when bare life, or what the Greeks called *zoē*, was "excluded" in the foundation of political order. According to Agamben, the primordial state of nature is what sovereign authority protects us from by excluding it from the political-legal order. However, that form of bare life is always *included* in the political sphere. The sovereign is defined not in terms of a positive order or rule but in terms of the exception, when "real life" breaks through normality—here Agamben followed Schmitt closely. The sovereign is always poised on the edge of law and nature, for Agamben, since the law produces from within its own normativity the very "exceptions" that the sovereign must then decide.

Agamben wanted to emphasize that sovereignty *produces* bare life by first excising it from political life, but insists that sovereignty at the same time includes it within the state as that which may be killed—this is, he claims, the origin of the traditional sovereign right to decide life and death, and also the origin of what Foucault called the "biopolitical body." Agamben will argue here that history has revealed a gradual, but inexorable move toward the "permanent state of exception," one where bodies are thrown into ambiguous and perilous conditions, subject to the arbitrary decisions of sovereigns now freed from the constraints of law, and simultaneously subject to all the technologies the state has produced to control life itself—this form of biopower emerges, for Agamben, as a corollary of sovereignty and not, as Foucault suggested, as its rival. Agamben claims that biopolitics is the logical consequence of a sovereign state of exception in which inside and outside are blurred, where *bios* and *zoē* are no longer distinguishable. The "killable" form of bare life, *homo sacer*, appears inside the law, and the sovereign, using its emergency authority to protect the law, may now put to death individual people (or even an entire people) in the guise of protecting human "life."

In his interpretation of Saint Paul's Second letter to the Thessalonians, Agamben emphasizes this crucial claim of sovereignty—that it must protect life in dangerous conditions. If the *katechon* is the one who arrests the coming of the "lawless one" who will herald the return of Christ, then, Agamben claims, "every theory of the State, including Hobbes's—which thinks of itself as a power destined

18 Giorgio Agamben, *Homo Sacer: Sovereign Power and Bare Life*, tr. Daniel Heller-Roazen (Stanford: Stanford University Press, 1998), 12.

to block or delay catastrophe—can be taken as a secularization of this interpretation of 2 Thessalonians 2."[19] For Agamben, however, it is crucial to pause here and note the fundamental ambiguity of the *katechon*. He suggests that by delaying the appearance of total *anomie*, this figure delays the "unveiling" of the essential mystery of Messianic time. Inspired by Benjamin, Agamben claims that the veiling of the foundational "lawlessness" is what occludes the essential "inoperativity" of all human law. By positioning the *katechon* in this negative light, Agamben attempts to cast the entire history of political sovereignty as a covering up of the radical, originary lawlessness that comes before all human law and therefore threatens its claim to protect order. As Agamben will repeat, the foundation of the political is the exception and not the norm because, as Schmitt already pointed out, there is no norm that will apply to chaos. Agamben's conclusion is that sovereignty is founded with the claim that this primordial chaos is only a *state of exception* that will be "returned" to a normal condition of security. But that normative condition—the rule of law, the constitutional order—has no positive foundation. This is why Agamben makes what might seem to be a rather dubious claim: that all state apparatuses are driven to *create* conditions of exception, because only with the reminder of ever-present potential chaos can the core justification for their power to "preserve" human order ever be properly activated.

This explains why Agamben turned to the liminal, exceptional space of the "camp," those places that are both inside and outside of the law—such as concentration camps, death camps, refugee camps, and the like—and where individual bodies become the object of arbitrary control because they are not governed by norms, only the essentially non-normative logic of emergency. The camp is therefore the "paradigm" of sovereignty, Agamben claims, because it is the production of this indistinct zone that blurs public political life and private forms of living that reveals the way in which all sovereign power devolves into a biopolitical nightmare. The goal, Agamben suggests, is to extricate bare life from this condition, not by returning it to "nature" (which is really just a fictional space created by sovereign power itself) but by constituting an (admittedly vague) "new form of life." The risk of not recognizing how sovereignty and biopolitics work together as logics of exception will be, he notes in his last sentence, "an unprecedented biopolitical catastrophe." This is a rather serious claim, given that the Holocaust has already served as one of his privileged examples in this book of catastrophe.

After 9/11, Agamben reiterated these arguments on sovereignty, which found traction in the congenial setting of Bush-era discourse and practice of emergency power. Agamben now boldly proclaimed the very end of law in a permanent (and global) "state of exception," noting how the new forces of "security" in states like

19 Giorgio Agamben, *The Time that Remains: A Commentary on the Letter to the Romans*, tr. Patricia Dailey (Stanford: Stanford University Press, 2005), 110.

the U.S. were just new appearances of biopolitical control and potential sites of new violence and exclusion.[20] In 2002 he warned:

> Nothing is therefore more important than a revision of the concept of security as the basic principle of state politics. European and American politicians finally have to consider the *catastrophic consequences* of uncritical use of this figure of thought. ... Maybe the time has come to work towards the prevention of disorder and catastrophe, and not merely towards their control. Today, there are plans for all kinds of emergencies (ecological, medical, military), but there is no politics to prevent them. On the contrary, we can say that *politics secretly works towards the production of emergencies*.[21]

Here we see that the very structure of political legitimation and authority inevitably leads to the appearance of catastrophic disorders, because the political can only thrive in a permanent state of exception. Thus is established a condition of "permanent catastrophe," according to Agamben at least.

In that same year, 2002, Roberto Esposito published his volume *Immunitas: The Protection and Negation of Life*, which took up these crucial themes—namely, the imbrication of theology, sovereignty, and biopolitics. Like Agamben, Esposito also zeroed in on Saint Paul and the idea of the *katechon*. His starting point was, however, the ambiguous place of religion in the human world. Citing the seminal work of René Girard on sacrifice, Esposito explained how the foundational violence of sacrifice was translated into law. By making the subject of "revenge" abstract, the essential violence of community formation can be contained—the revenge fury "folds up into itself and is exhausted."[22] Girard's theory was that in times of "overwhelming catastrophe" scapegoats are produced. But in ritualizing revenge, the community in essence "immunizes" itself from future outbreaks.[23] Esposito was interested in how the immunitary logic operates in modern political societies. As Girard had noted, in the historical "evolution from ritual to secular institutions men gradually draw away from violence and eventually lose sight of it."[24] (We might think here of Foucault's famous argument in *Discipline and Punish* that the spectacular but sporadic violence of the early modern sovereign gives way to the more systematic disciplinary tactics of modern states.) Still, as Girard noted, the

20 Giorgio Agamben, *State of Exception*, tr. Kevin Attell (Chicago: University of Chicago Press, 2005).

21 Agamben, "Security and terror," *Theory and Event* 5:4 (2002), my emphasis.

22 Roberto Esposito, *Immunitas: The Protection and Negation of Life*, tr. Zakiya Hanefi (2011), 40.

23 René Girard, *Violence and the Sacred*, tr. Patrick Gregory (Baltimore: Johns Hopkins University Press, 1977), 79.

24 Ibid., 307.

violence of the foundation never goes away—"this is why violence can always stage a stunning, catastrophic comeback."[25]

In the spirit of Foucault, Esposito highlighted in his work how the initial immunitary logic of the community, one that is necessary to protect individuals from the potential threat of the dangerous "other," inevitably produces new strategies and institutions of control—including the ultimate instrument of authority and coercion, the modern state apparatus. Indeed, it is the modern state, stripped of all other modes of legitimation, that reveals most clearly the link between self-preservation and immunity: in order to preserve oneself one must submit to sovereign power, which in turn must preserve itself and its subjects by containing the lawlessness inherent in any human community. As Esposito wrote, "it wasn't modernity that raised the question of the self-preservation of life, but that self-preservation raises itself in modernity's being, which is to say it invents modernity as a historical and categorical apparatus that is capable of coping with it."[26] Esposito's philosophical history is the exact inverse of Agamben's. Instead of an originary sovereign "exclusion/inclusion" that sets in motion the production of the biopolitical sphere of control, Esposito begins with the "immune paradigm" where individuals must be protected from the community they belong to; this is what it means to have law, to have rights. Yet immunity must assume the very thing it must negate, and therefore there is a continual effort on the part of the "immunizing force" of sovereignty to *control* the body of the community—which of course includes the very bodies being protected. Modernity is constituted by the "forms adopted by the immunitary logic in order to safeguard life from the risks that derive from its own collective configuration and conflagration."[27] So both sovereignty and biopolitical technologies emerge from the same logic of immunity. The question is this: how do we "immunize" ourselves from the very powers generated by the original, foundational act of immunization?

For Esposito, the biblical figure of the *katechon* is emblematic of this challenging condition. The restrainer, as we saw with Schmitt, kept at bay the lawlessness of absolute chaos, yet as Esposito sees it, the *katechon* must also *preserve* lawlessness in some form, because without it, the final victory will never come: "the *katechon* antinomically assigns a *nomos* to anomie, thus restraining its catastrophic unfolding." It protects the Christian body in two ways—it contains the evil threat, but just as important, this same figure "nurtures and is nurtured by iniquity, just as the body is nurtured by the antidote necessary to its survival."[28] For Esposito, the question of the *katechon* for our own age is tied to the prevalence of state sovereign power, which is still the main guarantor of order, law, and rights in human communities. And that power is still inflected by what he calls, with

25 Ibid.

26 Roberto Esposito, *Bios: Biopolitics and Philosophy*, tr. Timothy Campbell (Minneapolis: University of Minnesota Press, 2008), 55.

27 Ibid.

28 Esposito, *Immunitas*, 63–4.

Schmitt, "political theology." However, Esposito is less interested in the changing metaphysical aspects of power than in what he takes to be the fundamental relationship between religious figures of the infinite, and the finitude of mortal human beings.

Political theology "accomplishes and perfects the ancient function of the *katechon*" by incorporating within the political community the paradoxical logic of inclusion and exclusion. Citing Ernst Kantorowicz's seminal work on the king's two bodies (which was subtitled "a study in medieval political theology"), Esposito points out that the eternal, mystical body of the monarchy is what undergirds the concrete, but temporary and finite, powers of any specific monarch. Esposito is interested in how even in modern democratic states, the legitimation of power is still predicated on this logic of infinite/finite. Any political community is defined by a transcendent identity that exceeds those subjected to power, but at the same time, that transcendent force must be *embodied by these same subjects*. So, as Esposito writes: "nothing in modern politics … is understandable without reference to the political theology model … ."[29] The continuity of the political body, which is what gives security to the individual "immunized" from the threat of collective violence, is an essential theological dimension of any state power, and it will never disappear. The sovereign power takes the position of the *katechon*: not in the Schmittian sense of restraining chaos to protect life, and not, as with Agamben's *katechon*, in order to cloak the fundamental "groundlessness" of all law, but instead in order to *restrain* the threat of both lawlessness and law by creating a condition of normativity—a concrete order, we might say, but not one with pretensions to universality or eternity.

Here Esposito explicitly follows Foucault's sense that the contemporary era is defined as much by law as by *norms*. Unlike the law, the norm is not a transcendent category. The norm is only implicit in the activity that maintains it. Turning to George Canguilhem's theorization of the normal and the pathological, Esposito states that the pathological always precedes the norm that is established in its wake. How can that be? He writes that it is only in a state of imperfection, in a condition of "dis-ease," that the will to live, the survival instinct, ever comes to the fore in a body. In facing that perilous challenge, the organism must establish a new form of being that can adapt to the new conditions of life. Citing here the ideas of the neurophysiologist Kurt Goldstein (who had an enormous influence on Canguilhem's own theoretical work), Esposito asserts that the "healthy organism is measured by its capacity and willingness to experience the unexpected, with all the risks this entails, including the extreme risk of a catastrophic reaction."[30]

With these remarks, Esposito seems to be looking beyond the limits of the political theological model of sovereign authority, toward something along the lines of what I will call political physiology. Of course, Esposito's emphasis on the core category of "immunity" already suggests this turn; however it is also

29 Ibid., 71.
30 Ibid., 143.

the case that immunity was first a political concept, and not a physiological one. (That turn only happened in the late nineteenth century, with Elie Metchnikoff's highly motivated adoption of this term for his discovery biological self-defense.[31]) But Esposito's provocative rethinking of the relationship between organismic and machine models of the "body politic" in his book *Immunitas* opens up some interesting new approaches to the political that sidestep the permanence of the political-theological form, a form so problematic in our day because there is no serious conception of the "infinite" and eternal that could possibly ground a political metaphysics. A turn to political physiology would counter the rather extreme claims of someone like Agamben, namely, that that the fading of theological structures of authority has only intensified the production of violence in a permanent state of exception—because the state *must assert* its katechontic powers. As I noted, Schmitt already posed this question in 1922, when dominant modes of divine presence were already becoming untenable metaphysically.

To pursue the implications of this alternative tradition, political physiology and not theology, I will follow a suggestive clue in Esposito's work on the nature of norms. As he pointed out, both Canguilhem and Goldstein, working within the disciplines of medicine and physiology, were radically rethinking the relationships between unity, order, and norms within the organism. Instead of thinking of health as the central norm that was protected by the organism, they privileged concepts such as disease, crisis, and risk. It is clearly no accident that these thinkers were writing in the same period as Schmitt, who was concerned with parallel questions in the sphere of political and law—though this is something Esposito, strangely enough, fails to even mention.

My suggestion is that we can locate an important intellectual shift taking place earlier in the twentieth century, one that has been masked by the apocalyptic thinking that characterizes modern political theologies. The task of political physiology is to go beyond mere metaphors and to articulate the *structural* analogies between concepts of the organism and concepts of political community. However, the restricted aim here will be to generate some new insights into the nature of "permanent catastrophe" from the physiological perspective. Esposito has already indicated a starting point: I will begin by investigating what Kurt Goldstein called the *catastrophic reaction* of individuals facing extreme conditions.

31 On the complexities of the discourse surrounding the body's defense system, see Ed Cohen, *A Body Worth Defending: Immunity, Biopolitics, and the Apotheosis of the Modern Body* (Durham, South Carolina: Duke University Press, 2009). Other invocations of immunity and "auto-immunity," most notably in Jacques Derrida's interpretation of 9/11 in *Rogues* and elsewhere, are self-consciously metaphorical—that is, they are more conceptual heuristics than serious efforts to map physiological notions onto political ones.

Catastrophe and Crisis: Political Physiology in the Age of World War

When Hans Driesch began to interfere with various animal embryos in the late nineteenth century, he was only intending to demonstrate the principles of *mechanism* in biology. What he found, however, was that the embryonic organism was often able to resist extensive manipulation and even partial destruction: an embryo divided into two would become two whole organisms, for example, and damaged ones would regain their intended form despite the defects. If Driesch ultimately explained these surprising phenomena with recourse to a new form of vitalism (by postulating the existence of "entelechies" that guided development from beyond matter), what emerged in the wake of these investigations was an approach to biological form that was neither strictly mechanist nor wholly vitalist in the traditional sense. Rather, new orientations emerged from questioning the nature of organismic unity—how was it generated in the course of fetal development, and how it was protected and maintained in the face of threats to existence? Central to these debates was the role of shock, violence, and pathology, for the genuine question of unity was raised only when organisms had to refound their own identity when responding to the extreme challenges wrought by myriad forces of disorganization at work within and without.

In physiology work of this period, the fundamental problem of "homeostasis" was crucial. How did the organism maintain its various steady states (blood pressure, temperature, and so on, the *milieu intérieure*, in Claude Bernard's formulation) in a constantly changing environment? The dynamic quality of the physiological system was emphasized. For Walter Cannon, the American physiologist who coined the word homeostasis, the body had several internal institutions of control. His particular interest was seeing how the body could rise to sudden and unexpected challenges to its survival. In a book on the emotion system, he examined, for example, "the elemental experiences of pain and fear and rage that come suddenly in critical emergencies." He went on to detail just how these "*emergency functions* of the sympathico-adrenal system" preserved life in dangerous circumstances.[32] The body effectively entered a new form of being, with a new set of physiological norms, in order to prepare itself for battle or for rapid flight. As he wrote: "When the body goes onto what we have called a war footing, the physiological changes that suddenly occur are all adapted to the putting forth of supreme muscular and nervous efforts."[33] Cannon followed up these investigations with experiments on "traumatic shock," based on his medical work in the First World War, as well as animal studies on blood loss and the like. His main finding: "every complex organization must have more or less effective

32 Walter B. Cannon, *Bodily Changes in Pain, Hunger, Fear and Rage*, 2nd ed. (Boston: Charles T. Brantford, 1953), 194. Originally published in 1915.

33 Ibid., 385.

self-righting adjustments in order to prevent a check on its functions or a rapid disintegration of its parts when it is subjected to stress."[34]

This notion of shock was also developed in the field of neurophysiology, which was in fact founded on pathological inquiry, since the operation of the brain and nervous system only revealed itself (in an era lacking direct imaging of active brains) in dysfunction. Localization of functions, as well as more sophisticated holistic perspectives, relied on either animal studies using brain ablations, or postmortem dissections of human brains after monitoring behavior in the clinic. Constantin von Monakow's research on the brain was particularly interesting from the perspective of neuropathology. He argued that when the brain was injured (from external attack or internal failure, as with a stroke) it did not simply lose a specific function associated with that area. Influenced by John Hughlings Jackson, the great British neurologist, von Monakow believed that the brain and nervous system as a whole functioned as a connected, complex unity.[35] So in the crisis of injury, he suggested, what happened was a generalized shock to the whole system, since the initial failure disrupted the total normal operation of the brain of which it was a part. He called this phenomenon *diaschisis*. This reaction was only temporary however. The brain would recover its functions in the absence of failure by reorganizing itself in a new way.[36] This was no automatic, mechanical procedure.

> Any injury suffered by the brain substance will lead (just as lesions in any other organ) to a struggle [*Kampf*] for the preservation of the disrupted nervous function, and the central nervous system is always (though not always to the same degree) prepared for such a struggle; the participation in that struggle will depend on the tectonic relations between various nervous areas and the injured site and/or areas whose function is being threatened.[37]

As he expressed it in a later text co-written with the French neurologist Raoul Mourgue, the brain entered a zone of risky "combat" and emerged transformed:

> It is a matter of combat, of an active struggle for the creation of a new state of things that will permit a new adaptation of the individual with his environment. The whole organism participates in this struggle ... .[38]

---

34 Walter B. Cannon, *The Wisdom of the Body* (New York: W. W. Norton, 1932), 25.

35 On Monakow, see Anne Harrington, *Reenchanted Science: Holism in German Culture from Wilhelm II to Hitler* (Princeton: Princeton University Press, 1996), ch. 3.

36 Constantin von Monakow, *Gehirnpathologie* (Vienna: Alfred Hölder, 1905).

37 Constantin von Monakow, *Die lokalisation im grosshirn und der abbau der funktion durch kortikale herde* (Wiesbaden: J.F. Bergman, 1914), 30.

38 Constantin von Monakow and R. Mourgue, *Introduction biologique à l'étude de la neurologie et disintegration de la function* (Paris: Félix Alcan, 1928), 29.

The unity of the organism was not some vitalist supplement to the body's mechanistic components. Rather, unity was the expression of the organism's very life as a dynamic entity. The organism was capable of creating a new form of being because it was defined as an active principle of organization operative within specific organs and operations of the body, and not as a predetermined "form" or a vitalist "force" external to its materiality.

Kurt Goldstein's thinking integrated these two contemporary notions of shock: one linked with the different planes of homeostatic action, the other with nervous system plasticity and the recovery of complex functions in the wake of injury. Drawing on his extensive experience with brain-injured victims in the Great War, and in his interwar neurological practice, Goldstein theorized the relationship between shock and unity in his seminal 1934 book *The Organism*.[39] There he identified the difference between normal and pathological states as the distinction between ordered and disordered performances. He called the latter a "catastrophic reaction" (*Katastrophenreaction*) to the shock and stress of injury. In other words, the catastrophe lay in the inability of the body to respond to crisis—it was not capable of decision and reorganization. In normal conditions, the organism is continually responding to the challenge of the environment as it maintains its internal environment. With shock, the organism has no immediate response.

> Events in the outer world that do not permit this [adjustment] do not become effective in the normal organism, except when they are of abnormal intensity. In this case they do not lead to actual performances but to the phenomenon of shock of the whole organism, which endangers its continuity as a system and that I have therefore called catastrophic reactions.(105)

But as he went on to show with many examples from animal and human studies, the organism can recover its health, even in the midst of catastrophe. This process demanded explanation, for Goldstein believed that "these shocks are essential to human nature ... and life must, of necessity, take its course via uncertainty and shock." In the end, what Goldstein was arguing was that in both normal and pathological states, the organism sought the "closure" of unity. The catastrophic reaction, by temporarily interrupting normal response to a challenge, revealed most clearly this ability to re-found order even as it raised the possibility of the organism's death. But the most significant claim was this: the "normal" organism is in fact constantly repeating this same dialectic of catastrophic reaction to persistent "shocks." "The normal person, in his conquest of the world, undergoes, over and over again, such states of shock." That is, Goldstein was arguing that

39 Kurt Goldstein, *Der Aufbau des Organismus: Einfuhring in die Biologie unter besonderer Berucksichtigung der Ehfahrungen am kranken Menschen* (Hague, Martinus Nijhoff, 1934). References in the text are to the English translation: Kurt Goldstein, *The Organism: A Holistic Approach to Biology Derived from Pathological Data in Man* (New York: Zone, 1995).

every physiological action might be considered a response to a challenge of the environment, one that puts the being into question and temporarily produces a catastrophe, an interruption, because every challenge is unique and has no specific normative solution. There is never a "perfectly adequate configuration of the organism and the surroundings." This is also to say that every action of the vital being results is in essence a new organization. As Goldstein will say: the life of an organism is a series of "slight catastrophes" (*leichter Katastrophen*) that continually produce new adjustments and reorganizations. (227) Catastrophic situations are "constantly occurring"—the organism survives not in spite of but via the experience of *permanent catastrophe.*[40]

What Canguilhem took from Goldstein was this significant reversal of norm and pathology that takes place within the radical interruption that is the catastrophic reaction of the organism to shock and danger: "the organism, in facing risks, accepts the eventuality of catastrophic reactions." Goldstein demonstrated that shock was what defied any normative response. The creative solution was therefore an improvisation of a living creature, not the instantiation of a pre-existing physiological norm. For Canguilhem, the norm could even be an obstacle once the organism finds itself in a challenging environment. "Disease" marks the transformation of the organism into a creator of new norms. Health was radically redefined by Canguilhem in opposition to the idea that life obeyed predetermined norms—health, he insisted, was the capacity to *establish new norms* that would make possible the continuation of existence in those crises that provoked catastrophe in the organism.[41] In crises, organs could take on new functions or take over other functions. The living being for Canguilhem was essentially plastic.[42] The body did not return to a prior state "after" the struggle, but acquired a whole new order of being, one that may well be superior to the prior state.

Canguilhem did not hesitate in this work to express a version of what I am calling *political physiology*. He highlighted how biological notions of disease and abnormality could easily underwrite efforts to purge society of its own "ills" by returning it to its fundamental norms. But this notion of norm became obsolete, he says, once biological conceptions of disease were transformed in the course of the nineteenth century, by Claude Bernard and others. The political implication of Canguilhem's articulation of crisis physiology and the "catastrophic reaction" is clear: in moments of shock and danger, old norms and old structures, even the basic organs of society, may have to give way to new organizations and new norms, through the interregnum of catastrophe, the collapse of norms. If the body periodically must displace its "withered, obsolete, and perhaps soon to be

40 Kurt Goldstein, *Human Nature in the Light of Psychopathology* (Cambridge, Mass.: Harvard University Press, 1940), 109.

41 Canguilhem, *On the Normal and the Pathological* (New York: Zone, 1991), 126, 194–5.

42 Canguilhem, "Machine and organism," in *Knowledge of Life* (New York: Fordham University Press, 2008), 75–97.

extinct forms"(144), the same could easily be said of political organizations as they struggled to adapt to rapidly changing conditions in the age of world war and mass industrialization.

Cannon was even more explicit in suggesting a vision of a political physiology congruent with his own work on the "wisdom of the body." A political body, like the natural one, had both internal and external relations. If the natural body had both normal and emergency modes, so might the political order: the state of emergency might "disturb the internal environment, but renders the organism more effective in a contest that may issue in life or death."[43] On the other hand, the effective automaticity of normal internal regulations "frees" the body from attending to homeostatic operations, so that it might explore and engage the world for its benefit.

The structural homology between the political and the physiological was at the level of *organization* for Cannon: "we see that the analogies between the body physiologic and the body politic are so close and numerous as to suggest that there are, indeed, general principles of organization widely applicable to complex aggregations of collaborating parts."(24) Cannon believed that the current political forms of organization lacked effective "regulatory devices" to protect against "dangerous shifts of stability."(23) Yet Cannon refused to advocate a dictator figure for the political body. Leadership in the physiological sphere, though centered in the brain, was, he noted, "acutely dependent" on all the other organs. Political life was analogous to bodily existence in that both deploy complex organizations to meet the challenges of their environments. If, as Goldstein and Canguilhem argued, this body was in a repeated state of temporary shock, it was crucial that these regulatory devices be open and free. Catastrophe demanded not simply a response, but a refoundation of unity radically disconnected (at least in the formal sense) from previous organizations.

Cybernetics, Catastrophe Theory, and the Future of Political Physiology

Cannon's language was important. The idea of a "device" that could regulate complex systems pointed to another potential homology, one that intersected with the physiological sphere and would soon take hold of the political imagination in this period—namely, the homology between natural organisms and self-regulating technical systems. Cannon himself was the figure who introduced homeostasis into the new multi-discipline that was cybernetics, which might be defined along the very lines suggested by Cannon, as a "general" science of adaptive organizations. Cybernetic thinkers were working in computer design, experimental physiology, neuroscience, mathematics, and eventually even the social sciences. What is relevant to our preliminary outline of political physiology is that the cybernetic thinkers were not just interested in models of complete automation, despite their

43 Walter B. Cannon, "The body physiologic and the body politic," *Scientific Monthly* 79 (1954), 22. This essay was an edited version of a talk given in 1941.

privileging of the technological object in their concepts of adaptive "life." Like the physiologists of the early twentieth century, the cyberneticists were very interested in the plastic capacities of the organismic being—its ability to self-repair, to re-organize in the face of shock, its talent for improvisation, as Canguilhem put it.[44]

Nonetheless, cybernetics was broadly interpreted as an effort to "mechanize," albeit in a sophisticated way, the complex information and action systems of living creatures. But it is important to recognize that the reactions to cybernetics and "machine" theories of life were not grounded in some kind of romantic or regressive vitalism. At stake was the conceptualization of an organized, unified system that was capable of the kind of radical re-organization that was exemplified by the overcoming of what Goldstein called the "catastrophic reaction." If the organism was a system that was experiencing in effect *permanent catastrophe*, permanent violation of its normative order, how could that system maintain its unity as a material form of being? As the biologist and foundational "systems theorist" Ludwig von Bertalanffy put it, the living being is in fact *defined* by constant transformation, something that the cruder cybernetic systems, however sophisticated they might be, simply could not imitate. As he wrote, "the cybernetic model does not provide for an essential characteristic of living systems, whose components are continually destroyed in catabolic and replaced in anabolic processes, with corollaries such as growth, development, and differentiation."[45] In another work on theoretical biology, Bertalanffy also called attention to the fact that "a mechanized organism would be incapable of regulation following disturbances,"[46] which was at the heart of Goldstein's and others' work in the period. The capacity to regulate *after* shock meant that regulation was not always just a direct response to change but in fact a radical response to the *catastrophic reaction* that interrupted all normal operations. This capacity was, we might add, a fundamental attribute of any stable political order, at least in the sense that Schmitt and other interwar figures understood it.

It was precisely this puzzling connection between stability and ongoing transformation that prompted the development of catastrophe theory, a mathematical and conceptual modeling of complex systems undertaken by René Thom in the 1960s and 1970s. Building on early qualitative models of epigenesis (for example C. H. Waddington's "epigenetic landscape"), Thom attempted to explain how a unitary organismic system could, first of all, differentiate itself without any outside intervention into a complex of organs and subsystems, and then, in its mature phase, maintain that unity despite changing environmental

44 On this point see my paper, "Unity, plasticity, catastrophe: order and pathology in the cybernetic era," in Andreas Killen and Nitzan Lebovic (eds), *Catastrophe: History and Theory of an Operative Concept* (Berlin: De Gruyter, 2014).

45 Ludwig von Bertalanffy, *General System Theory: Foundations, Development, Applications* (New York: G. Braziller, 1968).

46 Ludwig von Bertalanffy, *Problems of Life: An Evaluation of Modern Biological Thought* (New York: John Wiley, 1952), 17–18. Originally published in German in 1949.

conditions and other shocks from both outside and inside of the organism. His insight was that one could describe the organismic being as a geometric object, identifiable as a four dimension space-time entity. The transformations of the object would be considered topological transformations (twisting and turning of the original structural relations) and not material changes. Stability would be an attribute of the system's abstract relational structure, not some external guiding principle. That is, Thom was one of the first to model the ways in which interacting determining factors can produce complex behaviors that are not entirely predictable or continuous but fundamentally stable. That was the heart of catastrophe theory, in fact. As Thom demonstrated formally, systems with a certain number of variables will *inevitably* display radical discontinuity that interrupts the previous continuous and linear behavior. If these singularities could not be exactly predicted, their inevitability could be proven. As Thom showed, if a system had four independent control variables (modeled in a four-dimensional space), then it would undergo a strictly limited set of catastrophic forms, seven to be exact.[47]

With this demonstration, Thom was suggesting a way of explaining the sudden discontinuous change of living beings as they evolved and adapted to pressures exerted on these different variables. Thom was adamant that this dynamic system could not be represented by any technological object (although he allowed that some mechanisms might provide models of individual subsystems in the organism). (200–201) This was because mechanical systems did not exhibit genuine unity—here Thom would explicitly acknowledge his debt to the theoretical biologist Jacob von Uexküll, who argued in his own work that living individuals were not composed of functionally specified parts, but unified by an integrated experience that gave meaning to all the functional parts. Thom rarely cited any other thinkers in his work, so it is significant in this context that he also mentions the name of Kurt Goldstein as another important influence on his theory. (In fact, Goldstein's work may well have been the source for Thom's very use of the term "catastrophe.")

Following these earlier theorists of the organism, Thom outlined a process whereby the system might recover from perturbation and even shock, by showing how the system could internally compensate for the deformation of one variable by changing others. This was no mystical event—the transformations would be explained in terms of the system's own dynamic. However, Thom would go on to speculate that living systems could experience something akin to Goldstein's "catastrophic reaction," when a normal adaptive compensation is not enough to maintain constancy—the affected organ is too damaged, and the system halts normal operation. The catastrophic singularity of the mathematical form represents the opening of the organism to the possibility of destruction. At this point the system must "enter a zone of qualitative indeterminacy" which results in a loosening of the behavior of the system. The healthy organs become super excited and ultimately will (if successful) find a new state that compensates for the

47 René Thom, *Structural Stability and Morphogenesis*, tr. D.H. Fowler (Reading, Mass.: W.A. Benjamin, 1975).

injury. The system enters a new topological space of organization. That is defined by Thom as the state of pathology, and we can easily see here concrete links to Goldstein and Canguilhem, for the pathological state is in essence a discontinuity, a "catastrophe," that does not so much generate new organization as it does interrupt one organization and thereby threaten its continued existence. And like these physiological thinkers, Thom will emphasize that even the "normal" dynamic of the system may be analogous to the more spectacular catastrophic reaction. As he noted: "our everyday life, on the physiological plane, may be a tissue of ordinary catastrophes," and death might be considered to be "a generalized catastrophe," when the discontinuity and rupture is not followed by some new continuity.[48]

Advocates of Thom's catastrophe theory—Christopher Zeeman in the United Kingdom was the most prominent[49]—immediately saw its potential for explaining myriad complex behaviors, from psychological conditions and animal reactions, to prison riots and the decline of civilizations.[50] Whatever the excesses of this application of Thom's rather abstract, even ethereal approach, the formal political physiology it engendered established a key point, namely, that complex social, economic, and political organizations were at once self-stabilizing systems *and* systems capable of sudden, catastrophic change. To be a self-stabilizing system, in the cybernetic sense of the term, would entail the inevitable appearance of catastrophes, sites of genuine rupture, because new organization had to be discontinuous with the prior state of being.

Historically and conceptually, we can see that Thom's mathematical version of the apocalyptic warnings pointed to a more general concern in the period with the permanent possibility of catastrophe. This concern hovers over the development of both poles of the "political physiology" dyad through the late twentieth century and into our present era. Physiological systems as much as human communities were subject to discontinuity, disruption, failure, and disorder, and this could produce catastrophic reactions, the inability to act in the face of impending disaster. At the same time, living bodies and living social systems alike repeatedly proved their ability to maintain and reproduce their unitary forms despite the impermanence and fundamental unpredictability of their constituent parts. The conjunction of what Francesco Varela and Hubert Maturana called "autopoiesis"[51] (the maintenance of a form of *organization*) alongside the theory of catastrophe (and related disciplines of complexity and chaos) would produce new understandings of the constitutive interrelation between structural stability and the inevitability of discontinuous change.

48 Ibid., 250–51.

49 Christopher Zeeman, *Catastrophe Theory: Selected Papers, 1972–77* (Reading, Mass.: Addison-Wesley, 1977).

50 See Peter Timothy Saunders, *Introduction to Catastrophe Theory* (Cambridge: Cambridge University Press, 1980).

51 Francesco Varela and Hubert Maturana, *Autopoiesis and Cognition: The Realization of the Living* (Dordrecht, Reidel, 1980).

Political and critical theory of the late twentieth century has vacillated between celebration and fear of that disruptive, catastrophic moment of rupture. What I want to suggest here in conclusion, is that a change in perspective—from political theology to political physiology—can help analyze what is at stake in the continuing life of our social and political bodies, because we can find some of the most meaningful metaphysical understanding of the supposedly theological notions of permanence and contingency (unity and plurality) within the sphere of life. Resistance to romantic political organicism and a suspicion of vitalist strains of thought have occluded the concepts I have traced so far. The problem of the life of the organism was concerned with the ability to create norms of existence and at the same time the capacity to abandon these norms in times of crisis. The concept of catastrophe pointed to the incredible risk of that moment. The decision to produce a new form of being was never guaranteed. The catastrophe was a turning point. We can say that there was a permanent condition of catastrophe in this sense: at no time is a living being not in question. Norm, crisis, exception, these were not clearly delineated. If catastrophe was the appearance of disorder, chaos even, the living being lived on the edge of that *anomie*.

So to modify Schmitt's earlier formulation, I would say that the most pregnant political concepts of the twentieth century were structurally analogous to physiological (not theological) concepts. At the very least, this hypothetical change in orientation will be productive because it will allow us to connect the work of twentieth century theorists who emphasize structural constraints and order, with those advocating radical contingency, to bring together into one intellectual zone the defenders of strict systems of legal control and neo-anarchists—Niklas Luhmann with Gilles Deleuze, so to speak—since the presumed analogy between the political and the physiological is predicated on the permanent threat of catastrophe, whichever side one chooses to emphasize. The current task of reinterpreting the question of the political—its location, its force, its future possibilities—is a historical task as much as a theoretical one; that much we can take from Schmitt's demonstration of the essential *mobility* of the political. But tying the essence of the political to a permanent theological condition is not only historically suspect, it is, I would suggest, also very limited conceptually.

Rather than restrict ourselves to categories derived from old and "withered" institutions and ideas, to borrow Canguilhem's description, a new understanding of political forms of community will have to address the evolution of systems of control, and the interaction and conflicts of these systems, but it will also have to pay attention to the elements within that systematicity that allow for sudden radical change and reorganization from within. Sovereignty and security are broad categories that hardly contain the complexity (and plurality) of political authority in our era. With open eyes attuned to the life of organization and the organization of life, we can seek out the *katechon* figure of the twenty-first century—those that delay the ultimate appearance of catastrophe, total devastation but only by keeping it alive in some form, within the very orders that perpetually try to contain it.

Chapter 5
Disaster, Ruin, and Permanent Catastrophe

Lewis R. Gordon

I come to this question of permanent catastrophe from my work in existential phenomenology, especially its African diasporic or Africana instantiation. An important element of existential philosophy is the primacy it gives to contingency. The human world is governed by the reality of that which could be otherwise. As a consequence, that which does not occur by accident is often simultaneously that which is not necessary. This leads to an additional view, that the notion of human nature should be abandoned in favor of a human condition. Essence, in other words, is that which is brought *into* the human world instead of being that which governs it. As a form of phenomenology, this approach raises the question of how one examines phenomena once one has bracketed, parenthesized, or, as I prefer, ontologically suspended one's naïve presuppositions. Such an act offers the unusual distinction of being able to articulate essence without essentialism. The first is a description while the latter is a prescription, a claim about what must be the way things are beyond the description. As a form of Africana philosophy, the descriptions that follow from this approach take into account a set of imperatives raised by the historical emergence of African diasporic peoples—namely, that something has happened in the modern world with regard to what it means to be human, to be free, and to engage in justificatory practices. The result is to take seriously the human condition under the lived-reality of the organizational practices that created such shifts, and these include colonialism and racism.

A catastrophe is something that occurs, which means there is a pre-catastrophic condition. So, the question is raised: Why, then, as something that comes into being it is not also what could go out of it? There is a peculiar symmetry implicit in this question: a changing world needs continued change for balance. But what if change is asymmetrical? What if there are some things that simply come into being and others that just go out of being? What if, in other words, there is a genuine end? We know there is such at least implicit in ideas about the universe or, if we will, pluriverse, that, for example, from a quantum of reality there was an explosion of energy expanding into our physical reality and it will eventually cool and all will end—at least as we understand it.[1]

1 See G. Lemître, "The Beginning of the World from the Point of View of Quantum Theory," *Nature* 127 (09 May 1931): 706–706. http://www.nature.com/nature/journal/v127/n3210/abs/127706b0.html, accessed May 6, 2015.

In a mundane sense, the eventual end of all there is haunts everyone's existence, but it does not do so for those of us who expect our own death to precede such events, which means it's a concern more for posterity or for those of us who hope to be remembered by such. A viable sense of permanent catastrophe requires, then, more modest concerns, despite the apocalyptic elements of the phrase. Given our specific history at the writing of this chapter, it behooves us to consider, at least, perspectives from which the world, in a word, ended, through which to understand permanent catastrophe in what ultimately may make more sense to us—that is, in ultimately human terms.

Wherein We Live

To say a permanent catastrophe is devastating in human terms would be an understatement. Immediate annihilation would leave nothing for reflection. Thus, realization of the event as such requires survivors or, from the perspective of the present, an imagined one who, comprehending its significance, laments the loss. Reflecting in such terms calls for an understanding of that plague on the human spirit and our efforts at its alleviation—namely, misery.

Sigmund Freud, in *Das Unbehagen in der Kultur* ("The Uneasiness in Culture"), known in English under the misrepresenting title of *Civilization and Its Discontents*, examines three sources of human misery. They are nature, our bodies, and other people. The first holds the terror and contingency of natural events such as actually being struck down by lightning or being swallowed up by a cyclone. The second is physically from within, as our genes, our physical frailty, and the reality of simply being mortal remind us. The third is the social world, in which constraints are placed in a dialectical tension with desire, wants, and social well-being. Unable to control others as one could a tool, and for others facing a similar problem regarding the self, the human world becomes, in Freud's Hobbesian model of life "brutish and short," a world of conflict in which individuals are subordinated at times by force and often by other means such as the stultifying weight of guilt. Yet guilt could only make sense where there is a sense of a deeply rooted good, and as this social world is one in which the challenges of nature and the limitations of our bodies could be, if not overcome, at least placed into some relief through the substitution of a human world, one in which the human being is at home, the effect of culture is, as Freud observed in its projection, almost isomorphically placed onto reality itself as a prosthetic god.

My aim here isn't psychoanalytical description so much as to affirm a shared observation of all humanists: the humanity of all human beings requires, tautologically as it is, a human world. This world is marked by a fundamental feature that bothered positivist adherents of inquiry, including Freud, and continues the same for their intellectual descendants who would prefer a neat reality of well-measured and precise phenomena. The lived-reality of meaning, however, does not behave as such. This aspect poses problems in one sense because of its fecundity. Where precision, a necessary element of scientific inquiry, is demanded, assertions of extension dominate over those of what philosophers of language call "intension." Abstract as this may be, it amounts to this: an extensional language has no gap between what is asserted and what is so in reality. It is in a one-to-one relation with what, proverbially, there is, which leaves no room for error. An intensional language is not in a one-to-one relation, which means an assertion could have other possibilities. The first would like to reduce the world to signs that simply point to "things." The second, however, addresses signs that point beyond signs and things. It is, in the language of Ernst Cassirer, "symbolic."[2] In his philosophy of culture, Cassirer reminds us that this term, whose etymology refers to throwing things together, a very synthetic term, is the basis of the peculiarly human world. It is a world lived through symbols and their forms, a world, in other words, of meaning.

Thus, for the human being, from this point of view, to lose culture, to be barred from it, to not enter it, to be outside of the framework through which it is made manifest, is to suffer disintegration, destruction, ruin.

Failing to enter culture, however, is something otherwise. It is, as Jean-Jacques Rousseau reflected in his *Discourses*, to be an animal, and a fairly intelligent one, but not a human being beyond the biological constellation of organic makeup. One could behave as such in a world of signs, as do so many other animals such as cats and dogs, but the vast constellation of meanings that make up the human world would not be on the horizon, for even "horizon" would, under conditions limited to signification instead of symbols, not make any sense. Culture, in this view, is thus a transcendental condition of a genuinely human reality.

Talk, then, of cultureless human beings is nonsense. This is because culture, in the radicalized philosophical sense, is isomorphic with human reality—or at least any reality that would be meaningful for a human being. Within this framework, there are organizations of meanings into what have been commonly called "folkways" and "mores." These elements, while features of culture, are not the sole determinants of it. Thus, it is fallacious to ascribe the absence of culture on the bases of difference along these lines. Folkways and mores may differ, but they stand, in the end, as manifestations of the same human condition and phenomenon.[3]

Yet it is coherent to talk about "a" culture as simply the expression of culture in ways that form the identity or fusion of a people. This is because individuals could meet under shared, meaningful conditions. This meeting, however, could transcend the singularity of chance encounter and become over time the formation

---

2 See his *Philosophy of Symbolic Forms*, 3 vols., trans. Ralph Manheim (New Haven, CT: Yale University Press, 1953–1955), and for a contemporary discussion of the relevance of his approach, see Drucilla Cornell and Kenneth Panfillio, Symbolic Forms for a New Humanity: Cultural and Racial Reconfigurations of Critical Theory (New York: Fordham University Press, 2010).

3 For a careful, methodic philosophical critique and discussion, see Kwasi Wiredu, *Cultural Universals and Particulars* (Bloomington, IN: Indiana University Press, 1996).

of a community. This fusion, so to speak, is conditioned by what existentialists call the lived reality of projects. Where meaning is exhausted, the consequence is decay.

Wherein We Die—of Catastrophe, Disaster, and Monstrosity

Decay, as we know, follows death, but it doesn't always have to. Sometimes, only a part of us dies and begins a process through which our impending death is paradoxically lived. This process offers symptoms through which its story could be told. Decadence, as Nietzsche showed, is a process of decay whose social symptom is nihilism.[4] He meant by this the emergence of anti-value as an expression of value. The latter, properly understood, is a living affirmation of life. The former pushes life to the side in an almost automated and dissociated performance of rules under the guise of "morals."[5] What is crucial about lived-values, however, is that they involve an active participation in the production of meaning, which brings to the fore the question of responsibility for what is produced. This classic existential model raises the question of meaning in life through which emerges also the meaning *of* life.

Jane Anna Gordon and I reflected on some of the consequences of this portrait of culture in our book *Of Divine Warning: Reading Disaster in the Modern Age*.[6] The title, while an accurate portrayal of our thesis and argument, turned out to be misleading since some readers took "divine" and "warning" to mean some kind of eschatological prophetic religious thesis. What we meant, however, was this; While disasters are discussed all across the globe, the question of the *meaning* of disaster receives scant attention. The matter becomes complicated, however, once we locate the category of thought into which such reflection belongs. To call an event a disaster, after all, is a judgment about a circumstance. The earth, after all, is a physical entity caught in the gravitational field of the sun, and as it relates to the gravity of other entities and its own internal physical structure, such things as volcanic eruptions, tidal waves, and climate change are part of the course. Whether life exists or not on the planet, the earth will continue to spin on its axis and revolve around the sun until the latter swells, incinerates it, and, if the conditions are right, much in this area of our galaxy collapses under the weight of its implosion, provided, of course, the remote chance of asteroid 2013TV135

4 See Part I of Nietzsche's *Will to Power*, trans. Walter Kaufman and R.J. Hollingdale (New York: Vintage, 1968).

5 See Nietzsche, *On the Genealogy of Morals*, trans. Walter Kaufman and R.J. Holingdale (New York: Vintage, 1967).

6 Jane Anna Gordon and Lewis R. Gordon, *Of Divine Warning: Reading Disaster in the Modern Age* (Boulder, CO: Paradigm Publishers, 2009).

colliding with our planet in 2032 doesn't prove otherwise.[7] All this is a different story, however, when life emerges in a form that asks: What would all this *mean*?

For one thing, it would mean, should that life aspire to persist, a catastrophe. From the Greek καταστρεφειν, the term literally means to fall down and come to an end. As we are not born standing, we experience catastrophe as falling back, which raises the question: Can we continue to rise again and again? Falling, however, is a mythic phenomenon in the sense of raising the question of meaning beyond its initial appearance. That meaning beyond signification makes the study of this phenomenon in the realm of the human sciences, where even the meaning of meaning receives scrutiny. The concept of disaster fits into this model well, since, as its etymology reveals—from the Italian *dis astro*, transformed through Latin from the Greek ἄστρον, which amounts to "fallen star or planet"—it is about that which literally falls from the sky, which we might as well call the heavens. And since falling from heaven isn't a good thing, the additional question becomes whether the fallen object has come to its end. A problem emerges, however, when witnessing such an event is an encounter with something portentous, which is why we often ask, upon seeing it, "What does it mean?" This question marks the event as a possible beginning.

Now, of course, if the fallen star's message is for the witness, then the event stops there. But if it is not, if it moves through the witness, then the sign, so to speak, continues. That means the event of "falling" is transformed into a series, which Jane Anna Gordon and I call "the sign continuum." What is striking about this continuation is that the witness is caught up into the sign and becomes, in effect, also a sign, and if it is a sign of becoming a sign for others, she, he, or they become a warning. As the origins are from the heavens, a location associated with divinity, this warning has the mythic quality of a divine warning.

A divine warning in Latin is issued in the word *monstrum*, which, in the infinitive is *monere* (to warn), from which we get, in English, "monster." Words such as "demonstrate," "remonstrate," "admonish," and "admonition," relate to this unusual phenomenon at the heart of which is disaster. The question in the face of monsters (and monstrosities), then, is: What do they mean? What are they telling us? If we think through the mythic structure of a message from the heavens, of what monsters signify, they mean, in a nutshell, that "we" (that is, whomever the sign is for) are doing something wrong or that there is something we are supposed to be doing to prevent the production of monsters. In effect, a disaster is a call for intervention, for action. The error, then, is to focus on the monster instead of what stimulated its appearance.

Returning to our initial Freudian triumvirate of nature, our bodies, and each other, the course of catastrophe, disaster, and monstrosity offers corrective possibilities in terms of natural science and technology for the first, medical

7 "Asteroid 2013TV135—A Reality Check," *NASA News* (October 17, 2013): http://www.nasa.gov/mission_pages/asteroids/news/asteroid20131017.html#.U3rSiLyCpZk, accessed May 6, 2015.

science and health regimens for the second, and social psychology and good governing for the last. But these are each technocratic responses that elide their deeper meaning, especially in terms of the last two. Responding to our limitations through corrections of the form of healthy behavior and systems of rules organizing those behaviors works the extent to which they are meaningful. What, however, if meaning itself suffers the catastrophe? What kind of disaster would that be? What are its monsters?

Once Whole, Left in Ruin

We come now to the focus of these reflections. In the words of Robert Ginsberg: "Humanity is the greatest ruin. Mythology and theology, philosophy's handmaids, identify us as fallen. The Golden Age preceded our history. It is the happy state we left behind."[8]

This happy state is, however, a presumed one, since we think of it as such only as a projection onto it. How can we, after all, remember a time of happiness when the conditions of its meaning—indeed, its even being meaningful—were absent? Wouldn't we need evidence, a "mark," as it were? This, of course, is one of the concerns Freud had about circumcision: the "memory" of the event is in the evidence of absent foreskin.[9] Men with their foreskin represent a former wholeness that those without now lack. The situation of course becomes more complicated with women since it could only work in a framework of bio-normality in which the male body becomes *the* human body. Under that circumstance, the lack for women becomes that of in effect never really being born. The matter is worsened for women as a form of "in the making" with the expectation of failed achievement—unless, of course, the subordination of this mythic meeting is achieved through technology, as we now see with the place of surgery. Yet women pose a possibility that could re-write male-centered psychoanalytical interpretation: If she becomes a woman, made whole, through losing her hymen, the notion of perfecting the male through circumcision would make foreskin the equivalent of the female membrane and its loss. Problems lurk, however, where becoming woman is not identical with becoming ethical. The folly of the matter emerges in the subversion of wholeness through, as in Judaism, ethical wholeness, where the absent foreskin becomes the mark of ethical potential. This leads, as we have seen in many countries today, to the normalization of circumcision to the point of making the uncircumcised the exemplification of lack. Ironically, this interpretation offers support for female

8 Robert Ginsberg, *The Aesthetics of Ruins* (Amsterdam, The Netherlands: Rodopi, 2004), 387.

9 See Freud, *Totem and Taboo* (1913), standard edition; trans. James Strachey (New York: W.W. Norton, 1990); *Analysis of a Phobia on a Five-Year-Old Boy* (Little Hans) (London: Hogarth Press, 1909); and *Moses and Monotheism*, trans. Katherine Jones (New York: Vintage, 1954).

circumcision and a form of equality of sexes for enthusiasts of the practice: Why should female wholeness be premised on male penetration instead of ritualistic surgery as it is for males? Wouldn't equality depend on both becoming "whole" at the same time—perhaps in transforming the foreskin and the hymen at the moment of heterosexual intercourse? Such is the way and continued folly of culture. For our purposes, however, the issue at hand is the presumption of prior happiness, even where the initial moment could have been premised on pain or mutilation. What, in other words, could make that prior state one of happiness?

If the presumption is that of no prior suffering, of the absence of suffering, as the model of happiness, then Nietzsche's counsel is a wise one: the best course is preemption—that is, never to have been born.[10] If that is the standard, then to be born is a disaster. It is to fall from the already fallen—to be a sign continuum—a catastrophe in which one is left ruined.

"Catastrophe" and "ruin" are intimately linked. The etymology of "ruin" is the Latin word *ruina*, which means to collapse or tumble down. We are already here witnessing a structure of sign continua, where a Greek word for falling to an end connects to a Latin word for falling down and then we move on to another Latin term, for "collapse" is from *collapsus*, which is the past participle of *collabi*, which literally means to fall together. The connection to *collaboration* is evident. This movement suggests a strong series of relations that many of us may wish to avoid—namely that embedded in our neighbor's catastrophe is our own.

A disaster, a fall from the heavens and its inaugurated sign continuum, always occurs somewhere at some time. A convergence of space and time in such a fall is a "disaster area." Such a place is in ruins. Somewhere, once teeming with life, at some point fell to the wayside, commencing a process of decay, perhaps from destruction, leading to the petrification of past hopes. The earth is littered with remains, historical in some cases, passing the eyes of most of us in others, many of which revealed a good fight against nature. Evidence abounds. Once lush fields turned desert. Ancient civilizations held out for as long as they could, because, after all, they thought they had forever on their side, but at some point, there were the eventual final steps, the last closed door, the last precious artifact taken, the final look (poetically offering the risk, as the Hebrew Bible attests, of turning into salt), a lamented memory, as the final dwellers moved on.

One emigrates to live, but as Jean-Paul Sartre reflected on exhaustion in *Being and Nothingness*, the point at which one abandons a project is not always due to an externally imposed necessity.[11] "I cannot go on!" is often cried when one could, after all, take at least another step. There is a point at which inhabitants

10 Nietzsche explores this in a variety of texts, but see his inaugural work, *The Birth of Tragedy from the Spirit of Music* (1887) in Raymond Geuss and Ronald Speirs (eds), *"The Birth of Tragedy" and Other Writings*, trans. Ronald Speirs (Cambridge, UK: Cambridge University Press, 1999).

11 Jean-Paul Sartre, *Being and Nothingness: A Phenomenological Essay on Ontology*, trans. with an intro. by Hazel Barnes (New York: Washington Square Press, 1956), 584–585.

abandon the project of the place, the point at which "here" becomes the place at which one can no longer live, the place at which the expectations for the self can no longer be realized. In other instances, the moment is cataclysmic. Death and destruction, as suffered by a village or city on a volcanic site, are instantaneous. In others, agents of destruction come in the form of human reapers of death, razing communities to the ground, decimating their infrastructure, with the rapidity of divine furies. And then there are plagues, infestations and disease eating away at life, spreading through the halls, infecting even the sociality of human life through the poisoning of proximity, rendering deadly the pleasure of touch and the warmth of breath. Such disasters at first leave a haunted presence of life in the wake of the flight taken by the uninfected, but in time, as abandoned homes, neglected streets, whole infrastructures, left to the ravages of bacteria, dust, and wind, decay, the ruined remains no longer stand as a site of sudden flight but instead as an above ground necropolis, indistinguishable from many other dead places beneath dirt, dust, sand, or the cold, barely livable, oxygen-deprived deepest depths of the sea.

Hubristic Hopes of Eternal Cities and Valuable Values

The marriage of science, technology, and language in the projected world of culture offers a seductive message of divine resistance. It enables human beings to forget we are not gods. If the city or empire could become eternal, so, we convince ourselves, could we achieve immortality. The existential term for this is *the spirit of seriousness*.[12] It refers to a form of bad faith, self-deception, in which we convince ourselves of a pleasing falsehood (in this case, our eternity or immortality) in an attempt to evade a displeasing truth (our mortality). The spirit of seriousness is an attitude in which values are materialized as devoid of human agency. This attitude tends to have a reflexive element, where the externality of the values, their objective credence, supposedly absolves responsibility for them. This view fails on two counts. Even if our values were objective, that doesn't absolve our responsibility for them since we ultimately must choose to adhere to them or not. In effect, the responsibility is also reflexively *for responsibility*. This ultimately makes their objective status irrelevant. But let us suppose they are objective and relevantly so. The question of why they are so, of their status *as values* comes into play. Seriousness would, then, make our relation to such values irrelevant.

12 Originating in Buddhist thought (which encourages self-detachment in the form of not taking one's self too seriously), this concept followed a path through Arthur Schopenhauer and Nietzsche to its more systematical examination in Sartre's *Being and Nothingness* and Simone de Beauvoir's *The Ethics of Ambiguity*. I expanded this concept at the methodological level to problems of disciplinary formation, especially in the human sciences. See Lewis R. Gordon, *Disciplinary Decadence: Living Thought in Trying Times* (Boulder, CO: Paradigm Publishers, 2006). Michel Foucault also explores this concept, although not explicitly so, in his "Technologies of the Self."

But then, placed out of relations, the effect becomes our own irrelevance. Human presence or not, the values would live on. Placed in the framework of culture, the problem returns of human relations to human institutions. Without human beings, such institutions lose their animus. They become mere artifacts. Values, human institutions, in other words *live* as manifestations of human relations. We return to the human paradox: not to be ruined means to be a god. But that means not to be human. So the human being becomes, as Sartre famously put it, a "useless passion": namely, to be a god with aspirations and realizations that could only have emerged from not being one.

All this is, however, on an abstract level. Concretely, we are haunted by this realization each day. I recall my youngest child's response to pictures of our family before he was born. He was perplexed. "Where," he asked, " is Mr. [his nickname]?"

The answer, though true and logical, was nevertheless disturbing: "Mr.— did not yet exist."

The child's apprehension is honest. How could my youngest see as the family's good times any period in which he did not exist?

His consternation is, however, our condition. We know there was a time when none of us existed. So even as we press on, as we struggle for some sense of permanence, the other side of the equation haunts us as well: There will be a time when we no longer exist. And even more radical, there could be the paradox of a time, as theoretical physicists argue, when time no longer exists.

Our passion is made concrete in our material objects and also in the variability of those relations the Germans call *Geist*, that is, "spirit." We'll conclude with the latter. But let's begin with the former.

A ruin is a peculiarly human phenomenon. It is the remains of a human project that has ceased. Our planet is littered with ruins. Gravestones, markers for the dead, also decay. Fossils, strewn about, portend our future. The earth moves on, and gravestones—representatives of solidity and stability—eventually slant, chip, topple over, or rot beneath a bed of weeds as they sink, slowly and assuredly into the fate of the fossil. Buildings go through decay and eventually fall into ruin. Across the planet, large-scale efforts for humanity to triumph over the forces of nature—"eternal cities" as some have been called—lie in ruin. They depend on the proverbial kindness of strangers to take pity on them, even in the form of maintaining them as ruins. Think of the ancient Roman city of Pompeii. Once vibrant, it reputedly became a necropolis within a day. Ginsberg defines ruin as "the irreparable remains of a human construction that, by a destructive act or process, no longer dwells in the unity of the original, but may have its own unities what we can enjoy."[13] In ruins, time has come to a halt. "Pompeii," Ginsberg observes, "has ruined time. Its walls are timeless wells. We dip into their absoluteness of being, beyond categories of time and purpose. The innate brickness of the bricks has all the time in the world to educate our sensibility to it. Roman civilization recedes

13 Ginsberg, op. cit., xvii.

in consciousness, as we give ourselves over fully to this civilization of bricks."[14] What Ginsberg is getting at here transcends the facts of the materials scattered at a disaster area and left in ruin. He is pointing to, in his reference to "civilization," the living community that once animated them with meaning. Culture, and the societies in which it is made manifest, requires human beings for its continuation; it is, then, an expression of human beings in the peculiar recognition of the same dynamic of being born from another while being responsible for itself and producing others. This dimension of human existence shared by its macro, societal correlate is its fundamental incompleteness. As with a human life, where there is birth, maturation, decline, death, there is a cyclical dynamic in societies, where, in the fervor of youth, they are lived as though they will do so forever. Whether the Coliseum in Rome, the Parthenon in Athens, Inca Pyramids across Peru or Aztec ones in Mexico, these ruins remind us of civilizations that once expected to last forever. They are testaments to the inevitable decay of all empires, cities, towns, villages, and homes. None of these live forever because no one lives forever, and even where such expectations are hoped for through memory, even the latter depends on the longevity of others. We are not, in ourselves, the children by whom we are remembered. At some point, there will be none.

Existentialists echoing Jean-Jacques Rousseau, such as Jean-Paul Sartre and Albert Camus, have written of the human being as a figure condemned to freedom. Although this freedom is a manifestation of our responsibility for how we live, it is also an understanding of our incompleteness. Each human being faces her or his self and correlative communities as a bastion of possibilities, but in each lived moment, many possibilities are dried up, and potential shrinks to the point of reflection on a narrative, if one is afforded such a luxury, of what could have been and what might still be possible. The message in life, Ginsberg argues, channeling Schopenhauer, is not happiness but for us to make ourselves ready when it is our time to die, which, paradoxically is happiness because of having lived a life worth living. To achieve one's goals in life, to have done what one sets out to do, transforms the threat of death. The odd rationalization of not having done X or Y no longer holds force. It is strange reasoning, however, since it presumes death has priorities. In the second volume of *The World as Will and Representation*, Schopenhauer writes:

> There is only one inborn error [in humankind], and that is the notion that we exist in order to be happy .... We are nothing more than the will-to-live, and the successive satisfaction of all our willing is what we think of through the concept of happiness. So long as we persist in this inborn error, ... the world seems to us full of contradictions.... We may still try to put the blame for our individual unhappiness now on the circumstances, now on other people, now on our own bad luck or even lack of skill, and we may know quite well how all these have worked together to bring it about, but this in no way alters the result, that we

14 Ibid, 7.

> have missed the real purpose of life, which in fact consists in being happy. The consideration of this then often proves to be very depressing, especially when life is already drawing to an end; hence the countenances of almost all elderly persons wear the expression of what is called *disappointment* .... Pains and sorrows, ... prove very real, and often exceed all expectations. Thus everything in life is certainly calculated to bring us back from that original error, and to convince us that the purpose of our existence is not to be happy.[15]

Schopenhauer draws the argument to its conclusion in a meditation on death:

> Dying is certainly to be regarded as the real aim of life; at the moment of dying, everything is decided which through the whole course of life was only prepared and introduced. Death is the result, the *résumé*, of life, or the total sum expression at one stroke [of] all the instruction given by life in detail and piecemeal, namely that the whole striving, the phenomenon of which is life, was a vain, fruitless, and self-contradictory effort, to have returned from which is a deliverance. Just as the whole slow vegetation of the plant is related to the fruit that at one stroke achieves a hundredfold what the plant achieved gradually and piecemeal, so is life with its obstacles, deluded hopes, frustrated plans, and constant suffering related to death, which at one stroke destroys all, all that the persons has willed and thus crowns the instruction given him by life (637).

Ginsberg probably had passages like that in mind when he declared: "To philosophize is to ruin the human being."[16] Living a life worth living is, after all, no easy task. This was ironically something of which ancients were aware. Socrates' lover Alcibiades, for instance, described the great philosopher and his practice in Plato's *Symposium* as "intoxicating," a form of poison, which Derrida rightly reminds us is pharmacological, despite its medicinal effects.[17] Philosophy doesn't happen without a change from one state to another, without transformation, which means, as well, a form of gain through loss, especially where what are lost are our naivety and innocence. Some philosophers respond to this realization with sensible admission of its being what it is, while others are troubled by this phenomenon and attempt to overcome it. They attempt to lose the loss. Ginsberg prefers Schopenhauer's counsel: "We are the species living under the death sentence ... that it has passed against itself."[18] And he adds the existential situation of humanity in the new millennium: "The one constant truth for all humanity has been that we are each going to die. What differentiates the present generation from

15 Arthur Schopenhauer, *The World as Will and Representation*, Vol. 2, trans. E.F.J. Payne (New York: Dover Publications, 1958), 634–635.

16 Ginsberg, op. cit., 419.

17 See Jacques Derrida, "Plato's Pharmacy," in Dissemination, trans. with introduction and notes by Barbara Johnson (Chicago, IL: University of Chicago Press, 1981).

18 Ginsberg, op. cit., 439.

our predecessors is that we also bear the cross of destroying the species. If such a thing as sin exists, this is it. Killing a god might be forgiven by humanity, but we cannot forgive killing humanity" (ibid).

Killing Humanity

Although we are all condemned to death, it makes all the difference to each of us whether that shared fate is something any of us, in our life story, deserves. Karl Jaspers has written of this problem as *Die Schuldfrage*, "the guilt/blame/responsibility question."[19] The term *Schuld* is related to the German word *Schule* (school), which reveals the educational dimension of the concept. The notion of guilt without learning is pointless and, in many instances, pathological. Jaspers was thinking through the disaster wrought by the actions of the German government, many of the German people and their allies, and the general responsibility shared by German citizens leading up to, during, and after World War II. They left countries and nations in ruins, and in some cases, given their genocidal intentions, suffering bio-cultural catastrophe, the result of which, although difficult to see today, was a Germany seemingly left in ruins. Jaspers outlined four kinds of guilt with correlated responsibilities: metaphysical, ethical and moral, legal, and political. The first pertains to one's relationship with the Absolute or existence throughout the universe; the second is a relationship with the rules and mores of one's society and one's relationship with one's self; the third is a matter of positive law; and the last is the responsibility every member of a society has for the actions of its government. The last, as he addressed it to his fellow Germans at the end of World War II, raises the question of whether a people's government has acted in a manner that affords a good case for mercy in the instance of its defeat. Jaspers counsels every government to remember that it is the people, its citizens, who will suffer the debt, and in some instances the sentence of death, of such a trial. Returning to Schopenhauer and Ginsberg, if life is about preparing for not deserving to die, would it not be a catastrophe for a government or a society to have failed to offer the same for its people? Ginsberg admits:

> We are responsible for our extermination. Efforts exist to attribute the blame to the culprits among us: the rules, greedy, hostile, thoughtless, doctrinaire, military, otherworldly, Other. But they are our fellows. The blame is upon us for failing to control them or guide them to the light. Looking for an escapegoat, we also cast blame on the System, economic order, communication gap, uneven distribution of resources, violence of television, limitations of education, inhibitions of tradition, intolerance of religion. Yet, at heart, we know that human beings are

19 See Karl Jaspers, *Die Schuldfrage. Von der politischen Haftung Deutschlands* (Munich, Germany: Piper, 1965), available in English as *The Question of German Guilt* (New York: Fordham University Press, 2001).

> victims of ourselves, not of circumstances. We allow circumstances and systems to get in our way ... . The destruction of the world falls upon our head, if we fail to stop it ... . You and I are obligated to save the world .... To be human requires action to save the world. Such action is without expectation of success. It need not be accompanied by hope.[20]

We come, then, to the underlying theme of these reflections, the one that stimulated the Freudian reflection and which is the animus for culture, the prosthetic god, which, as we know, needs to be fed and preserved because of the threat faced by all—namely, the ultimate catastrophe, not only the end of the world but also that of *all worlds*.

Empires, those mighty organizations that eroded national boundaries in their effort to achieve eternity through reaching across space and time, deceive their constituents with such a promise, which is achieved, no doubt, because people want to be deceived. Evidence, the remains of past empires, mock such fantasies, yet hegemony, if not empires, continues, and any society that achieves such continues to be beguiled by delusions of its own necessity. We in the U.S. need simply use ourselves as the example. Ask most—and, oddly enough, even many from other countries—about what the demise of the U.S. would mean, and they will no doubt speak honestly, though not truthfully: the end of the world.

The world could, however, end not in a great cataclysm but through a quiet and perhaps unnoticed whimper. Our earlier meditations of culture pointed to a possibility suffered by many and forgotten by most: What can a society do when the sign continuum of the end of the world is the death of its form of culture?

The events since Christopher Columbus landed in the Bahamas in October 1492, inaugurating a period of expansion that transformed Christendom into Europe and much of the rest of the world into colonies, include the rapid death of whole continents of peoples and their ways of life—the death, in other words, of worlds. In many cases where the genetic material of the people survived, the symbolic life either disappeared or was mutated into a new kind indigenous to the world constituted by new sets of relations. This struggle is not, however, new, as similar questions marked struggles of similar kind in antiquity and even earlier as a forgotten time of different *species* of hominids reveal. Earlier hominins such as Neanderthals and Denisovans appear to us as fossilized zoological ruins, even though traces of them exist in the transformed populations we now know as Europeans, Asians, and sub-Saharan Africans who mixed with them. There are also cultural practices connected to whatever genetic adaptations they afforded with their descendants' environments. Although to some extent an "us" that is a new kind of "us," the basic conclusion remains that some genes remain where once robust cultural life of another kind existed. In relatively more recent times, Greece and then Rome offered for ancient Judeans the challenge of modernization the result of which was the emergence of Christianity and Rabbinic Judaism, the

20 Ginsberg, op. cit., 439.

complex intellectual and spiritual struggle of reconciling the Hellenic, Roman, and Israelite worlds, and a debate on the cultural location of Judaism to this day. Similar concerns abound on the place of the Arabic world in North Africa, the varieties of Mainland Northeast Asian civilizations on the Pacific islands, including the indigenous peoples of what is today Japan. And in the Americas, this problem of cultural disaster unfolded in the genocidal practices that reduced the numbers of Native populations through the cultural hegemony of Spain and Portugal in the South and England and France in the north, with brief instances of Holland and Denmark. There are still speakers of these languages, but many fear, as speakers diminish even where the population (genetic material) continues, the looming cultural equivalence of the end of the world.

For some, cultural disaster takes the form of a ruined existence. There are, all over the world, people living through cultural ruin or culture on the verge of ruin. The struggle of continuation is Promethean. For some, the struggle for cultural continuity drags cultural practice out of the stream of mundane life to the level of sacrifice and fanatical devotion. Religious fundamentalisms are the perverse bedfellows of cultural preservation. How could certain cultural practices become relevant across all time without war on the future? If subsequent generations must be bound to past ones in an eternal circle of the same, would not the effect become one of never truly having been born? There are many myths about parents refusing the birth of the next generation: Among the ancient Greeks, Ouranos (sky) refused to let his children emerge from the birth canal of their mother Gaia (earth). Kronos, one of the sons, took the option of castrating his father and throwing his genitals into the sea from which sprang Aphrodite. Among the Israelites, disobedience in the form of eating from the fruit of knowledge leads to expulsion from paradise, and an endless chain of sacrifices of children to elders, which offers a narrative of election as the responsibility to preserve and protect the ethical expression of the *Imago Dei* on earth. There, prayers as sacrifice remind younger generations that theirs is to give, the giving, the *Mitzvot*. The holy source of giving also demands much. What happens to Judaism, many Jews worry in the wake of *Shoa* and the emergence of Israel, when generations emerge who wish no longer to give but to take?

Permanent Catastrophe in Human Terms

All over the world, the youth are losing their youthfulness. The burden of living one's life is already unbearable. To add the weight of one's people and one's culture, as has been the lot of colonized peoples, beckons the dreaded tide of lost horizons. Exhaustion lurks.

Cultural disaster leads to a rallying of forces against the future. It demands sacrifice of the young. Richard Fenn, in *The Secularization of Sin*, reads modern burdens on the youth through ancient grammars of sacrifice devoid of their original telos or purpose.[21] Using the Daedalus myth as inspiration, Fenn argues against institutions of authority that deploy mystifying practices to hold sway over the youth. This bars, he contends, possibilities of growing into responsible adulthood. Recall that Daedalus was the gifted technician who built the labyrinth to hide the Minotaur, the offspring of Pasiphaë's (King Minos's queen's) lusty union with the white bull given to Minos by Poseidon for sacrifice to the gods. Fenn reads the myth as a tale of insatiable greed with consequences so ugly that additional precautions of subterfuge were needed. Minos' greed led to his withholding the bull instead of returning it to the gods. Pasiphaë's lust and greed were such that she masqueraded as a cow to satisfy her desire for union with the bull. The offspring, the Minotaur, born of greed, inhabited the labyrinth where he consumed unfortunate youths lost there. These calamities didn't abate Minos' untrustworthiness and greed. Hoping for permanent access to Daedalus' technical genius, he imprisoned Daedalus and his son Icarus in a tower overlooking the sea. Daedalus then devised their escape by fashioning wings of feather and wax with which they flew over the open sea. Securing the wings with wax carried the danger of their melting when exposed to heat, so Daedalus warned Icarus not to fly toward the sun, and not to fly close to the sea where he could be swept up by the waves. As we know with myth, Icarus didn't stand a chance. He might as well have been Eve looking at the fruit of knowledge. Lost in the joys of flight, he flew too high, whereupon the sun's heat melted the wax and he plummeted down and into the hungry sea.

The myth of Daedalus, Fenn contends, offers a tale of sacrifice, purification, and the pressures of older generations on the young: Icarus is warned by his father (no doubt appearing monstrous as an admonition) not to fly too high or too low but to follow him, as many exemplars of patriarchal authority, what Fenn calls the Daedalus Complex, do. Icarus' fall reveals two poles of purification, namely, fire and water. Thus, there is the greed manifested in institutions of power, the king and the queen, which consumes the people, and then there is the sacrifice by which purification is sought for the debt of consumption.

In the modern world, where the mythic foundations of rituals of purification have been lost, a legitimation crisis emerges for institutions that demand sacrifices of the people, especially across generations and across communities. "When the Minotaur is clearly the government or banking system, there is no abiding reason for either tribute or sacrifice. The Protestant miracle is that so many are still willing to make their sacrifices to the larger society."[22] Writing at the end of the Reagan era of unbridled greed, Fenn's ruminations portended the pyramid scheme behavior in the financial and real estate markets that led to the situation of world financial ruin by the end of the George W. Bush administration and the dawn of Barack Obama's. The sacrifices are many, and who else will inherit the large debts for the bailout of the banking industry and other aspects of economies, not only in the

21 Richard Fenn, *The Secularization of Sin: An Investigation of the Daedalus Complex* (Louisville, KY: Westminster John Knox, 1991).

22 Fenn, ibid., 163.

U.S. but many worldwide, but everyone else, especially subsequent generations? As greed has spread to financial derivatives, where betting on the future has led to debt beyond the imagination of the present, the possibility of human foreclosure is hardly a fantasy. For our purposes, the divine warning represented by economic monsters, which oddly enough in the age of neoliberalism is socialism, is the dimension of the self, of the avowed better system, pushed from sight in a maze of confusion similar to the financial instruments used to bamboozle much of the public worldwide. As things fall apart, further distance is placed from the self through claims of adulteration: Somehow, the system has been polluted and purification is called for.

Overlooked in the inevitable search for culprits, Fenn observes, is the demise of the individual as person versus institutional actors—in other words, the human relation to human institutions. What many of those who selfishly took from the system and its correlative institutions knew was that the latter would sacrifice them at the slightest threat. They, as expendable, followed the paths against being swallowed up. "This leaves the individual as *person* a mere survivor of the labyrinth."[23] Purification demands rooting out purveyors of the pollution that has spread throughout the community, which in this case extends across the globe, and the expected rituals of cleansing, which in the past involved fire (burnings, electric chairs), water (drowning or rebirth through baptisms and conversions), or burial and resurrection (prison time). The accused continue to be the usual suspects: immigrants, social pariah, and other members of the damned of the earth. But those are ultimately not enough to erase the burden placed on those rendered distant in the obfuscation of international hysteria, namely, the young and subsequent descendants. "Any community that seeks to restore primordial unities, to pay the debt of the individual to those who have gone before and to the world itself," writes Fenn, "is inevitably going to stimulate demands for an unbroken harmony with both the natural and social orders. That harmony will always be threatened by the young and the old, by aliens and intruders, and by those who represent impurities in the ideological or social system."[24] What, however, about those whose domain is the future? "Certainly the young, who like Icarus 'impede their fathers at their work' and seem to play when the serious rites of the community are at stake, can be scapegoated as a source not only of innovation but of threat to the community as a whole."[25]

There is, then, the yoking of the young, discussed in the struggle against cultural disaster, brought to the understanding of debt in even the dominating society. Subsequent generations, in effect, forced to be the parents of those from whom they have descended by virtue of the debts they bear. Beyond the constraints of economic ensnarement are the cultural presuppositions lived in each generation as though permanent. Implicit in such presumption is the same cultural fear pushed

23 Ibid, 170.
24 Ibid, 178.
25 Ibid, 181.

to subconscious levels: indebted to the past but without a future, what else do they sense, with fear and trembling, but the end of the world?

The message from dying cultures, suffered in relations of the old to the young, is that all cultures ultimately die, and their signals, as divine warnings, are for what all must learn, that despite avowed preservation for the sake of children and subsequent generations, the disaster of contemporary society, its sign continua, is that by not facing our responsibilities we are ruining the future *as future* and are thereby making the case for what Jaspers lamented—namely, a deserved vanquishing of humankind. It is stupid for humankind to expect to live forever. Schopenhauer, Ginsberg, and Fenn remind us, however, that life as a preparation for death involves taking seriously what one must do for the sake of life. A society that fails to do such wastes what little time it has at the expense of others. Ignoring the signs is perilous. The testament to the unheeded divine warning of our age may be an epitaph of admonition from desperate final efforts. The worst would be for the youth to suffer exhaustion, for they would then eventually offer nothing, and what is the absence of effort but the permanent catastrophe of a world well lost?

Index

For Product Safety Concerns and Information please contact our EU representative GPSR@taylorandfrancis.com
Taylor & Francis Verlag GmbH, Kaufingerstraße 24, 80331 München, Germany

www.ingramcontent.com/pod-product-compliance
Ingram Content Group UK Ltd.
Pitfield, Milton Keynes, MK11 3LW, UK
UKHW011019180926
475701UK00004B/822

* 9 7 8 1 1 3 8 3 8 4 0 6 4 *